China, the U.S., and the Power-Transition Theory

A critique

Steve Chan

Routledge
Taylor & Francis Group

LONDON AND NEW YORK

First published 2008
by Routledge
2 Park Square, Milton Park, Abingdon, Oxon OX14 4RN

Simultaneously published in the USA and Canada
by Routledge
270 Madison Ave, New York, NY 10016

*Routledge is an imprint of the Taylor & Francis Group,
an informa business*

Typeset in Times New Roman by Keyword Group Ltd
Printed and bound in Great Britain by TJ International Ltd, Padstow,
Cornwall

British Library Cataloguing in Publication Data
A catalogue record for this book is available from the British Library

Library of Congress Cataloging in Publication Data
Chan, Steve.
China, the US and the power-transition theory: a critique/Steve Chan.
p. cm.
Includes bibliographical references and index.
1. China–Foreign relations. 2. United States–Foreign relations.
3. International relations. I. Title.
JZ1734.C52 2007
327.51–dc22
2007006406

ISBN10: 0–415–44023–8 (hbk)
ISBN10: 0–415–44024–6 (pbk)
ISBN10: 0–203–94066–0 (ebk)

ISBN13: 978–0–415–44023–3 (hbk)
ISBN13: 978–0–415–44024–0 (pbk)
ISBN13: 978–0–203–94066–2 (ebk)

What made [the Peloponnesian] war inevitable was the growth in Athenian power and the fear this caused in Sparta.[1]

To forestall or prevent . . . hostile acts by our adversaries, the United States will, if necessary, act preemptively.[2]

Among precautions against ambition, it may not be amiss to take one precaution against our *own*. I must fairly say, I dread our *own* power and our *own* ambition: I dread our being too much dreaded. . . . It is ridiculous to say we are not men, and that, as men we shall never wish to aggrandize ourselves in some way or other . . . we say that we shall not abuse this astonishing and hitherto unheard of power. But every other nation will think we shall abuse it. It is impossible but that, sooner or later, this state of affairs must produce a combination against us which may end in our ruin.[3]

Contents

Tables

Preface

In recent years we have witnessed a series of truly momentous events in international relations. The end of the Cold War, the collapse of communism, the reunification of Germany, and the expansion of the European Union are watershed developments promising to define a new era for international relations. Concomitantly, the September 11 (2001) terrorist attack against the U.S. and the ensuing campaign by the U.S. to combat global terrorism introduced a new set of challenges and dynamics to international relations. At a moment of its unipolar predominance, Washington's decision to invade Iraq in March 2003 turned out to be especially controversial both domestically and internationally. Whether Operation Iraqi Freedom eventually succeeds or fails will have profound and lasting effects in the Middle East and on U.S. relations with the Muslim world.

This book turns its attention to a different region of the world. It is anticipated that by the year 2025, seven of the world's ten largest economies will be located in Asia. The center of global political economy will increasingly move away from Western Europe and North America to the Asia Pacific region. Because of its size and the speed of its growth, China leads these upwardly mobile states. In the past quarter century, China's economy has attained an average annual growth rate of 9 percent, quadrupling its people's average income. No other country has ever been able to achieve and sustain this rate of growth over a comparable period of time. If the recent past is a prologue for the immediate future, China's economy may triple again in the next fifteen years. In a recent cover story entitled "China's Century," *Newsweek* projected that this country's economy could overtake Japan's by 2015 and that of the U.S. by 2039.[1] Accordingly, the emergent importance of the Asia Pacific and especially the rise of China rank among those unfolding processes with a potential to bring about a fundamental transformation of the global political economy. In the words of one thoughtful analyst, "whether for good or ill, the most significant bilateral international relationship over the course of the next several decades is likely to be that between the United States and the PRC [People's Republic of China]."[2]

The prospect or, to some, the reality of China's ascent as a great power has not escaped the attention of scholars and officials. Many Americans have been drawn to ponder about the implications of China's rise for the security of their country and, more generally, the peace and stability of the international system.

Some have looked to history for analogies, seeking to draw possible lessons especially from Anglo-German interactions a century ago.[3] Others have turned to broader theoretical formulations attending to the rise and decline of nations, hoping thereby to develop a more sound understanding about their general sources and implications. One especially popular formulation comes from the power-transition theory.[4] The amount of attention accorded to this theory reflects the serious scholarship that has thus far been undertaken to investigate its propositions and the cumulative evidence that has been produced by this program of research. This theory has been a focus of discussion in both the U.S. and China.[5] In brief, it proposes that the danger of war increases when a dissatisfied challenger catches up with or even overtakes an existing hegemon. Because of this theory's popularity and its obvious policy relevance, I frame my discussion in its context. This discussion presents a series of concerns, suggesting why the standard applications of this theory to Sino-American relations are often problematic or misleading. I take issue with this theory and the received wisdom typically associated with it not because of a wish to be dismissive or disrespectful, but precisely out of a desire to treat it with the seriousness it deserves.

This book presents a synthesis of ideas from research undertaken over several years. Many of these ideas have appeared in previously published articles while others come from working papers. I offer here a more coherent and comprehensive set of arguments on the implications of China's recent growth for Sino-American relations and for global and regional peace. My arguments present contrarian, even controversial, propositions that systematically challenge the currently dominant views as they tend to be captured by the power-transition theory and its derivations. Like colleagues who work in the tradition of the power-transition theory, I draw my arguments from contemporary social science research and historical analysis. Thus our differences cannot be attributed to disagreements about epistemology or methodology. Indeed, although I often reach conclusions contrary to generally accepted views in U.S. scholarship on international relations, I draw my theoretic logic and empirical evidence from sources that are familiar and common to this scholarship.

Scholars, no less than other opinion leaders, play an important role in interpreting international developments, in propagating and legitimating these interpretations, and in framing them for consumption by government officials and the general public. They are thus as much engaged in the social construction of reality as are other political entrepreneurs. Some views gain a dominant status. When they are taken as evidently natural and reasonable by a large number of people, they form "a hegemony of ideas."[6] That China's recent growth augurs an impending power transition between it and the U.S. and that this development is likely to alter the existing international order are widely accepted by many informed Americans and Chinese. More dangerously, the current U.S. administration has announced a strategy seeking to prevent the emergence of any rival power – forever,[7] and there appears not to be a shortage of Chinese who believe that the U.S. is actually determined to act according to this premise. This book examines the assumptions and implications behind these views, and submits them to critical inquiry.

Mao Tse-tung remarked that people's class background determines their outlook. As social scientists, we strive to be objective in our study of international relations. Still, as colleagues writing about feminist theory, dependency theory, and social constructivism remind us, we cannot be completely successful in immunizing ourselves from particular biases or prejudices even if unconsciously. It is therefore not surprising that international relations theories tend to reflect the perspective of the dominant states or those that have won past wars. This does not mean that these theories are necessarily wrong. It does mean, however, that we should also listen to alternative perspectives which challenge the prevailing views. Which competing interpretation is more satisfactory should ultimately be determined on the basis of logic and evidence.

The power-transition theory obviously offers a great deal of policy relevance. It calls attention to the management of a strategic competitor seeking international primacy.[8] In so doing, it reminds us not to overlook the differential rates of national growth and the revisionist agenda of a prospective challenger. A leading cause of the Peloponnesian War was Sparta's alarm over the rising power and ambition of Athens. Similarly, the accumulation of power by the Habsburg family and its perceived hegemonic design were among the chief motivations that inspired a league of opponents in the Thirty Years' War. More recently, on the eve of World War II, British leaders Neville Chamberlain and Winston Churchill disagreed not so much about Germany's strength as its leader's intentions.[9] Did Adolf Hitler have limited demands that could be reasonably accommodated, or was he bent on conquering Europe? As these illustrations imply, judgments about relative power shifts and policy intentions have serious consequences. It is dangerous to mistake an ascending state with an expansion plan for a status-quo power. It is also dangerous to make the opposite error of suggesting a power transition when there is limited evidence supporting this claim, or taking for granted that a rising latecomer is inevitably dissatisfied with the existing international order. Both types of mistake can produce unwarranted policies, resulting possibly in self-defeating or self-fulfilling prophecies.

In different ways the propositions advanced in the following discussion may not resonate with the hopes or expectations of either the Chinese or the American people. I argue that despite China's recent growth, it is still far behind the U.S. and that it will assume a relatively low profile in international relations, trying to avoid and postpone a direct confrontation with the U.S. I also argue that despite self-characterization as a satisfied status-quo power, the U.S. seeks to transform the international system. Moreover, I contend that absent extreme provocation, the neighbors of a rising power do not generally organize themselves into a balancing coalition. In addition, contrary to the power-transition theory's expectation, wars are more likely to be initiated by a declining power than by a rising state. Whereas the Anglo-German rivalry prior to 1914 has provided a popular example among many Americans concerned about the destabilizing dynamics of real or prospective power transitions, the analogy suggested by Germany's worries about an emergent Russian/Soviet colossus has received less attention. Some historical parallels are more easily recalled and provide more congenial ideational construction than others.[10] Presumably, one is more inclined to invoke or apply those analogies that are graphic (even traumatic), occurred recently, and reflect direct personal experience (or involving one's close associates).

To the extent that there are people in Beijing and Washington who share a common belief in an ongoing power transition leading to a likely or even inevitable showdown, it is critical to examine the relevant historical precedents and analytic logic involved in their reasoning. As already noted, I offer alternative interpretations to the conventional wisdom. My hope is that these alternative interpretations make good sense and can hence help to avoid misperceptions contributing to conflict.

I thank several anonymous reviewers and colleagues who have offered suggestions and comments on earlier drafts of this work in whole and in parts. As noted in subsequent citations, some of the ideas discussed below have originally appeared in the pages of *Asian Survey, Conflict and Cooperation, International Relations of the Asia-Pacific, Issues & Studies, Security Studies,* and *World Affairs.*

1 Introduction

The basic arguments

States rise and fall in their international status. Some emerge as the premier powers and even hegemons of their day, while others drop out of the ranks of leading states and even suffer a loss of their statehood. In contrast to the fate of Spain, Italy, Austria-Hungary, and the Ottoman Empire, others sometimes manage to recover their great-power position as Germany did after World War I and China appears to be doing now. Naturally, the processes and consequences of changes at the top of the international hierarchy are a matter of significant interest to officials and scholars alike. There was, for instance, in the 1970s a debate about the extent and implications of America's relative decline, a debate that has ironically been replaced in the 1990s by questions about the endurance of the U.S. "unipolar moment."[1] As suggested by popular titles such as *Le Défi Américain* and *Japan as Number 1*,[2] it is not unnatural for concerned observers to call policy and public attention to foreign rivals seemingly poised to mount a serious challenge to one's global position.

Surely, efforts aimed at understanding better the rise and fall of nations have been a central and enduring part of research on comparative politics and international relations, involving colleagues from different disciplines. Max Weber's account of the Protestant ethic and Paul Kennedy's explanation of imperial overstretch come to mind as leading examples of scholarship addressing the causes of national growth and decline.[3] Others, such as political scientists Charles Doran and George Modelski,[4] have inquired about the consequences that follow from the differential rates of expansion or contraction of national power, especially with respect to the danger of global war.

This book is concerned about the international implications of China's rapid rise in recent years. What does this development augur for Sino-American relations and for global stability? I plan to pursue this inquiry by taking advantage of leading theories in international relations, thereby treating the case of China in the context of national comparisons and historical patterns. At the same time, I hope to address critically the extent to which the standard interpretations offered by researchers can satisfactorily inform our understanding about China. On several matters of fact or interpretation, I propose a revisionist perspective departing from the prevailing wisdom in both international relations research and China studies.

Historical analogies can provide a useful basis for understanding. Some have suggested that those in charge of contemporary Sino-American relations can benefit from studying the dynamics of Anglo-German rivalry a century ago.[5] Others have tried to synthesize a larger number of historical episodes in order to formulate a more generalizable statement. Among such formulations, the theory of power transition has offered a leading analytic perspective and a robust research program.[6] The respect and popularity accorded to this theory follow from a substantial number of studies seeking to validate its empirical derivations.[7] Thus, it seems natural that Sinologists as well as others with different field specializations are drawn to this theory. This attraction extends not just to Americans but also to their Chinese colleagues, therefore suggesting a common framework of reference for their dialogue.[8] This book focuses on this discourse pertaining to power transition, and seeks to develop and clarify further the relevant analytic logic and conceptual basis in the hope of understanding better the policy and theoretical implications of China's recent ascendance in the international system.

What is the central claim of the power-transition theory? It contends that when a revisionist latecomer overtakes an erstwhile leader of the international system, war looms. War is likely to be precipitated by the faster-growing upstart in its attempt to displace the declining hegemon. The Anglo-German rivalry is supposed to exemplify this dynamic that eventually ended in the outbreak of World Wars I and II. Similarly, France's decline relative to Prussia is taken to have set the stage for their war of 1870.[9] Contrary to the view that a balance of power between the major states provides a basis for peace and stability, the theory of power transition argues that the approach to a more symmetric relationship and especially the occurrence of a positional reversal between the two top states augur increased bilateral tension which in turn has the potential of engulfing other countries in a system-wide conflict. The logic of the power-transition theory naturally raises the concern that China's recent rapid growth portends more turmoil for the international system and the danger of heightened discord, even military collision, between Beijing and Washington.[10]

The brief stylized account given above presumes a shared understanding about what makes a state powerful. It would of course be difficult to assess relative changes in national power absent an agreement about the nature of this power. Therefore, when people speak about an ongoing or impending power transition, it is pertinent to inquire about the empirical indicators they are using. That is, what is the nature of their evidence? Although territorial or demographic size may be a factor, it would surely not be a decisive one because, according to these measures, Russia and China would remain the most powerful countries throughout the contemporary era. If one chooses to emphasize military power, for example by focusing on the number of a country's military personnel or the size of its defense budget, the U.K. has never been the world's premier power according to these criteria. Moreover, the entire notion of any ongoing or pending power transition involving the U.S. becomes far-fetched, as this country has been spending more on the military than the rest of the world *combined*.

One could perhaps turn to economic size or productivity as another way to track changing national status. It is worth noting, however, that the U.S. had overtaken the U.K. as the world's largest economy before World War I. According to this criterion, prior to 1914 a power transition had occurred between the U.S. and the U.K. and not between the U.K. and Germany, if one is to focus on the displacement of a previously dominant state by a latecomer. Moreover, the Anglo-American transition was peaceful, even though it was not entirely without acrimony. Measured by their respective economic size, Germany prior to World War II and the USSR since that conflict never came close to challenging the U.S. lead. It also does not appear that the U.S. economy is in any imminent danger of being overtaken by the Chinese economy (certainly not in terms of per capita income which may be used as an approximation of a citizenry's productivity), even though the latter's size has recently grown rapidly from a relatively low base. Finally, if one emphasizes a state's pioneering and dominant status in developing leading economic sectors, one would again be hard pressed to argue that China is capable currently or in the foreseeable future of competing with the U.S. in fostering scientific discovery and technological innovation.[11]

These issues naturally require those concerned about power transitions to be more specific about the capability attribute(s) they have in mind when speaking about power shifts among the world's leading states. Without a clear specification of these attributes, one can hardly begin to assess when power transitions have occurred historically and whether any is currently taking place in Sino-American relations. Vague and/or shifting empirical referents cause confusing and even arbitrary arguments about when power transitions occur and what consequences they entail. Although people can have reasonable disagreements about which indicators give the most valid or reliable information about national power, it is necessary for them to be clear and consistent about the ones they do use to reach their judgments. In Chapter 2, I explore different measures of national power for any evidence of an ongoing or impending power transition involving China. This analysis shows that the U.S. has a vast lead in those capabilities that are critical in determining future economic growth and productivity. It is also militarily much stronger than China or, for that matter, any other country or conceivable combination of countries.

Just as important as the need to be explicit about the nature of national power to be used for monitoring any approaching power transition, one would want to know the identity of those states whose changing status is supposed to affect global peace and stability. Changes involving the relative positions of minor states would not presumably precipitate a transformation of the entire international system. The original formulation of the power-transition theory addresses the relative positions of the world's two most powerful states or, at most, those three states that are designated as the main contenders in the "central system" of international relations. It seems, however, a little odd for this formulation to deny this status to the U.S. before 1945, as Washington's entry to both World Wars was arguably the most important determinant of these conflicts' eventual outcome. Indeed, by the 1870s the U.S. had already overtaken the U.K. as the world's largest economy and the home for its most dynamic industries.[12] Does contemporary China qualify for the status of a contender for world leadership in view of the denial of this status to the U.S. until 1945? Do Japan, Germany, and Russia qualify today? These questions are not idle because had the U.S. been recognized as a central contender prior to 1914, Germany's overtaking of the U.K. would not have qualified as a positional reversal between the world's two largest economies. Moreover, if the theory's domain is extended to address the upward or downward mobility of the lesser great powers, one would then have to account for Russia's economy being recently overtaken by those of Japan, Germany, and China without engendering any threat of a war occurring between these pairs of countries. One is therefore led to infer that some power transitions (e.g., the Anglo-German case) are more dangerous for the world's peace and stability than others (e.g., the Anglo-American case).

But why should this be so? Presumably this is because states make strategic choices, and officials and scholars construct realities. The issue of which states should or should not be accorded the status of a central contender in the international system involves more than just a matter of definitional consistency. It reflects the strategic conduct of statecraft and the interpretation of social reality by officials and scholars alike. When faced with potential challengers in the Western Hemisphere and Europe, the U.K. chose to appease the U.S. and oppose Germany. These decisions by London are supposed to reflect its closer cultural or political affinity with the U.S. than with Germany. But the argument of affinity will hardly suffice to explain London's decision to recruit Japan as a junior partner in the Asia Pacific during the late 1800s and early 1900s, or why it found itself supporting Czarist Russia in World War I. It has also been argued that the status-quo orientation or the democratic characteristic of a rising power's regime should make its ascendance less threatening to the leading state and less destabilizing for the international system.[13]

These propositions, however, would naturally raise the question of what should be the appropriate indicators for status-quo orientation and democratic governance. How can one distinguish a status-quo power from a revisionist power? In what sense was the U.S. more status-quo oriented than Germany in the last three decades of the nineteenth century? In addition, when is the democratic nature of an upstart regime supposed to preserve peace, and when is it likely to precipitate war? One would presumably want to stipulate *ex ante* these attributions as opposed to engaging in *post hoc* construction after the occurrence of war when the identity of the belligerents has become known.[14] Whereas the U.S. and the U.K. settled the Venezuelan and Alaskan boundary disputes peacefully in the late 1800s, Washington sought a confrontation with Spain in an effort to displace the latter's influence in the Western Hemisphere. Spain has been classified as a great power with even some democratic institutional features,[15] but its being overtaken by the U.S. was hardly peaceful. How can a rising power's regime character account for the different outcomes of the Anglo-American and Spanish–American transitions? In Chapter 3 I address how the application of the logic of power transition may be influenced by political and ideational motivations.

The power-transition theory sees the faster-growing latecomer as inclined to challenge the status quo and, therefore, to pose a threat to international stability. The concept of status quo and the related ideas of satisfaction and dissatisfaction with the international system, however, are fraught with ambiguity.[16] In Chapter 3 I argue that contrary to the suggestion of power-transition theory, one should not automatically assume that a hegemon wants to defend and preserve the status quo. American officials have declared publicly their intent to transform the international system in the interest of spreading democracy and promoting capitalism. Whether one agrees or disagrees with these goals, Washington's stated agenda of seeking "regime change" abroad does not quite correspond with the attribution of a "status-quo orientation" according to this term's conventional meaning. In contrast to Washington's avowed objective of encouraging congenial changes in other countries' political and economic systems, China professes its allegiance to the Westphalian precepts of state sovereignty, territorial integrity, and non-interference in others' domestic affairs. If the officials' public statements mean anything, they would suggest a reversal of the standard attribution made by American writers, designating the U.S. as a status-quo power and China as a revisionist power.

In Chapter 3 I discuss how one may be able to discern the status-quo orientation of different great powers. Besides looking for indicators showing the extent to which a country is in or out of step with the international community and the extent to which it is committed to multilateral diplomacy and global norms, I offer some survey data that provide a glimpse of how people in other countries perceive the threat to world peace posed by Washington and Beijing respectively. As will be seen, the standard designations offered by American scholars of international relations, including those applying the power-transition theory, are at substantial odds with these data. Whereas it is typically taken for granted in standard American scholarship that the U.S. is a satisfied power committed to the existing international order and the stability of the international system, this view is not supported by the available empirical evidence or by the perceptions of people living in other countries. Rather than seeing China and even the so-called rogue states (Iraq, Iran, and North Korea) as the principal threat to world peace, the public in even those European states traditionally friendly to the U.S. tends to locate the source of this danger in Washington.

Power-transition theory suggests that wars are caused by a rising latecomer's challenge to the existing hegemon in a bid to capture the latter's pre-eminent position in the international system. But why would this latecomer want to precipitate a confrontation if, with the passage of time, differential growth rates would make it more powerful than the erstwhile leader? It seems that a rational challenger would want to postpone such a confrontation in the hope that it will become stronger over time. It may even be able to achieve hegemony without having to incur the costs of waging a war if the erstwhile leader accepts its inevitable decline. In contrast to this putative challenger, a hegemon in relative decline would have an incentive to start a preventive war. Assuming that the challenger's hostility is unalterable and expecting that its own position will suffer a deep and irreversible setback, the dominant but declining power should prefer to fight an earlier rather than a later war. This state's relative power will only deteriorate further if it postpones an inevitable showdown with the upstart. This logic argues that wars tend to be started by a declining but still stronger hegemon, and not by a rising challenger. This attribution is controversial because it reassigns the source of instability from the latecomer to the dominant power. It certainly contradicts the prevailing view that systemic war is more likely to originate from the former than from the latter. Yet, as I argue in Chapter 4, this prevailing view departs from rationalist explanations of war, and it also contradicts what we know about how people respond to prospective gains and losses in their personal lives.[17]

In Chapter 5 I take up several historical cases in order to show how structural conditions influenced a declining state's decision to wage a preventive war or, alternatively, to seek accommodation and retrenchment. I offer a revisionist interpretation of World Wars I and II, arguing that these conflicts can be more reasonably explained as an attempt by Germany to confront Russia/the USSR's rising power rather than that country's challenge to British dominance.[18] At the same time I show that preventive war is not the only or even the most likely policy available to a state whose power has peaked. Whereas Germany was motivated by the logic of preventive war in 1914 and again in 1939, the U.K. chose to appease the U.S. in the Western Hemisphere from the 1890s on and, more recently, the USSR under Mikhail Gorbachev accepted retrenchment and concessions to the West. The historical circumstances surrounding these different responses to relative decline point to the influence of structural conditions in shaping policy choices. I conclude Chapter 5 by arguing that power transitions do not always end in war. Whether these processes turn out to be peaceful or violent, however, does not appear to be related to the nature of the overtaking regime or the one being overtaken. Contrary to popular expectation, an authoritarian regime does not necessarily resort to war when faced with the prospect or reality of facing a sharp demotion in its international status. Conversely, even in the absence of an ongoing or impending positional reversal working to its disadvantage, a democracy can attack a weaker adversary by recourse to the logic of preventive war.[19]

I return to the concept of "satisfaction" or "dissatisfaction" in Chapter 6. It is puzzling why the accumulation of power by a rising latecomer and its improved status in the international hierarchy do not turn it into a more satisfied country. That is, why does this country remain dissatisfied even after it has joined the ranks of the most powerful states in the world? In the standard rendition of the power-transition theory and other similar formulations, rising states such as Napoleonic France, Wilhelmine and Nazi Germany, Czarist Russia and communist USSR, and militarist Japan remained unhappy with their international status despite their upward mobility, and their unmitigated dissatisfaction and enormous ambition motivated them to initiate war. Imperial Britain and democratic U.S., however, are typically seen as satisfied or status-quo powers during their periods of initial ascendance and subsequent dominance, and they are therefore not supposed to present a threat to the other states or to destabilize the international system. This attribution seems odd in view of the fact that both the U.K. and the U.S. made huge territorial acquisitions after 1815 (the year of the Congress of Vienna, marking the beginning of the modern international system), and have been involved in more wars and militarized interstate disputes than the other great powers.[20]

In Chapter 6 I argue that the ideas of "satisfaction" and "dissatisfaction" should be linked more specifically to the benefits a state is receiving from the international system. A state may be dissatisfied with its pay-off under the current system without necessarily raising fundamental objections to its rules. Thus, the ideas of "dissatisfaction" and "revisionism" (or anti-status-quo orientation) should not be conflated. Power-transition theory proposes that when a dissatisfied state is poised to overtake the hegemon, the danger of systemic war heightens. I formulate a different argument, claiming that the combination of dissatisfaction and rising power is not the basic cause for war. Rather, I submit that wars will not pay for any state (including the ascending latecomer) unless it expects to improve its current benefits from the system. Whether or not this expectation is warranted depends on the extent to which its current benefits are less than what its current power assets would entitle it to. The greater this discrepancy, the more a state can expect to gain from going to war. I explore the implications of this formulation, including the application of appeasement by a declining hegemon and the decision by a surging latecomer to defer the full adjustment of its benefit share.[21] One of the more important and, in some ways, contrarian propositions derived from this discussion is that a latecomer still experiencing rapid growth is more easily appeased than one whose growth has slowed or even stopped. Thus, China's continued growth should introduce a stabilizing rather than destabilizing influence for international relations.

Given the prevailing view that international instability originates from a rising, revisionist state, it is unsurprising that much of the discourse in current U.S. commentaries emphasizes efforts either to check China's power ascent or to reform its regime and society. In Chapter 7 I take on a critical examination of the premises pertaining to the competing advice to contain China or to engage it.[22] The proponents of containment appear to face several constraining considerations. Domestic factors tend to be more important sources of national growth than external factors. Moreover, the Phoenix phenomenon suggests that states previously defeated in a war are usually able to resume their prewar growth trajectory in a reasonably short time. In addition, the neighbors of a rising state do not typically form a coalition in order to balance it. This coalition usually results from repeated aggression by a state whose pattern of behavior leaves its neighbors no option but to fight back, or when such behavior exacerbates these neighbors' security concerns to such an extent that they are energized to abandon their neutrality.[23] As for the proponents of engagement, their logic is often (though not always) based on the hope of influencing a target regime's values and interests, or to create points of bargaining leverage in order to obtain political compliance or conformity. The propositions that increased economic and cultural contact with the U.S. will bring about a change in Beijing's policy agenda and priorities, and that the implied threat to suspend this contact may be used to extract concessions for reform, raise important empirical and even normative issues. The discussion in Chapter 7 introduces considerations derived from studies on the application of economic statecraft for political power, and also those more closely associated with Marxian ideas about economic dependency, social penetration, and cultural cooptation.[24]

Standard U.S. analyses, especially those coming from the "China threat" school, tend to assume that as China becomes stronger, it would adopt a more active and confrontational posture in opposing U.S. interests and resisting American domination.[25] In Chapter 8 I submit that Beijing's management of U.S. hegemony will not likely follow the typical emphasis placed on "internal balancing" (that is, armament) or "external balancing" (that is, alliance formation) in standard realist writings on how states seek to enhance their security.[26] Rather, I expect Beijing to pursue stratagems aimed at deflecting direct U.S. pressure and avoiding a frontal collision. Evasion, entrapment, and even engagement are hypothesized to represent the more salient aspects of Beijing's efforts to cope with U.S. hegemony. If this prognosis is correct, the Chinese leaders will not behave in the fashion of a cocky, rash upstart portrayed in some discussions of power transition. They would want to avoid provoking the U.S. Should a confrontation occur, it would not be because Beijing has wanted to challenge the U.S. Rather, it would be because Beijing has been unable to prevent the U.S. from becoming engaged. A parallel may be drawn from War World I. Far from seeking a confrontation with the U.K., Germany had wanted but was unable to keep the U.K. on the sideline. In Chapter 8 I attempt to show that my characterization of Beijing's strategy for dealing with Washington's pre-eminence and for managing its own ascent in the international system accords with some strong strands in traditional Chinese thought and with the revised logic applied to the power-transition theory.

Major wars in history typically stem from third-party conflicts that escalate and engulf the two most powerful states rather than from head-on confrontations between them as suggested by the power-transition theory. The Peloponnesian War, the Thirty Years' War, World War I, and World War II all share this similarity. In Chapter 9 I analyze how failures in extended deterrence have contributed to the contagion of major wars in the past, and study the seemingly puzzling position adopted by the U.S. with respect to Taiwan. Washington's posture of "strategic ambiguity" is obviously contrary to the emphasis placed on either "sunk costs" or "tied hands" in standard discourse on deterrence strategy.[27] I argue that significantly, this posture implies tacit bargaining and mutual partisan adjustment by the U.S., China, and even Taiwan. My interpretation implies a common awareness by all parties about the constraints imposed by the others' domestic politics and realistic policy adjustment in view of these constraints. Although the danger of escalation cannot be overlooked, the parties have also seemed to become increasingly adroit in their communication and coordination to avoid a breakdown of relationship. If correct, this view suggests learning and adaptation so that the insecurities and rigidities characteristic of some past deterrence encounters may be more easily managed, if not entirely overcome. Still, I argue that both history and logic suggest that an extended deterrence can fail even if the defender has both the capability and the will to intervene on behalf of its protégé. What is missing in much of the current discussion is the expected gain a challenger may hope to achieve by making a move, even in the face of its knowledge of a defender's power and resolve, and its expected loss if it decides not to act. By applying the logic of selection, I advance several propositions about extended deterrence in the Taiwan Strait that tend to differ from, if not necessarily contradict, the prevailing wisdom.

Chapter 10 summarizes the main theoretical propositions and policy implications from the previous discussion. I advance an epistemological argument and a substantive argument. I argue that epistemologically, it is important not to treat China's rise as an isolated or special case. Rather, it behooves us to analyze this case in a comparative and historical context, seeking to understand the capabilities and motivations of China's contemporary counterparts and the experience of ascending and declining states that had preceded China's recent re-emergence. Substantively, I argue that the U.S. is likely to continue its historically unprecedented preponderance, and that predictions of a Sino-American power transition are unlikely to materialize in the next three or so decades at the earliest, if at all. Yet, even in the absence of a power transition, China may clash with the U.S. over Taiwan – and not because Beijing is dissatisfied with the current trends or because it doubts Washington's capabilities or resolve to defend Taiwan. A desire to avoid a serious loss of domestic support and legitimacy in the context of increased mass political participation and elite competition is likely to reduce Beijing's inclination to accommodate or negotiate if Taipei declares *de jure* independence. As a growing power that seeks a stable environment to continue its growth, I contend that Beijing is unlikely to want to disturb the international or regional status quo or the one prevailing over the Taiwan Strait. A challenge to the latter status quo is more likely to originate from Taipei during an administration of the Democratic Progressive Party than from Beijing. In the concluding Chapter 10, I also explain why the power-transition perspective offers a useful framework to conduct a general discussion of international relations. Moreover, I show important areas of agreement between this study and earlier formulations of the power-transition perspective. Finally, I offer some policy implications from my study.

The power-transition theory blends structure and agency in developing its explanations, predictions, and implied prescriptions.[28] This combination offers a healthy antidote to a common tendency by people to use different interpretative logic when explaining their own behavior and the behavior of others. People are inclined to offer situational reasons when accounting for their behavior that others dislike, but are instead likely to resort to dispositional attributions when interpreting others' unwanted behavior.[29] Thus, one tends to blame circumstances beyond one's control for dictating a course of action that others find objectionable, but is prone to see malevolent intention ("inherent hostility" or "bad faith") when someone else behaves in a similar manner. For example, notwithstanding obvious geographic similarities and parallels in attempts at extended deterrence, Chinese military and diplomatic moves against Taiwan are usually seen to be motivated by coercive and offensive intents whereas far more aggressive actions taken by the U.S. against Cuba (e.g., invasion at the Bay of Pigs, blockade against Soviet missiles, repeated assassination plots against Fidel Castro, protracted and ongoing economic embargo) are typically explained by recourse to structural imperatives such as the need to oppose a hostile neighbor, resist external encroachment, and preserve hegemonic influence in one's home region. The relative emphasis given to situational and dispositional attributions is often reversed when interpreting actions that may be construed as friendly. For instance, non-violent power transitions may be attributed to one's own peaceful disposition in one case (e.g., the U.S. overtaking the U.K. in the 1870s) but to the other's limited capabilities in another (e.g., the USSR being overtaken by Japan more recently). When such biases are pervasive, it is difficult for either side of a relationship to reassure and conciliate with the other.[30] In the following discussion, I present views of international relations structure and agency that are often at odds with the prevailing wisdom. My hope is that this presentation will encourage constructive theoretical and policy debates, resulting in a more balanced perspective and sound understanding of international relations and, hopefully, also more prudent statecraft by the officials of those powerful states that dominate these relations.

2 Power scores and the identity of central contenders

Power-transition theory is about a contest for world primacy by the most powerful states and, as such, it is concerned with these states' power positions in the global context. It is concerned with relative national power. As a result of this concern, it requires researchers to have access to some reasonably intersubjective and accurate indicator(s) of "power."[1] In the absence of such indicator(s), one would not be able to gauge and track the relative positions of states.

There is a voluminous literature discussing the sources and exercise of national power, for example a state's ability to influence others' decision processes and shape their policy agendas, or possession and production of tangible and intangible assets. I eschew a thorough discussion of national power, and present in the interest of conserving space a straightforward profiling of states in terms of those attributes commonly taken by people to represent the basis for status and influence in international relations.

A good place to begin our inquiry would be to turn to the Correlates of War (COW) Project. This project has produced a systematic data series consisting of several pertinent national attributes dating back to the Congress of Vienna in 1815.[2] The COW researchers sought to collect data on the size of a state's total population, its urban population, its military personnel, its defense expenditures, its iron and steel production, and its energy consumption. They determined a state's relative share of each of these indicators of national power in the international system, and took the average of these shares to come up with an aggregate measure called Composite Index of National Capability (CINC).[3] Table 2.1 gives the CINC scores for the world's ten largest economies in 2004, after adjustment has been made for purchasing-power parity. These scores are given for the years 1860, 1880, and 1900, and then at every five-year interval from 1946 on.

At the end of the CINC time series in 2001, the U.S. still had the highest score (15 percent of the global aggregate) although China (with 13.4 percent) was not far behind. Both countries were substantially ahead of the third-ranking state, India. Over the period 1946 to 2001, the U.S. lead over China had shrunk significantly from approximately a three-to-one advantage in favor of the U.S. to a rough parity. This change, however, was due more to a relative decline experienced by the U.S. than a successful catch-up by China. Whereas the U.S. was vastly more powerful than the other major states in 1946 (commanding 36.4 percent of the

Table 2.1 Composite Index of National Capability

Year	U.S.	China	Japan	India	Germany	U.K.	France	Italy	Brazil	Russia
1860	.077	.174	.025	—	.052	.276	.122	.029	.008	.089
1880	.125	.163	.021	—	.106	.218	.108	.032	.009	.104
1900	.188	.120	.029	—	.132	.178	.075	.028	.009	.109
1946	.364	.133	—	—	—	.116	.031	.018	.013	.123
1951	.320	.104	—	.050	—	.059	.033	.018	.012	.173
1956	.261	.098	.032	.045	.038	.049	.033	.018	.011	.170
1961	.211	.105	.039	.049	.041	.040	.030	.020	.013	.174
1966	.209	.110	.043	.052	.037	.035	.026	.021	.015	.167
1971	.171	.112	.054	.053	.034	.028	.024	.021	.018	.172
1976	.143	.116	.055	.054	.033	.027	.024	.020	.020	.176
1981	.139	.118	.051	.052	.029	.025	.022	.019	.023	.169
1986	.137	.111	.049	.057	.026	.023	.018	.017	.026	.174
1991	.137	.114	.053	.062	.030	.026	.021	.019	.024	.102
1996	.143	.126	.052	.067	.030	.025	.023	.019	.027	.059
2001	.150	.134	.051	.068	.028	.023	.020	.018	.025	.055

Source: National Material Capabilities (v3.0) available at http://cow2.la.psu.edu.

Note
Figures from 1951 to 1986 refer to West Germany.

global aggregate of the CINC tallies), its share had diminished to only 15 percent in 2001. Conversely, China's CINC score was basically unchanged between 1946 and 2001 (13.3 percent vs. 13.4 percent). The important impression conveyed by Table 2.1, however, is that the U.S. and China are indeed the two most powerful states in contemporary international relations, and that the distance separating these two states' power positions has clearly narrowed over recent years. In other words, the CINC data would support the view of an ongoing process which, if not arrested, will produce a reversal of positions between the U.S. and China in the not-too-distant future.

The data reported in Table 2.1 also tell, or fail to tell, several other important details. The CINC scores for Russia would suggest that the USSR had overtaken the U.S. by 1971, and that the USSR was the most powerful state in the world (in 1986) shortly before the collapse of the Soviet empire in Eastern Europe. The CINC data gave no hint of the protracted stagnation and subsequent severe decline experienced by Moscow during the 1970s and 1980s, and they only reported Russia's misfortune after the fact (in 1991, when the Soviet Union itself disintegrated).

The CINC data were obviously not very sensitive to relative economic performance. Thus, not only did they miss the contraction of the Soviet economy, they also overlooked the rapid growth achieved by Japan and West Germany in the 1960s and 1970s. Japan's CINC score was actually lower in 2001 than in 1971, and the score for a reunited Germany was lower in 2001 than West Germany's score in 1956. According to the CINC scores, these countries' relative power had fallen during the intervening years.

While the CINC data appear to suggest an impending power transition between the U.S. and China, they also show that such positional reversals had already taken place among some other pairs of states included in Table 2.1. For example, China overtook Russia in 1991, and in 1996 India and Brazil overtook Russia and the U.K. respectively. Earlier, the U.K. also suffered a loss of its lead to Germany by 1961 and to Japan by 1966. Going back further in history, China led the U.S. in CINC scores during much of the nineteenth century. The U.S. managed to edge out China only by 1890, with a score of 16.5 percent versus 15.6 percent.

Given imperfect data and the fallibility of human judgment, one could hardly claim any precision in locating the exact moment when one state became more powerful than another. One could only reasonably point to general trends and approximate rates of change pertaining to the various components of national power. Nevertheless, the discussion thus far helps to underscore three points. First, positional reversals have occurred rather frequently in history if one is willing to consider such changes beyond just the two most powerful states. Second, most power transitions between pairs of great powers did not result in war. Thus, although a power transition may be a necessary condition for war, it is certainly not a sufficient condition.[4] Third, the CINC data contradict our historical understanding in important ways, such as when they miss the downturn in Soviet power and when they suggest that the USSR was more powerful than the U.S. during the 1970s and 1980s. Surely the nature and sources of national power have changed since the nineteenth century. As a result, several components that went into building the CINC measure have become obsolescent, and they contributed to creating misleading impressions about relative national influence and capabilities.

Because of their large population and territory, China and Russia/the USSR are accorded a higher value by the CINC measure of national power than they deserve. The other components of the CINC measure (specifically the amount of iron and steel produced, the amount of coal and fossil fuel consumed, and the number of personnel enlisted in the armed forces) tend to have the same bias, causing an increasing distortion over time. Economic competitiveness in contemporary times has come to depend more on human capital and information technology. Similarly, preparation for modern warfare nowadays requires the development and deployment of smart weapons. Thus, one may argue that whereas the CINC measure provides a reasonable basis for gauging relative national power in the nineteenth century and perhaps even in the first half of the twentieth century, it has lost much of its validity at the start of the twenty-first century.[5]

As an alternative, one may consider a country's gross domestic product (in U.S. dollar equivalent of purchasing-power parity (PPP)), its military expenditures (in current U.S. dollars), and its total number of internet hosts. These variables represent approximations of the economic, military, and technological dimensions of national power in contemporary international relations. Table 2.2 presents estimates reported by the U.S. Central Intelligence Agency (CIA).[6] These figures show that the U.S. and China had the world's largest economies in 2004. The U.S. economy, however, was about 1.6 times larger than China's.

Table 2.2 Three dimensions of national power, 2004: economic, military, and technological

Country	Gross domestic product in PPP (trillions)	Gross domestic product in current $ (trillions)	Military expenditures in current $ (trillions)	Internet hosts (millions)
U.S.	$11,750	$10,949*	$371	115.3
China	$7,262	$1,591	$67	0.16
Japan	$3,745	$4,301	$46	13.0
India	$3,319	$663	$17	0.09
Germany	$2,362	$2,403*	$35	2.7
U.K.	$1,782	$1,795*	$43	3.4
France	$1,737	$1,757*	$45	2.4
Italy	$1,609	$1,468*	$28	1.4
Brazil	$1,492	$470	$11	3.2
Russia	$1,408	$553	n.a.	0.6
Canada	$1,023	$857*	$9	3.2
Mexico	$1,006	$626*	$6	1.3

Sources: The 2005 *World Factbook* at www.cia.gov/cia/publications/factbook, and World Development Indicators available at http://devdata.worldbank.org/dataonline.

Notes
*2003

Even when China's economy is combined with Japan's (the world's third largest economy), the U.S. economy would still be bigger. Similarly, the U.S. economy was bigger in 2004 than the combined economic size of all the twenty-five countries belonging to the European Union.

Turning our attention from size to rate of change, one may wish to ask how long it would take China to overtake the U.S. given the different assumptions about their respective future rates of growth. If the U.S. economy were to remain at the level estimated by the CIA for 2003 (in other words, assuming no growth at all for the U.S. economy), and if the Chinese economy were to grow consistently at an annual rate of 5 percent, it would take ten years for the latter to overtake the former after adjustment is made for purchasing-power parity. Alternatively, if one assumes that the U.S. economy were to expand at a rate of 3.5 percent and the Chinese economy were to grow at 8.5 percent, it would take eleven years for this overtaking to occur. Under both sets of assumptions, a power transition appears to be likely in the near future. According to the power-transition theory, the overtaking of a dominant state by a latecomer "may take several decades."[7]

It is important to recognize that the extrapolations given above rely on estimates of purchasing-power parity. These estimates are notoriously difficult to make, and analysts using different methods and assumptions may reach very different figures.[8] Table 2.2 includes the gross domestic product of the leading states without adjusting for purchasing-power parity. Stated in current U.S. dollars, the World Bank estimated the Chinese economy to have reached $1,591 trillion in 2004. This figure was raised by about 450 percent if the CIA's conversion for purchasing-power parity is accepted. In the absence of this conversion, the gap separating the U.S. and Chinese economies would be much larger. Whereas this disparity was 160 percent in favor of the U.S. in 2004 when stated in purchasing-power parity, it increased to about 690 percent in terms of current dollars. Accordingly, one's assessment of the occurrence of a power transition and the speed at which this transition is occurring depend to a very large extent on the validity assigned to the procedures for estimating purchasing-power parity. In their original work, the authors of *The War Ledger* accepted gross national product unadjusted for purchasing-power parity as the most appropriate indicator of national power.[9]

Most projections of China's gross domestic product show that it will probably reach a size comparable to that of the U.S. by 2050.[10] Under some postulated scenarios, it is projected that the Chinese economy could become larger than the U.S. economy by that year. However, under all the alternative scenarios examined by Emilo Casetti, the U.S. gross domestic product per capita is projected to remain higher than the Chinese figure. This means that the Americans will continue to enjoy a much higher productivity level than the Chinese.

Because experts tend to disagree among themselves about the most appropriate approach to be used for making these estimates, it seems all the more reasonable to introduce additional measures that can complement economic variables such as gross domestic product. Accordingly, Table 2.2 also presents the leading economies' military expenditures (in current U.S. dollars). These estimates, again based on the CIA, show that in 2004 the U.S. outspent China by over 550 percent. Indeed, the U.S. committed more resources to defense spending than the combined total for all the other countries included in Table 2.2. To the extent that military expenditure serves as a useful proxy of a country's ability to defend itself against physical coercion or, conversely, to apply physical coercion against others, the U.S. is in a very enviable position. It is the only power that has a truly global reach. No other state – or combination of states – even approaches the pre-eminence enjoyed by the U.S. in military assets. Analysts generally agree that China will remain in the foreseeable future substantially behind the U.S. on this dimension of national power.[11]

Table 2.2 introduces yet a third indicator of national power, one that seeks to gauge a state's technological capability in the information era. The number of internet hosts provides an approximate measure of this capability. Again, on this dimension of national power, the U.S. commands a huge lead over the rest of the world. It had almost 900 percent more internet hosts than Japan which ranked second on this variable. The U.S. had about 720 times more internet hosts than China. Again, no other country – or combination of countries – could even come close to matching the U.S. on this dimension of information technology. Because modern economies and armed forces depend heavily on the application and development of such technology, this U.S. advantage augurs well for its continued dominance in economic and military competitiveness. Scholars such as George Modelski and William R. Thompson have argued that a leading state's ability to foster innovative technologies has been the key determinant of its global status.[12] Global leadership has historically been derived from and sustained by technological pioneership rather than by a large military presence or population – or even a large economy. Therefore, in the words of one leading analyst, "China's ability to catch up with American economic and strategic power is very much in doubt." Rather than being faced with a power transition, "the combination of U.S. technology and military policy is expanding America's comprehensive superiority over China."[13]

Of course, national power can also consist of more intangible qualities such as the extent to which foreigners find a country's mass culture, political institutions, and education system especially appealing or congenial. These qualities point to a country's "soft power" to coopt or convert others so that they are disposed to share its beliefs and adopt its practices.[14] In Table 2.3, I report two indicators that tend to reflect a country's "soft power." The number of foreign students studying in a country offers an approximate indication of the attraction of its education system. In this regard, the U.S. has clearly been the premier destination for those who wish to study abroad. American institutions of higher learning have attracted far more foreign students than have their European counterparts. The number of foreign tourists and visitors hosted by a country presents another informative, albeit imperfect, measure of its attraction abroad. Again, the U.S. ranks very high on this variable even though it is more difficult for foreigners to travel to the U.S. than to those European countries located in close physical proximity to each other. Moreover, in the wake of the 9/11 terrorist incident, stricter visa requirements would also have reduced the number of tourists and visitors arriving in the U.S. Yet, as may be seen from Table 2.3, more foreigners traveled to the U.S. in 2002 than to any other country except France.

Table 2.3 Foreign students and tourists/visitors

Country	Number of foreign students	Number of foreign tourists/visitors (in 1000s, 2002)
U.S.	453,785 (1995/96)	41,892
China	n.a.	36,803
India	n.a.	2,384
Germany	165,977 (1996/97)	17,911
U.K.	198,839 (1996/97)	24,180
France	138,191 (1995/96)	77,012
Italy	24,858 (1996/97)	39,799
Brazil	n.a.	3,783
Russia	73,172 (1994/95)	7,943
Canada	n.a	20,057
Mexico	n.a.	19,667

Sources: *UNESCO Statistical Yearbook 1999* (Paris: UNESCO Publishing and Bernan Press, 1999), vol. II, pp. 486–499; and *United Nations Statistical Yearbook 2004* (New York: United Nations, 2004), pp. 766–773.

To the extent that an emphasis on the quality rather than quantity of national assets is warranted, the most succinct indicator (albeit one that is not without distortions, such as when applied to the oil-exporting countries) is a country's gross national product per capita. This indicator summarizes the productivity of a people. Obviously, if a smaller population produces as much as or more economic value than a larger population, then members of the former group must be better at doing what they do.[15] The leading states in earlier eras, such as Portugal, the Netherlands, and the U.K., were not distinguished by their physical or demographic "bulk." Rather, these states excelled because their institutions encouraged and promoted entrepreneurship, innovation, and efficiency.[16] Therefore, despite their smaller size, they were able to reach the forefront of the international rank. Among the world's ten largest economies in 2003, gross domestic product per capita was far highest in the U.S. Compared to Japan and the Western European countries, the U.S. figure ($37,562) was over 130 percent higher. This U.S. advantage becomes very large when judged against the Chinese figure ($5,003). Although China has grown rather rapidly in the past several decades, most of its large population remains very poor by Western standards. It is still lagging far behind the U.S., which has a per capita income (adjusted for purchasing-power parity) that is 750 percent higher. By this latter measure, it is very premature to speak of a power transition between the two countries.

Of course, per capita income speaks to current economic productivity. Future economic productivity, however, is of greater concern in gauging the possibility of a power transition decades from now. Those states that enjoy a competitive advantage in current productivity may not be able to sustain this advantage in the future. Technological innovations buttress and accelerate economic growth in the pioneering state, whose leading economic sectors in turn enable it to stimulate and maximize benefits from global trade and to develop capabilities necessary to gain global reach (historically in the form of large navies).[17] It goes without saying that predicting future productivity and growth is a challenging business. Nevertheless, we know enough about national productivity and growth to say that they benefit from certain facilitative factors. Some of these factors (such as the rate of national savings and educational achievement) are easier to measure, whereas others (such as the entrepreneurial élan of a people) are more elusive. Most people, however, would agree that the quality of a nation's human capital is a critical determinant of its future economic performance and, by extension, its acquisition of a variety of assets that constitute national power.

The idea of human capital speaks to the health and literacy of a people, its work ethic and achievement orientation, its mastery of modern information technology, its capacity to engage in technical innovation, and its ability to advance the frontier of knowledge about science and technology. In addition to reporting gross domestic product per capita (stated in purchasing-power parity), Table 2.4 presents some evidence on the relative positions of the ten leading economies with respect to those human resources necessary for supporting future economic growth and productivity. Life expectancy, internet usage, and the number of mobile telephones offer a glimpse of a people's average level of health and

Table 2.4 Economic productivity, human capital, and technological command

Country	GDP p.c. PPP, 2003 ($)	Internet user per 1,000, 2003	Life expectancy at birth, 2003	Mobile phones per 1,000, 2003	Resident patent application, 2002	Science & technology articles, 2001
U.S.	37,562	551*	77	543	198,339	200,870
China	5,003	63	71	215	40,346	20,978
Japan	27,967	483	82	679	371,495	57,420
India	2,892	17	63	25	220	11,076
Germany	27,756	473	78	785	80,661	43,623
U.K.	27,147	423*	78*	841	33,671	47,660
France	27,677	366	79	696	61,959	31,317
Italy	27,119	337	80	1,018	4,086	22,313
Brazil	7,790	82*	69	264	6,521	7,205
Russia	9,230	20#	66	249	24,049	15,846
Canada	30,677	513*	78	417	n.a.	22,626
Mexico	9,168	118	74	291	627	3,209

Source: World Development Indicators at http://devdata.worldbank.org/dataonline.

Notes
*2002
#2000

technical skill. All these indicators put the U.S. ahead of China, sometimes by a huge margin (for example, the number of internet users was 874 percent higher in the U.S. than in China).

Perhaps the most revealing information contained in Table 2.4 pertains to the number of patent applications by residents and the number of journal articles published on science and technology. In 2002, the number of patent applications by residents was about 2.5 times higher in the U.S. than in Germany, and five times higher than in China. Only one country, Japan, had a higher number than the U.S. – and significantly so (371,495 for Japan compared to 198,339 for the U.S.). The U.S., however, remained head and shoulders above the other countries in the advancement of basic knowledge (as opposed to applied knowledge as indicated by the number of patent applications submitted). It published more journal articles on science and technology than Japan and the four members of the European Union (Germany, the U.K., France, and Italy) combined. Compared to China, the U.S. was about ten times stronger according to this measure pointing to the development and dissemination of knowledge with potential application for future economic growth and productivity.

The combined implication of the evidence presented thus far warrants the conclusion that China derives its relatively high ranking on traditional measures of national power as a result of its "bulk." The sheer size of China's population and territory is among the chief reasons for its international prominence, and this country's mass production of consumer goods with relatively low technology content has helped the rapid expansion of its economy in recent decades. It is not clear, however, that this growth can be self-sustained in the sense that China has developed sufficient human capital and innovative capacity to proceed to the more advanced stages of value-added production, in contrast to expanding its exports of consumer non-durables with high labor content but low technology content.

Although the U.S. appears to have suffered a relative decline according to some of the statistics presented above, this decline is to some extent to be expected because its predominance during the years immediately following World War II reflected the wartime devastation suffered by the other leading states. With the economic recovery of Europe and Japan, a diminishing U.S. advantage seems natural and, indeed, inevitable. To the extent that this recovery was one of the avowed objectives of postwar U.S. foreign policy, this phenomenon also reflects the success of U.S. policy.[18]

A less imbalanced situation still favoring the U.S., however, does not mean a loss of U.S. hegemony or an impending power transition. The U.S. today possesses far more coercive power than any other state. Only the U.S. is capable of launching and sustaining a military operation outside its home region. No other state, or combination of states, can match the overwhelming advantage possessed by the U.S. in military capabilities. Equally significant, the U.S. enjoys a huge lead in its capacity to forge scientific development and technological innova-tion.[19] According to this criterion again, there is little hint in the available evidence that the U.S. will be supplanted by China or, for that matter, by any other country at any time in the near future.[20] Because scientific development and technological innovation hold the key to an economy's future dynamism, the U.S. advantage in these areas suggests that concerns about an impending power transition involving China are greatly exaggerated. According to Michael D. Swaine and Ashley J. Tellis, even assuming the most favorable circumstances, China is unlikely to even *begin* to approach the U.S. power position until 2015 to 2020 *at the very earliest*.[21] The Chinese are not unaware that despite their country's recent economic growth, it is still very much behind the U.S. They tend to view exaggerated claims of China's strength and warnings about an impending power transition as an attempt by foreigners to contrive the existence of a "China threat" and to mobilize support for a campaign to contain China's influence.[22]

We have thus far compared the power status of a number of leading states as if the growth trajectories of all these states would matter equally for the stability of the international system. Power-transition theory was originally formulated to explain wars among the most powerful states.[23] These wars are fought out at the pinnacle of the international system in a struggle over which state(s) should dominate this system in the future. Accordingly, one would necessarily have to identify those states whose changing power status is the focus of concern for the power-transition theory. Which states fall within the analytic domain of this theory, and which are located outside its domain?

This determination is important because even though the U.S. had become economically the most powerful state by the 1870s, this country was not designated by the power-transition theory as a "contender" in the "central system" of international relations before either World War I or World War II.[24] Because the U.S. was denied this status as a central contender for international supremacy,[25] both World Wars could be characterized as resulting from the conflict dynamic set off by Germany's overtaking of the U.K.

It is therefore important to determine which countries qualify for "contender" status before one can decide whether the changing gap separating any pair of states is or is not consequential for the power-transition theory. Changes in the relative positions of minor powers would not imply the same serious system-transforming consequences that a power transition among the leading states can have. Yet, although it is clear that the power-transition theory has as its major and original focus those great powers positioned at the pinnacle of the international hierarchy, the question about which states qualify for membership in this select club remains somewhat murky.

In applying the power-transition theory to the world before 1890, A.F.K. Organski and Jacek Kugler designated the U.K., Russia, and France as "contenders" in the "central system" of international relations.[26] From 1890 on, Germany replaced France as the third contender in the "central system." The designation of these European countries as competitors for international dominance is important because, as mentioned in Chapter 1, it draws attention to the Anglo-German rivalry preceding both World War I and World War II. At the same time, this designation excludes the U.S. as a contender even though the U.S. economy had already surpassed the British economy by the 1870s.

Because the U.S. was not considered a contender, the power transition between it and the U.K. represents a non-event for the theory. The failure of this transition to occasion war does not appear to suggest an important puzzle to be analyzed.[27] Of course, had the U.S. been designated a central contender before 1914 and again before 1939, there would not have been a power transition between the two most powerful states prior to both World Wars. The U.S. had become the world's dominant power by the beginning of the twentieth century. Since then, its premier status never came close to being challenged by Germany or any other state.

The U.S. was not considered a central contender for international supremacy because of its ostensible self-professed isolationist inclination. Yet U.S. actions during the century before 1945 contradict this isolationist characterization. There were wars initiated against Spain and Mexico, and competition with the U.K. for influence in the Western Hemisphere. As William R. Thompson remarked, even

> [the year] 1898 is a bit late as the beginning of American great power status. While it is true that the United States never played much of a role within the nineteenth-century *European* regional system so closely associated with the other great powers, it was an actor of some importance on North, Central, and South American issues throughout the nineteenth century [emphasis in the original].[28]

Considering that U.S. military intervention was arguably the most important factor in deciding the ultimate outcome of both World Wars, the denial of this country as a leading candidate for international dominance in the years before 1945 does seem quite baffling.[29] As already mentioned, one can claim that power transition among the strongest states leads to war only by excluding the U.S. from this select group. Naturally, if the U.S. did not qualify for this designation before 1945, which states warrant this designation today? What should the criteria be for making this designation of leading contenders for global supremacy?

One possibility is to apply the "largest drop-off" rule. Douglas Lemke and Suzanne Werner offered an example.[30] If A is the leading state and B, C, and D have respectively 92 percent, 83 percent, and 46 percent of A's power, then A, B, and C would be considered contenders but, given the largest drop in power capability between C and D, D would not be recognized as such.

The "largest drop-off" rule may be applied to the states listed in Table 2.2. Let us consider the six largest economies positioned immediately after the U.S.[31] After adjustment has been made for purchasing-power parity, China's economy is about 61.8 percent of the U.S. size. The figures for the others are 31.8 percent for Japan, 28.2 percent for India, 20.1 percent for Germany, 15.1 percent for the U.K., and 14.7 percent for France. The distance separating each of these countries from the one above is 38.2 percent, 30.0 percent, 3.6 percent, 8.1 percent, 5.0 percent, and 0.4 percent, respectively. Accordingly, the gap between the U.S. and China constitutes the largest drop-off. According to this criterion, only the U.S. qualifies for contender status. The predominance enjoyed by the U.S. is such that the other states do not qualify as a peer competitor for the U.S.[32]

One can repeat this exercise by examining the distribution of military power as indicated by defense expenditures. As it turns out, the U.S. enjoys an even more striking predominance on this dimension. China spent only about 18.1 percent of the U.S. defense outlay, and the figures for the other states are, respectively, 12.3 percent of the U.S. total for Japan, 4.6 percent for India, 9.4 percent for Germany, 11.6 percent for the U.K., and 12.1 percent for France. Again, by the logic of the "largest drop-off" rule, only the U.S. qualifies as a contender for international dominance. The other states are hardly in the same league with respect to their expenditure on military instruments.

The third variable reported in Table 2.2 pertains to the number of internet hosts in each country. The leading position of the U.S. on this dimension is even more pronounced than on the previous two dimensions. China has only 0.1 percent of the U.S. total, whereas the figures are 11.3 percent for Japan, 0.1 percent for India, 2.3 percent for Germany, 2.9 percent for the U.K., and 2.1 percent for France. The largest drop-off on this variable applies to the distance separating the U.S. and Japan (a whopping difference of 88.7 percent). This result confirms the conclusion suggested by the data on gross domestic product and military expenditures that none of the other states truly qualifies as a contender capable of competing for international influence against the U.S. The U.S. has such a huge edge on all these dimensions of national power that it represents a select club of one. Indeed, this assessment is warranted according to not only the largest drop-off criterion, but also the stipulation indicated in the original formulation of the power-transition theory that to qualify as a challenger, a state must be at least 80 percent as powerful as its rival.[33]

To be considered a great-power contender, a state must also have intense interactions with the other great powers. In the original formulation of power-transition theory, this state must have extensive involvement in international relations, especially as indicated by its military alliances with the other powers. Accordingly, another seemingly reasonable way to identify today's great-power contenders is to examine the candidate states' military deployment abroad and the security commitments they have taken up to defend their allies. Table 2.5 provides some pertinent information on these aspects. It becomes immediately clear from this table that the U.S. is again the only truly global power. Whether judged according to the number of troops stationed abroad (without counting those deployed offshore or committed to peacekeeping missions), the number of countries or locations where these troops are deployed, or the number of defense pacts signed to support foreign allies, the U.S. has maintained a far more active and prominent profile than the other candidates for possible great-power status.

For example, whereas the U.S. maintained 405,000 troops abroad, the U.K. (which ranked second behind the U.S.) had only 44,650 soldiers stationed on foreign soil – or just about one-tenth of the U.S. level. Moreover, the U.S. had a military presence in more places around the world and had entered into more defense pacts than any of the other countries listed in Table 2.5. China does not have any troops deployed abroad. In contrast to the U.S. that has several multilateral alliances covering large regions and involving many countries

Table 2.5 Global military presence, 2004

Country	Troops deployed*	Countries deployed in	Defense pacts[#]
U.S.	405,000	30	6
China	0	0	1
Japan	1,000	1	1
Germany	1,290	6	1
U.K.	44,650	19	2
France	24,900	10	3
Russia	17,150	7	0

Source: Data on foreign military deployment are from Bruce Russett, Harvey Starr, and David Kinsella, *World Politics: The Menu for Choice* (8th edn) (Belmont, CA: Wadsworth/Thomson Learning, 2005), p. 236; and data on formal alliances are from http://cow2.la.psu.edu.

Notes
*Foreign deployment does not include U.N. or other peacekeeping missions, or military personnel stationed offshore.
[#]Only counting those formal alliances in effect as of December 31, 2004.

(e.g., the North Atlantic Treaty Organization, the ANZUS pact with Australia and New Zealand, and the Rio Pact with the countries in the Western Hemisphere), China has only undertaken one security commitment, with its immediate neighbor North Korea. The evidence reported in Table 2.5 again supports the conclusion that the U.S. is the only legitimate contender for global dominance. No other country, not even the U.K., has the same intensive and extensive military involvement in different parts of the world that the U.S. has.

Naturally, military involvement offers only one kind of indication of a state's plausible qualification for great-power contender status. In Table 2.6 I present two other measures. The first refers to the total value of foreign trade (imports and exports) in goods and services. Despite China's rapid rise as a trading state,

Table 2.6 Foreign trade and membership in intergovernmental organizations

Country	Exports and imports of goods and services, 2003 (billions of current US$)	Membership in intergovernmental organizations, 2000
U.S.	2,538	92
China	934	73
Japan	981	82
Germany	1,651	107
U.K.	964	102
France	907	126
Russia	255	80

Sources: Data on foreign trade are based on World Development Indicators available at http://devdata.worldbank.org/dataonline; and data on intergovernmental organizations are available from http://cow2.la.psu.edu.

its volume of foreign commerce in 2003 was only about 37 percent of the U.S. level. Alternatively, the U.S. traded roughly 270 percent more than China. China's trade volume in that year was somewhere between the levels for the U.K. and France. The second indicator reported in Table 2.6 refers to the number of inter-governmental organizations (IGOs) in which each state held membership. As recently as 1970, China belonged to only two IGOs. It did not become a member of the United Nations until October 1971. Therefore, its increased participation in various regional and global multilateral institutions since then has been quite impressive. Nevertheless, China still does not belong to as many IGOs as the other states included in Table 2.6. Naturally, the European countries have formed and joined a larger number of these organizations due to the dense web of institutions fostered by the European Union. However, China has had less of a presence in IGOs than Japan and Russia. In addition, the U.S. has been a member of more IGOs than all these three countries, even though it has belonged to fewer IGOs than the U.K., Germany, and France.

Which empirical criteria should be applied to identify those great powers that are contenders for international supremacy? As discussed above, one approach is to differentiate the contenders from the non-contenders by the distance separating their physical assets, using the largest drop-off rule. This rule indicates that on practically all those dimensions of national power considered, the largest drop-off applies to the gap between the U.S. and the second-ranking power. Another possible approach presented in this chapter is to consider the scale and spread of a country's international involvement. A great-power contender should, almost by definition, be actively engaged in many parts of the world. The U.S. again stands out in the intensity of its interactions with other states and in the geographical range of these interactions. No other state can even come close to matching 80 percent of the overseas military deployment or foreign commerce involving the U.S. With the exception of membership in intergovern-mental organizations, the available evidence points to the conclusion that the U.S. enjoys a predominant position in international relations. It is difficult to argue that any contemporary state qualifies as a peer competitor that can mount a credible challenge to, or seriously contend with, the U.S.[34] Unlike perhaps the situation prevailing before World War I when one might describe the U.K. and Germany as reasonably matched rivals, we have today the nearest thing to a unipolar world since the zenith reached by the Roman and Chinese empires in their respective regions. To the extent that there may be a contender for U.S. hegemony on the horizon, it would not be a single state. Only the aggregate assets and reach of the European Union would entitle this entity to the status of a contender.[35] Put alternatively, the gap separating the U.S. and the other states individually is such that there is scant evidence pointing to a power transition. There is little possibility of the U.S. being displaced from its position of pre-eminence by China or by any other state in the foreseeable future. An influential Chinese scholar observed, "for a long time to come, the United States is likely to remain dominant, with sufficient hard power to back up aggressive diplomatic and military policies."[36] While emphasizing that arrogance and a myopic pursuit of hard power could diminish America's soft power, a leading U.S. academic and official noted: "China is a long way from posing the kind of challenge to American preponderance that the Kaiser's Germany posed when it passed Britain at the beginning of the last century."[37] In Joseph Nye's view, "American preponderance will last well into this century – but only if we learn to use our power wisely."[38] China's recent rise points more to its relative ascent as a regional power rather than its arrival as a global contender. Yet the distinct focus of the power-transition theory has been on a supposed contest for systemic primacy and competing designs for world order. Those armed conflicts, such as World War I and World War II, that motivate this theory are about a struggle for global domination. One might add moreover that even as a regional power, Beijing's influence today is hardly as dominant as Washington's in the Western Hemisphere in the late 1890s. The U.S. had by then, if not earlier, successfully established a regional hegemony, a feat that no other country has been able to achieve in the modern era.[39] Rather inconsistently, analysts of the power-transition theory have dismissed the U.S. as a global power contender before both World Wars even though it had already become the strongest country by 1900, while treating China today as a peer competitor even though it falls far short of this status.

A recognition that China qualifies only as a regional power is therefore tantamount to acknowledging persistent U.S. world dominance. Although China has been getting stronger, the U.S. is not in the process of being overtaken, globally or regionally. Hence, suggestions of an ongoing or impending power transition between these two countries appear greatly exaggerated. Even though the validity of the individual indicators of national power used in this chapter may be questioned in specific respects, the collective implication to be drawn from the ensemble of such indicators can hardly be denied. China's sheer physical size and the rapid rate of its recent growth can be an obvious cause for concern by other states regardless of the extent of its relative power gain. Yet, even though China's recent economic growth has been rather impressive, a focus on *just* China overlooks the continued global pre-eminence enjoyed by the U.S. in a variety of measures of national power. Of course, concerns about China's rise stem not just from its recent growth but tend to be, more importantly, motivated by perceptions of Beijing's intentions. Would China's increased capabilities be put to pursue its security or used to expand its power? This question turns on a judgment about a country's likely intention to adhere to or challenge the prevailing international order. We turn to this topic in Chapter 3, and discuss how one may be able to differentiate status-quo from revisionist states.

3 Revisionist impulse and the incumbent's strategic selection

The data presented in the last chapter show that there have been occasions in the past when a power transition has occurred peacefully. For instance, Russia/the USSR and the U.K. were overtaken by Japan, Germany, India, and/or China in recent years. These changes in their relative position, however, did not result in war. The failure for war to break out on these occasions does not necessarily invalidate the power-transition theory. This theory can explain the non-occurrence of war on at least two grounds. First, these power transitions did not apply to the central contenders for international dominance. Second, the regime characteristics of some states make any power transition involving them less likely to result in war. Having already taken up the first rationale, I address the second consideration in this chapter. Concerns expressed by those who subscribe to the "China threat" school and by those who call attention to the perils of power transition are based on the view that China is not a status-quo power. In the words of the current U.S. Secretary of State, "China resents the role of the United States in the Asia-Pacific region. This means that China is not a 'status-quo' power, but one that would like to alter Asia's strategic balance in its own favor."[1] This remark implies that a country's status-quo orientation is to be judged by its support of or opposition to the dominant power, and that the dominant power is itself not tempted to create a more favorable strategic balance for itself.

In its original version, the power-transition theory postulated that the danger of a serious conflict exists only when a "dissatisfied" power overtakes an international leader.[2] Conversely, when a "satisfied" power is poised to replace this leader, this danger can be avoided.[3] The reason behind this hypothesis is that a satisfied latecomer does not seek to undermine the international status quo. A dissatisfied latecomer, however, is fundamentally upset with the rules and principles underlying the existing order. Therefore, the emergence of such a revisionist state poses a great threat to both the existing leader and the international system as a whole. According to this reasoning, because the U.S. was a status-quo power in the late 1800s and early 1900s, its ascendance did not threaten the U.K. as much as the menace coming from a rising Germany. London was willing to accommodate the ascending U.S., thus making the power transition between these two countries a peaceful process. A revisionist Germany, however, could not be easily accommodated, because it sought to change the existing international order rather than just to improve its status within the framework provided by this order.

The stylized account offered above immediately raises two questions. First, how can one discern a status-quo oriented power from a revisionist one? What verbal and non-verbal indicators can one use to differentiate between these two types of states? Presumably, we would not want to attribute a revisionist motivation to a state simply because it had fought a dominant power, thus committing the error of circular reasoning. In addition, presumably the dominant power and the international system are not synonymous, so that challenging the former is not the equivalent of challenging the latter.

Second, because a declining dominant power often faces several rising states simultaneously, how does it decide which ones to confront, accommodate, or even join forces with? Does the perceived status-quo orientation of the latecomers or some other factor(s) play a more important role in shaping its reaction to the latter countries' ascendance? A hegemon in relative decline does not necessarily have to prepare for an inevitable confrontation with all the revisionist latecomers.[4] By the end of the nineteenth century the U.K. had all but conceded the Western Hemisphere as a region of exclusive U.S. power. Besides coming to terms with the U.S., London settled accounts with Japan in 1902, with France in 1904, and with Russia in 1907, thereby isolating Germany as its chief antagonist.[5] Thus, the eventual alignment of states in World War I was already becoming visible prior to 1914. Instead of just stressing that the U.S., France, and Russia eventually joined the U.K. to fight against Germany's bid for hegemony, it would not be unreasonable to also suggest that by accommodating these rising states, the U.K. had sought to court or at least neutralize them in anticipation of a possible war with Germany.

These two questions are interrelated, and a good place to start our inquiry would be to examine Anglo-American relations in the late 1800s. Even if one should acknowledge that the U.S. had already become a central contender in international relations by that time, the power-transition theory can still explain its peaceful displacement of the U.K. as the leading power by pointing to Washington's democratic regime and its status-quo orientation.

This attribution, however, overlooks the fact that Anglo-American relations had been rather acrimonious during much of the nineteenth century. The U.S. and the U.K. had fought a war in 1812, and had come close to blows in the Oregon dispute in 1845 to 1846. London had also considered intervening on behalf of the Confederacy in the U.S. Civil War in order to contain the American colossus and to enhance the defense of Canada. As a historian noted,

> The United States remained an enemy of Britain's calculations . . . until 1895-96. Until after the Venezuelan affair any increase in the territory and strength of the United States was regarded as a direct threat to the British possessions and British power and influence in the western hemisphere.[6]

The two countries were rivals for territorial, commercial, and political influence not only in the Western Hemisphere but also in the Asia Pacific.

The U.S. and the U.K. (which was in control of Canada) were hostile neighbors during much of the 1800s, even though their governments shared some democratic attributes. Yet to the extent that the character of their governments remained largely constant during the nineteenth century, this similarity in regime attributes cannot be used to explain a change to more cordial relations following the settlement of the Venezuelan Boundary Crisis in 1895. As William R. Thompson remarked, "the most difficult position to defend is the extreme argument that democratization was primarily responsible for the decline in Anglo-American conflict."[7] It seems also a stretch, at least by contemporary standards, to describe either country as a democracy since suffrage for women and minorities was not allowed for quite some time to come.[8]

Moreover, if the concept of status-quo orientation is meant to describe a stance aimed at maintaining a state's existing possessions, this characterization would hardly apply to the U.S.[9] As John Mearsheimer remarked, "the United States was bent on establishing regional hegemony, and it was an expansionist power of the first order in the Americas."[10] He quoted Henry Cabot Lodge saying that the United States had "a record of conquest, colonization, and territorial expansion unequaled by any people in the nineteenth century."[11] The U.S. had expanded its territory fourfold during the first half of the nineteenth century and, by the century's end, it had realized its regional hegemony in the Western Hemisphere. The territorial gains made by Washington through wars against its neighbors (e.g., Mexico, Spain) and the indigenous people, or through foreign purchases (e.g., France, Russia), and its military interventions in the "near abroad" are a familiar part of the doctrine of Manifest Destiny. By the time Commodore Matthew Perry attempted to "open" Japan in 1853, the U.S. was already trying to expand its influence in the Asia Pacific. At the turn of the twentieth century, it was pushing for an "open door" policy in China, and took part in the military intervention to put down the Chinese Boxer Rebellion against foreign penetration. In the process of acquiring the Philippines as a colony, it had waged a bloody campaign against nationalist insurgency in that country. By the then prevailing standards of behavior, it is difficult to argue that Russia's expansionist drive in Central Asia, Germany's bid for influence in Central Europe and Africa, and Japan's territorial ambitions for acquiring Korea and Taiwan were any more egregious or "anti-status quo."[12] As Dale Copeland noted, from 1898 to 1913, the U.S. gained seven times more colonial territory than imperial Germany.[13]

Of course, the concept of status-quo orientation does not have to refer to a state's acquisitive ambitions and its desire to improve its relative status in the international system. It may be assumed that all states would have these motivations and, in that sense, all may be described as "dissatisfied."[14] A state's status-quo orientation, however, may be used to indicate its basic attitudes toward the prevailing institutions and rules of conduct in international relations. To what extent can a state (or, more precisely, its regime) be said to have been "normed" according to the customs and conventions shared broadly by the international community? An anti-status-quo state would presumably be one that opposes and seeks to replace the existing institutions and rules. It is in this sense that republican France and communist Russia (after their respective revolutions in 1789 and 1917) may be characterized as revisionist states. Their regimes professed an ideology that challenged the values, expectations, and ordering principles espoused by the existing international system.[15]

We sometimes only recognize the states' revisionist agenda in retrospect. Germany's complaints about its war reparations imposed by the Versailles Treaty, its limited sovereignty in Danzig and the Rhineland, and the treatment of ethnic Germans in Sudetenland hardly amounted to a fundamental challenge to the international system. These grievances could not be easily interpreted to suggest that Germany was a revisionist state bent on overthrowing the existing order. Indeed, Neville Chamberlain and Winston Churchill were not acting unreasonably when they disagreed about Adolf Hitler's intentions. Did the Führer have limited demands that could be accommodated or exorbitant ambitions that must be resisted? While both leaders recognized Berlin's dissatisfaction, its behavior prior to the invasion of Prague (in 1939) would be compatible with either interpretation.[16] The certainty of hindsight belies the ambiguities of the time.

What do people mean by a status-quo orientation that supposedly favors the maintenance of the existing order? Presumably, they have in mind those values, expectations, and ordering principles pertaining to matters such as the legitimacy of ruling elites, the rules of warfare, the mechanisms for making territorial adjustments, and the mutual observance of spheres of influence. In their effort to gain international recognition, Japanese reformers in the Meiji era were eager to introduce and adopt Western institutions and practices. Ironically, however, even though imperial Japan played the game of colonial conquest and territorial aggrandizement according to the then-prevailing diplomatic and military proto-col, their ambitions for expansion on the Asian mainland were thwarted by the Western powers.[17] In the words of one scholar, this country "proved an example *par excellence* in conforming its government institutions, legal system, and general international practices to the interests, rules, and values of 'civilized' international society, as prescribed by Western nations."[18] Conversely, the U.S. made up its own rules in the Western Hemisphere by unilaterally declaring the Monroe Doctrine in 1823 and forcing a showdown with the U.K. in 1895 over this self-declared mandate. It is therefore difficult to argue, again, that imperial Japan – or for that matter, Wilhelmine Germany or Czarist Russia – acted more outside of the international community than the U.S. In other words, it is hard to make a case that these states' objective behavior warrants their different classification according to their support for or commitment to shared institutions and codes of conduct.[19]

In designating states as status-quo oriented or revisionist, analysts often fail to engage in comparative analysis and are instead prone to simply assert as if it is self-evident that a rising U.S. was a status-quo power whereas the others (e.g., Germany, Russia, Japan, and China today) were/are motivated by a revisionist agenda. They do not address as a matter of empirical puzzle why in the case of the U.S., a rising power was status-quo oriented, whereas in the other cases the rising powers remained revisionist despite their improving position in the international system. By exempting the former from a revisionist motivation while attributing to the latter this same motivation, one often substitutes assertion for analysis. Moreover, in implying that in all the cases except the U.S., a rising power continues to have a revisionist agenda even though it is making gains in its power (and status) under the existing order, one is in effect treating the revisionism of latecomers as an analytic constant rather than as an empirical variable, and is accordingly introducing a tendency to focus exclusively on relative power shifts. It is not hard to grasp the policy implication of such a tendency – the management of latecomers should aim at containing or blocking their power since efforts to alter their revisionist impulses are unlikely to succeed or are at least difficult to achieve.

As already noted, the U.S. and the U.K. were involved not only in disputes over Venezuela's border but also in other contentious issues such as the demarcation of the Alaskan territory from northwest Canada and the construction of the Panama Canal. These acrimonies, however, were all eventually settled in favor of the U.S., with the U.K. making unilateral concessions without any expectation of U.S. reciprocity.[20] Constrained by geographic distance, fiscal stringencies, and multiple rivals, British officials were hard pressed to keep up with rising American power.[21] They chose to appease Washington in recognition of the inevitability of U.S. dominance in the Western Hemisphere, and in recognition of other emergent challengers posing a threat to its interests (such as Germany in Western Europe, and Russia in Afghanistan and the Far East). They reduced their naval presence in the western Atlantic and the Asia Pacific region in order to concentrate their forces closer to home. Whether by deliberate choice or a process of trial and error, the British decided in the end to confront Germany rather than the more distant U.S.[22]

The peaceful displacement of the U.K. by the U.S. as the dominant regional power in the Western Hemisphere underscored the inexorable rise of the latter country as much as it reflected the former country's strategic predicament. The U.K. faced strained resources in responding to its perception of multiple threats to its global empire. Accommodation and reconciliation with the U.S. were part of London's strategic alignment of forces to cope with a rising Germany. The degree of threat as indicated by geographic distance – rather than in regime characteristics or cultural affinity – is better able to explain this choice. After all, the U.K. also promoted ties with Japan in the Asia Pacific in its attempt to contain Russia. This attempt by London to recruit Japan as a junior partner could hardly be explained on the ground that Japan was a democracy or that it shared Britain's culture.[23]

The upshot of this stylized account is that with its economic resources and military forces increasingly stretched to defend its many positions in different parts of the world, London had to eventually undertake a strategic retrenchment. It essentially decided to yield to a rising U.S. in the Western Hemisphere and to ally with an emergent Japan in the Asia Pacific, so that it could face more effectively the challenge emerging from Germany and, to a lesser extent, Russia that were located closer to the British Isles. It was not the case that there was only one emergent power, namely Germany, that threatened to displace the U.K. from its pre-eminent position in the international system. There were several rising powers qualifying as potential competitors for the U.K. That the Anglo-German rivalry became a topic of much historical interest reflected in part the choice made by British officials to focus on Germany and to appease or even ally with the U.S., Russia, and Japan. This rivalry, in other words, reflected as much the dynamics of differential change in national power emphasized by the power-transition theory as the calculated policy on the part of British officials. That some power transitions turned into heated rivalries whereas others passed peacefully has something to do with which potential threats the officials of a declining power chose to confront and which ones to accommodate.

Contrary to conventional wisdom, this differential treatment cannot be fully explained by the supposed status-quo orientation of a rising power, or by its regime characteristic or national culture. As Ido Oren observed, although Imperial Germany is typically characterized in contemporary literature as an aggressive autocracy responsible for starting World War I, it was lauded by leading Americans (even Woodrow Wilson) before that conflict as an advanced constitutional state, admired for its efficient administration, and accepted as a leading member of the superior Aryan/Teutonic race.[24] Conversely, as William R. Thompson noted,

> In the late eighteenth century and early nineteenth century, the British ruling elite had seen the United States as a revolutionary challenger to the status quo, both internationally and potentially within the British domestic politics. The Americans, for their part, did not consider the British political system of the same period to be particularly democratic.[25]

These observations point to the risk of *post hoc* attempts to use cultural and regime attributes to describe status-quo orientation or to explain global wars. They also remind us that the designation of allies and adversaries can and does often reflect socially constructed identities and elite-manipulated symbols.[26] The identification of in- and out-groups and the attribution of amity and antipathy have an ideational basis separate from objective material conditions and actual behavioral conduct.

Until recently, quantitative studies attempting to test the power-transition theory have either overlooked the status-quo variable or treated the dominant state and its allies as being status-quo bound by definition. In the latter case, the analyst takes for granted that a hegemon is *necessarily* content with the existing international order, because it is assumed that as the dominant power, the hegemon derives the most benefits from the existing order and has the greatest incentive to defend and maintain it. In making this assumption, the analyst does not consider whether, given its overwhelming power, a hegemon may be motivated to change the existing order to further advance its political and economic interests. That a hegemon has already attained the largest share of benefits from the existing international order should not preclude it from trying to gain even more benefits. Contrary to the existing tendency in the relevant literature to treat the hegemon as a status-quo power *by definition*, it is quite plausible for this country to pursue a revisionist agenda in order to transform the international system in a direction that it finds even more congenial than the current situation.[27]

How can one tell whether a state is trying to introduce and promote new rules, norms, and morality for international conduct? One may listen to official pronouncements made by a government for some pertinent indication. China's current government professes its adherence to the principles of the Westphalian system with its emphasis on state sovereignty, territorial integrity, and non-interference in the domestic affairs of others. Conversely, the current U.S. administration has openly declared its intent to seek "regime change" and to insist on its right to initiate preventive strikes against any source of perceived threat. Whatever one thinks about the political prudence or the moral ethics regarding the proliferation and use of weapons of mass destruction, the public justification advanced by George W. Bush and other senior U.S. officials for invading Iraq goes against the traditional presumption that each state is entitled to decide its own means of national defense. Similarly, whether one agrees or disagrees with Washington's goal of spreading democracy and capitalism globally, it is difficult to argue that this self-declared agenda is intended to maintain the international status quo.[28] One can therefore be baffled when colleagues applying the power-transition theory characterize hegemons in general and the U.S. in particular as status-quo powers.

It is necessary again to clarify that the concept of status-quo orientation does not refer to whether or not a state is interested in improving its current status or stature. Since every state may be expected to have this interest, this concept would be quite trite if used in this way. Rather, an anti-status-quo orientation should suggest a fundamental objection to and challenge of the rules of the game, and not just how these rules can produce a different distribution of benefits. In this sense, then, the concept of status-quo orientation may be understood to refer to whether a state stands inside or outside of general agreements shared by most members of an international community. In describing the power-transition theory, Kenneth Organski and Jacek Kugler were quite explicit in stating: "it is a general dissatisfaction with its position in the [international] system, and a desire to redraft the rules by which relations among nations work, that move a country to begin a major war."[29]

One possible, though hardly perfect, way to gauge a state's status-quo orientation in the sense described above is to examine its participation in intergovernmental organizations (IGOs).[30] Membership in IGOs offers prima facie evidence that a state is in principle willing to abide by the rules and procedures of the relevant multilateral institutions and to be bound by the outcomes of their collective decision processes. Thus, joining an IGO signifies a minimum amount of concession on a state's autonomy and a disposition to coordinate its affairs with others. Membership in IGOs indicates an investment by states as participants in a broader community in what Robert Keohane and Lisa Martin described as "focal points of international cooperation" and what Harold Jacobson called "networks of interdependence."[31] Other things being equal, one would expect that the larger number of IGOs a state belongs to, the more it identifies with the international community and the more it supports the existing international order.

Table 3.1 presents some comparative statistics about the number of IGOs that the U.K., France, the U.S., Germany, and Russia/the USSR belonged to during the period 1890 to 1945.[32] Until about 1910, Germany's participation in IGOs was quite comparable to that of the U.K., and was somewhat higher than that of the U.S. Therefore, by this measure, Wilhelmine Germany was no less status-quo oriented than the U.K. and the U.S. However, as a likely sign of its disaffection, Germany's membership in IGOs (relative to that of the other great powers) started to fall in the years immediately prior to World War I. During the 1920s and 1930s, Germany continued to belong to fewer IGOs than the U.S. and the U.K. Our logic of inference would suggest that Germany was becoming increasingly alienated from the international community.[33] Note, however, that the USSR's relative participation in IGOs fell to an even lower level following the Bolshevik Revolution, thus hinting at the new communist regime's international isolation. Compared to their earlier scores, the ratio of Germany's and the USSR's IGO membership in relation to that of the U.S. and the U.K had acquired a more anti-status-quo orientation by the time World War I broke out or shortly thereafter. This same measure would point to France rather than the U.S. or the U.K. as the most status-quo-oriented country in this group during the entire time period reported. These inferences correspond reasonably well with our general historical understanding. From 1890 on, France was on the strategic defensive, seeking mainly to forestall its weakening position in Europe even though it

Table 3.1 Ratios of IGO membership held by major-power contenders, 1860–1949

Year	Compared to U.S. as denominator				Compared to U.K. as denominator			
	U.K.	France	Germany	Russia/ the USSR	U.S.	France	Germany	Russia/ the USSR
1890–94	1.40	1.60	1.50	1.20	0.71	1.14	1.07	0.86
1895–99	1.25	1.58	1.33	1.17	0.80	1.27	1.07	0.93
1900–04	2.10	2.30	2.20	1.70	0.48	1.10	1.05	0.81
1905–09	1.16	1.28	1.20	1.04	0.86	1.10	1.03	0.90
1910–14	1.23	1.38	1.15	1.07	0.81	1.13	0.94	0.88
1915–19	1.04	1.33	0.89	0.70	0.96	1.29	0.86	0.68
1920–24	1.47	1.53	0.88	0.47	0.68	1.04	0.60	0.32
1925–29	1.57	1.53	1.03	0.63	0.64	0.98	0.66	0.40
1930–34	1.33	1.31	0.93	0.52	0.75	0.98	0.70	0.39
1935–39	1.18	1.22	0.91	0.49	0.85	1.04	0.77	0.42
1940–44	0.91	0.81	0.52	0.42	1.10	0.90	0.58	0.46
1945–49	1.10	1.01	—	0.28	0.91	0.92	—	0.25

Source: Steve Chan, "Can't Get No Satisfaction?," p. 223.

continued a program of colonial expansion in Africa and Asia. As noted above, the drop in the Russian data series captures the Soviet revolution and the new regime's revisionist orientation. Significantly, in line with our earlier argument, imperial Germany (in contrast to Weimar or Nazi Germany) did not appear to be any more revisionist than the U.K. or the U.S., according to the data in Table 3.1.

The United Nations offers the closest approximation to the contemporary international community. The political distance that separates a state from its counterparts can be indicated by the extent to which it finds itself in the minority in voting on resolutions presented to the General Assembly or the Security Council. These votes should be informative about which states are in or out of step with the rest of the world. Although these votes are hardly perfect indicators of a state's support for or defiance of the prevailing international rules and norms, such behavioral evidence would be an improvement over an analyst simply stipulating, by definition, that any particular state is or is not status-quo oriented. To the extent that this orientation refers to the standard aspirations and expectations of the global community, a status-quo power is more likely to agree with and support the international consensus than to oppose it.

Table 3.2 reports the number of times each of the five permanent members of the Security Council had cast a veto since 1976. By definition, a veto is an attempt to block a majority that would have otherwise carried the day. In recent years, the U.S. has found itself resorting increasingly to this form of blocking action. Of the 110 vetoes recorded between February 1976 and January 2006, the U.S. accounted for 68 (or 62 percent of the total). The U.K. had the second highest number of vetoes (19, or just over 17 percent of the total). During this same period, China had cast a veto on just two occasions. Compared to the frequency of U.S. vetoes, it is hard to argue from this measure that China has been more out of step with the international community than the U.S.

The incidence of vetoes by the permanent members of the Security Council of course does not address directly the extent to which these states may have an anti-status-quo orientation. The Charter of the United Nations gives the veto prerogative to the permanent members in recognition of their status as great powers, and the exercise of this prerogative certainly conforms to "the rules of the game." It is, however, also true that the incidence of vetoes speaks volumes about the extent to which a state is willing to defer to majority sentiments and is committed to the norms of multilateral diplomacy. A frequent resort to this attempt at blocking majority preference cannot be easily reconciled with the U.S. officials' tendency to assert rhetorically that they speak for "the world."

Washington's abrogation of the Anti-Ballistic Missile Treaty and its decisions to oppose other international conventions would not on a prima facie basis lend support to attributions of its status-quo commitment or adherence to emergent international norms and principles. Those international agreements rejected by the U.S. in the recent past include "the Comprehensive Test Ban Treaty, the Land Mines Convention, the Law of the Sea Convention, the International Convention on the Rights of the Child, and the treaty to establish a permanent International Criminal Court, and the Kyoto Protocol on global warming."[34] Regardless of whether one feels these decisions have merit, they do not suggest a record of joining and promoting international regimes aimed at coordinating shared expectations and encouraging common standards of behavior. Presumably, whether a state adheres to these regimes is pertinent to the determination of its status-quo orientation; that is, its adherence to the general expectations and behavioral standards of the international community. Is a state willing to subscribe to these general expectations and to allow its own behavior to be scrutinized according to common standards? Declaratory support for these expectations and standards of course does not suggest actual compliance. An unwillingness, however, to even extend this declaratory support may hardly be construed as evidence of being integrated into the international community and accepting (if only in theory) its prevailing norms and principles.

Nico Krish reported one pertinent indicator.[35] Thirty-eight treaties have been deposited with the U.N. Secretary-General. More than half of the world's states are parties to these treaties (that is, more than 95 states have ratified them). The U.S. is a party to only 24 of these 38 treaties – compared to 32 for China and Canada; 35 for Russia, France, and Japan; 36 for the U.K.; and 37 for Italy and Germany. As David M. Malone and Yuen Foong Khong remarked, the U.S. has often taken an active and leading role in negotiating international treaties, but has tended to recoil from the prospect of being bound by these treaties' obligations.[36] Washington's reactions to the League of Nations, the Universal Declaration of Human Rights, and the Havana Charter on the International Trade Organization come to mind. More recently, it has sought to commit other states to international rules on human rights, war crimes, and weapons proliferation, while trying to exempt itself from these same rules. In these instances as well as other cases such as its invocation of the exceptionalist reasoning in justifying its preventive war against Iraq, the U.S. declines to conform to the standards and principles that it wishes to impose on other states.[37]

The U.S. finds itself joined by China in objecting to international agreements such as the International Criminal Court. In these cases, both countries are out of

Table 3.2 Veto frequency by permanent members of the Security Council*

	China	France	USSR/Russia	U.K.	U.S.	Total
1976–85	0	9	6	11	34	60
1986–95	0	3	2	8	24	37
1996–2006	2	0	1	0	10	13
Total	2	12	9	19	68	110

Notes
* February 16, 1946 to January 17, 2006; updated summary with the data for February 1946 to August 1997 drawn from Sydney D. Bailey and Sam Daws, *The Procedure of the UN Security Council*, 3rd edn. (Oxford: Clarendon Press, 1998), p. 239; and for September 1997 to February 28, 2002 from Steve Chan, "Power, Satisfaction, and Popularity: A Poisson Analysis of U.N. Security Council Vetoes," *Cooperation and Conflict* 38 (2003): 347. United Nations news releases (at www.un.org/News/Press/doc) report the voting record of Security Council resolutions.

step with the rest of the world. However, when compared to the conduct of other states (including the U.S.), China's words and deeds do not suggest an obvious case of revisionist agenda. After considering a variety of pertinent evidence, one scholar remarked:

> It is hard to conclude that China is a clearly revisionist state operating outside, or barely inside, the boundaries of a so-called international community. Rather to the extent that one can identify an international community on major global issues, the PRC has become more integrated into and more cooperative within international institutions than ever before.[38]

Another colleague offered a similar view, stating: "the evidence so far suggests that although China has outstanding territorial disputes with a number of countries, it has neither revisionist nor imperial aims."[39] Still a third prominent Sinologist noted: "most nations in the [Asia] region now see China as a good neighbor, a constructive partner, a careful listener, and a non-threatening regional power."[40] Such views from specialists of China or Asia often stand in considerable contrast to those of international relations theorists. Indeed, if a country's record on territorial disputes can be used to indicate any revisionist ambition, Beijing's recent behavior would again challenge such characterization. It has settled 17 of its 23 territorial disputes on the basis of substantial compromises that have usually given China less than 50 percent of the contested land.[41]

One would not naturally want to imply that a state's ratification of international agreements and its participation in intergovernmental organizations are necessarily indicative of its commitment to the general rules and principles shared by the international community. Surely, a state can profess allegiance to these rules and principles without actually complying with them. It is, however, more difficult to argue that a rejection of international agreements and intergovernmental organizations may be construed as support for the international community. It is therefore especially telling that although Washington has castigated other countries (including China) for violating human rights, it does not itself have a very impressive record of ratifying international covenants for the observance of these rights (see Table 3.3). One would presume that the values and principles embodied in these legal instruments represent the most basic and common aspirations of the international community. Again, formal ratification of these agreements does not guarantee faithful observance. It is, however, difficult to reconcile Washington's proclamation to place human rights at the core of its foreign policy with its ratification record compared to that of other states. This record, in addition to Washington's refusal to join the other international agreements mentioned earlier, does not quite indicate a status-quo orientation if one can define this orientation as an allegiance to and support for norms shared generally by members of the international community.

Most Americans and U.S. scholars of international relations tend to take for granted the idea that the U.S. is a status-quo power and, by implication, a stabilizing force for international order. Foreigners, however, do not necessarily share

Table 3.3 Ratification of major international human rights instruments*

	China	France	Russia	U.K.	U.S.
International Convention	yes	yes	yes	yes	yes
On the Elimination of All Forms of Racial Discrimination					
On Civil and Political Rights	no	yes	yes	yes	yes
On Economic, Social, and Cultural Rights	yes	yes	yes	yes	no
On the Elimination of Discrimination Against Women	yes	yes	yes	yes	no
Against Torture and Other Cruel, Inhuman or Degrading Treatment or Punishment	yes	yes	yes	yes	yes
On the Rights of the Child	yes	yes	yes	yes	no

Source: Steve Chan, "Realism, Revisionism, and the Great Powers," *Issues & Studies* 40 (2004): 154.

Note

*Updated from United Nations Development Programme, *Human Development Report 2000* (New York: Oxford University Press, 2000), pp. 48–51, including China's ratification of the International Covenant on Economic, Social, and Cultural Rights in 2001.

this view, especially in the wake of the U.S.-led invasion of Iraq in 2003. Even among the citizens of the closest allies of the U.S., there is significant skepticism about whether U.S. policies have the intent or the effect of promoting international peace and stability. The European Commission undertook an opinion poll in 2003, asking the respondents to indicate whether or not in their opinion a particular named country presented a threat to peace in the world. Table 3.4 gives the results from this survey.

Significantly, in every one of the 15 European states where the survey was conducted, more respondents indicated that the U.S. presented a threat to world peace than that China posed such a threat. Not in a single country did a majority believe that China presented a threat to world peace, whereas in every country there was such a majority pointing to the U.S. as the source of this threat. In about half of the countries surveyed, those who held the latter view outnumbered those holding the former view by a margin of two to one. Even in the U.K., a country that has historically been most closely aligned with the U.S., 55 percent thought the U.S. posed a threat to world peace compared to 40 percent who thought in this way about China. For the European Union as a whole, 53 percent of respondents thought the U.S. presented a threat to world peace compared to 30 percent who expressed this belief about China.[42] Those who thought Russia posed such a threat represented an even smaller segment (21 percent) of the European public. Significantly, the E.U. average suggests that the number of Europeans who thought the U.S. was a threat to world peace was about the same as those who held a similar belief about Iraq, Iran, and North Korea – the three "rogue states" singled out by Washington as the "axis of evil."

Table 3.4 Eurobarometer: Answering "yes" to whether the named country presents a threat to world peace

	U.S.	China	Russia	Iraq	Iran	North Korea
Austria	63%	32%	24%	45%	49%	69%
Belgium	59%	29%	21%	54%	54%	49%
Denmark	52%	36%	23%	50%	55%	63%
Finland	63%	31%	29%	53%	48%	57%
France	52%	24%	20%	50%	55%	49%
Germany	45%	26%	19%	57%	57%	65%
Greece	88%	28%	23%	27%	26%	30%
Ireland	60%	37%	31%	54%	54%	66%
Italy	43%	27%	16%	55%	58%	42%
Luxembourg	55%	36%	27%	56%	62%	65%
Netherlands	64%	43%	25%	61%	64%	70%
Portugal	53%	39%	30%	59%	56%	59%
Spain	61%	27%	19%	42%	41%	37%
Sweden	54%	27%	19%	54%	54%	59%
U.K.	55%	40%	27%	54%	54%	59%
E.U. 15	53%	30%	21%	52%	53%	53%

Source: "Iraq and Peace in the World," commissioned by the Directorate General Press and Communication of the European Union, November 2003, p. 78

The interests of the dominant power are not identical to the interests of the international community as a whole. While current or past dominant powers were largely responsible for constructing the rules and conventions of the international system, these states are obviously not synonymous with the international community. As John Vasquez has put it succinctly, "states need only to be dissatisfied with each other and not with the way the system is being ruled in order to have a major war."[43] Although officials of the current U.S. administration under George W. Bush often appropriate for themselves the prerogative to speak for "the world," their actual conduct betrays a disdain for international public opinion and a decided preference for unilateralism. To the extent that American scholars take it for granted that as the world's premier power, the U.S. "must" be a status-quo power committed to the defense and maintenance of the current international system, this assumption is not widely shared by people abroad. As noted above, public opinion in other countries and to a large extent Washington's self-professed policy goals and its actual conduct suggest that far from committing to defend the status quo, the U.S. wants to promote changes in the domestic politics and economies of other countries and to transform the international system in an even more congenial way. Unless people have in mind something other than the customary meaning of words such as "status quo" and "revisionism," the actual behavior and declared agenda of the U.S. are the opposite of the standard characterization found in the U.S. literature.[44] That a dominant power has received a lion's share of benefits from the current system does not mean that it would stop trying to claim even more benefits.

None of the indicators used in this discussion for inferring revisionist motivation is without flaw. Readers do not have to accept them, and can surely develop and propose their own empirical measures in order to gauge the extent to which a particular state stands inside or outside of the international community. These measures can include but are not limited to indicators such as the degree of a state's discordance with a majority of other member states in the U.N. General Assembly, the incidence of its military interventions abroad, and the frequency of its overt or covert involvement in destabilizing or overthrowing hostile foreign regimes. One may also wish to examine the size of territories won or lost, the number of wars fought, the extent of troop deployments abroad, and the relative size of the national defense burden. Some colleagues have suggested that indicators such as a state's observed behavior in terms of its treaty commitments, arms procurements, or alliances, can provide clues about its future behavior.[45] Collected systematically over time and applied consistently across countries, this evidence can help one gain a general sense about which countries have been on an expansionist path and which have been trying to mount a defense on their home turf. Such data are likely to show that France and China are more status-quo oriented than the U.S. or the U.K.[46]

The debate between offensive realists and defensive realists offers a possible basis for an exploration of the kind suggested above. Whereas offensive realists argue that all states are driven to maximize their power, defensive realists contend that most states seek instead to maximize their security.[47] According to defensive realism, states realize that their aggressive pursuit of power can exacerbate the security dilemma and thus cause other states to take counter-actions that end up making them less rather than more secure. Because defensive realism does not deny that some states may be driven to maximize their power rather than their security, the critical challenge for analysts and officials alike is how to recognize these two types of states. How can those security-minded states signal to reassure others about their defensive interests, and thus to distinguish themselves from those that are power-hungry? In order to be credible, these signals have to entail actions that would be too costly for the power-hungry type to undertake.

Andrew Kydd's work is instructive for discerning whether states are primarily interested in maximizing their security or power.[48] He argued, persuasively, that democracies are more likely to disclose their true preferences because their policy processes are more transparent. All things being equal, democracies' declarations and actions should be more credible. Kydd offered examples of costly signals both democracies and autocracies can undertake to reassure others that they are "security seekers" rather than "power maximizers." For instance, both can moderate an official ideology that may be perceived by others as antagonistic and even threatening. Their treatment of domestic dissidents and ethnic minorities can project an image abroad about how they are likely to act toward other states. A willingness to tolerate dissidence and accept autonomy among one's weaker neighbors can offer another way to signal one's benign intentions to the broader international community. Finally, states' military policies can communicate to others their intention to seek security or pursue power. Do they accept agreements for arms control, forsake opportunities to extend strategic advantage, and invest in force structure and advanced weapons with primarily a defensive orientation?

Under Mao Tse-tung's leadership, especially during the Cultural Revolution, China espoused an ideology of people's war and revolutionary insurgency that threatened its neighbors. It was also guilty of horrendous abuses of human rights against millions of its own citizens, outrageous persecution of political dissidents, and harsh suppression of Tibetan resistance. Although technologically backward, China had a large army and fought several border wars with its neighbors. Moreover, during the 1960s and 1970s, Beijing was involved in several serious territorial disputes. Quite understandably, such behavior was not reassuring to other states which were concerned that Beijing was motivated by power expansion rather than by security amelioration. In the last quarter century, however, Chinese foreign policy has undergone a fundamental transformation. Beijing has moderated its ideology to promote international engagement, joined multilateral efforts to control armament and the spread of weapons technology, and introduced socio-economic reforms that extended personal freedom and individual rights to its citizens to a far greater extent than during the Maoist years. As noted above, it has also settled most of its border disputes on terms generally favorable to its counterparts.

How would foreigners judge the U.S. on similar grounds as suggested by Kydd? The Bush doctrine emphasizes an aggressive, unilateral assertiveness, and acknowledges openly "the basic strategy of the United States *must* [emphasis added] be to prevent the emergence of any rivals – forever."[49] As already noted, whereas Beijing now professes to support the Westphalian principles of state sovereignty, Washington seeks to promote regime change abroad according to its vision of democracy and capitalism. Whereas, unlike China, the U.S. has not engaged in massive and flagrant domestic violation of its people's physical integrity and civil rights,[50] there are nevertheless legacies of racial segregation, internment of citizens of Japanese descent, and sharp and persistent disparities in the physical quality of life along racial and ethnic lines.[51] The legal and physical treatment of "enemy combatants" and terrorists, be they U.S. citizens or not and whether held at home or abroad, tends to alarm rather than reassure other states. Similarly, frequent and unwarranted military intervention and political subversion against unfriendly but weak neighbors imply that Washington is more interested in the pursuit of power than in security. In addition to how the U.S. chooses to use its awesome military might, the nature of its armament-procurement and weapons-development programs can make a difference in projecting an image as a security seeker or power maximizer. Contrary to Washington's own definition of its wide-ranging security interests, its deployment of aircraft-carrier battle groups, long-range stealth bombers, and missile-defense systems are not likely to be construed by other states as an investment in defensive weapons intended for security protection rather than offensive instruments for power projection.

Naturally, other states' perceptions, such as those public opinions cited earlier, are just that: perceptions which may or may not correspond to reality. Nevertheless, these perceptions have consequences because others will act on them. The images held by non-Americans are often at odds with Americans' self-image.[52] The standard characterization by which a hegemon and, by extension, the U.S. are necessarily committed to the defense of the international status quo does not correspond with the country's historical behavior or with Washington's professed policy agenda. Such attribution, however, inevitably conveys a rhetorical bias in favor of maintaining the current international system, implying that the existing state of affairs is just and even natural. At the same time, this attribution casts any state that is unhappy with the hegemon in the role of challenging the entire international system. Therefore, the interests of the hegemon are treated as the equivalent of the interests of the international community as a whole. Challenges to the hegemon are seen to be tantamount to destabilizing the international system, whereas the policies pursued by the hegemon are presented as having necessarily the intent and the effect of defending the international system. Naturally, these claims should be better settled by empirical inquiry than asserted by assumption or definition.

Disagreeing with the conventional view, some American scholars have recently questioned whether the U.S. is threatened with a power transition and whether it is a status-quo state. They acknowledged that Washington is taking advantage of its historically unprecedented primacy in an effort to fashion new international rules and to advance its own nationalist agenda.[53] One noted that:

> the United States is in a position that is historically unprecedented, and that it has used its power to mold a world that would be compatible with U.S. interests and values. The United States has not acted as a "status quo" power: rather, it has used its position of primacy to increase its influence, to enhance its position vis-à-vis potential rivals, and to deal with specific security threats.[54]

Others described current U.S. officials as "assertive nationalists."[55] These comments offer a comparative context for interpreting typical U.S. scholarship on China with its singular focus on Chinese nationalism and China's use of power.[56]

4 Imperial overstretch and loss aversion as sources of war

Thus far, I have focused on the identification of any ongoing or past power transitions and the determination of the status-quo or revisionist orientation of states. These discussions have been about how one may seek to capture those empirical referents in the world of international relations that correspond to the central concepts of the power-transition theory. I now turn to the logic behind the causal attribution suggested by this theory. In brief, this theory hypothesizes that major wars happen when a revisionist challenger instigates a conflict to displace a declining hegemon from the pre-eminent position that the latter country has previously enjoyed.[1] According to this theory, major wars coinciding with or following from such a power transition are fought over more than just the distribution of benefits between the upstart and the hegemon; they are really contests about the rules according to which such distribution is to be made.[2] In other words, these wars are about who should control the international system and thus have the potential of transforming this system.[3]

The logic presented above suggests that the existing hegemon has status, prestige, influence, or whatever else that the upstart challenger wants, and the latter is emboldened by its increasing power to start a war in order to take away from the hegemon that which it (the challenger) covets. Accordingly, the source of danger to international peace may be traced to the latecomer's ambitions. This latecomer's dissatisfaction and its rising power combine to create the sufficient condition for international instability. This country has both the motivation and the capability to cause havoc.

This reasoning, however, overlooks two pertinent questions. First, if the hegemon realizes that the latecomer harbors dangerous ambitions, why should it (the hegemon) not seek an early confrontation before the latecomer becomes even stronger? That is, why should the hegemon not start a preventive war? Second, if their differential growth rates favor the latecomer over the hegemon, why should the latecomer not simply wait for history to unfold so that eventually it will end up as the top dog without having to fight for this status? Should not the latecomer prefer this course of action compared to a premature confrontation with the hegemon that can end badly for it (the latecomer)? Indeed, knowing that the hegemon would be wary about its ambitions and growing power, should not the latecomer try to convince the hegemon that it (the latecomer) does not seek to overthrow the existing international order? In doing so, the latecomer can try to avoid becoming the target of a preventive war waged by the hegemon. In this chapter I consider the ideas contained in these two counter-hypotheses. I examine these ideas first in the context of rationalist explanations of war, and then evaluate them from the perspective of prospect theory. A historical analysis will be postponed until the next chapter.

The rationalist perspective argues that wars are an inefficient way for settling disputes. Fighting a war is costly in blood, treasure, goodwill and, for top officials, their political career and even their life or liberty (just consider the fate of Saddam Hussein, Slobodan Milosevic and, from an earlier era, Adolf Hitler and Benito Mussolini).[4] Surely, if the leaders of the belligerent countries could anticipate the eventual outcome of their contest, they would have preferred to reach an agreement on the basis of that outcome without having to suffer the costs of actual fighting. That they were unable to agree on the terms of this settlement without having to fight implies that they had different expectations about how the war would end. In other words, they held different *ex ante* beliefs about their performance on the battlefield and therefore about the settlement terms to which they should be entitled. They must have believed they knew something about their likely performance on the battlefield that the other side did not, so that a resort to arms can help to persuade the opposition to make concessions that it would otherwise be unwilling to make in the absence of the information disclosed in actual fighting. The possession of such *private information* therefore constitutes one reason for wars to occur, despite their known inefficiency.[5]

Presumably, when the publicly known capabilities of the competing countries have become more equalized, private information plays a more influential role in their respective calculation. That is, secret knowledge about one's own strength and the other side's weakness in a potential military showdown is likely to matter more, when the contestants have become more closely matched in those power assets that are widely recognized and publicized (such as those discussed previously in Chapter 2 in regard to relative economic output and military expenditures). Conversely, when common knowledge indicates a large gap separating the contestants' power, private information pertaining to their capabilities is less influential in their respective estimation about how a military conflict will turn out and the likely terms of its eventual settlement.[6]

What do these observations imply? It would appear in the first instance that one does not need to privilege psychological factors such as anxiety, arrogance, or over-confidence in order to explain the outbreak of war during periods of power transition. The occurrence of war during these times can simply be due to the fact that, everything else being equal, private information will matter more in situations where the contestants' capabilities are becoming more equally matched (or when changes in relative national capabilities create a fluid and therefore more uncertain situation). This discussion implies, second, that the two opposing sides in a war cannot obviously both be right in their anticipation of how their conflict will end.[7] Had they been able to reach convergent expectations about the war's outcome, they could and should have settled on the basis of this anticipation, thereby sparing themselves the costs of having to fight. That Germany lost both World Wars in its supposed bid for international supremacy (or, at least, regional hegemony in Europe) would indicate that its leaders had miscalculated. Surely, the private information in Berlin's possession was not sufficient to assure its victory in these contests. This apparent mistake again recalls the enigma that Berlin did not wait for Germany's power to increase further. Why would Germany want to precipitate a confrontation in 1914 and again in 1939 when its position relative to the U.K. might have been expected to become even stronger with the passage of time? As Paul Kennedy has put it, why did Berlin refuse to choose "peace [which] must have brought Germany the mastery of Europe within a few years"?[8] Moreover, that Germany had lost both conflicts even when it was supposed to have already overtaken the U.K. must mean that the British had stronger allies than the Germans. These questions naturally turn one's analytic attention to the other great powers such as Russia/the USSR and the U.S., states whose relative power trajectories and alliance decisions were critical in explaining the initiation as well as the outcome of these global conflicts. I will address these questions in later chapters.

For now, I continue with the discussion about the rationalist perspective to explain war. As noted above, private information often inclines one or both disputants to believe that they are entitled to a better deal than the other side is willing to concede in the absence of the information revealed by fighting. A resort to arms provides a means to disclose, by way of relative performance on the battlefield, the "true" distributions of national capabilities and motivations, and hence the terms of a settlement in accordance with these distributions. In this view, wars become necessary because, by its very nature, private information cannot be publicly disclosed without in effect giving away state secrets about one's true capabilities and the strategic plans by which one expects to gain an advantage over one's opponent. Moreover, even if one were to announce publicly one's capabilities and plans, others would be reluctant to accept these declarations at their face value. This is so because leaders are well aware of the tendency for states to deliberately exaggerate their capabilities and resolve. Rationalist theories point to this known tendency by states to engage in *misrepresentation* as another reason for the occurrence of war. Because officials discount "cheap talk," actual combat and performance on the battlefield are taken to be more credible indicators of a state's true strength and its real intentions.

Why would states want to engage in misrepresentation? One common reason is to get the other side to concede by creating an appearance of being stronger or more determined than is actually the case. How does this discussion relate to the power-transition theory? The stronger a country is compared to its potential adversary, the greater would be its temptation to bluff about its intentions. Precisely because the weaker side is faced with an asymmetric situation tilted to its disadvantage, it must overcome greater foreign skepticism when it professes a willingness to confront the stronger side in a showdown. The stronger side does not face the same credibility problem and, therefore, is more disposed to believe that its bluffs will work.[9] If valid, this reasoning implies that a declining hegemon, a state that still holds a stronger hand in bilateral relations even though its advantage is slipping, is more prone to engage in this sort of misrepresentation. It can be expected to exaggerate its interests in other parts of the world and its resolve to defend these interests, when it may in fact lack both the capabilities and the intention to defend these declared interests. That others, including those states whose power is on the rise, are not unaware of this tendency leads to another implication, which in turn creates a paradox. Knowing that the dominant state's power is on the wane and that it may be tempted to misrepresent its ability and readiness to defend its interests abroad, latecomers are in turn more likely to call these bluffs. Significantly, although a dominant state was originally bluffing, it might subsequently change its mind and decide to stand behind its publicized commitment if challenged.[10] That is, once its reputation becomes engaged, it may decide to stand firm after all. This series of interactions can increase the danger of getting the disputants locked into a situation from which it is difficult for them to disengage.

As a partial example of this dynamic, the U.S. really did not want to commit itself to the defense of the offshore islands of Quemoy and Matsu. However, once Beijing began its campaign of bombardment against these Kuomintang outposts in 1958, it became more difficult for Washington to back down in the midst of an escalating crisis. Similarly, the U.K. found itself facing this predicament in its confrontation with Argentina over the Falklands (or the Malvinas) in 1982. Even though London had originally not insisted on controlling these islands and had not wanted to fight a war over their status, Buenos Aires's invasion engaged Margaret Thatcher's reputation and motivated her to resort to arms to recover them.

Naturally, attempts at misrepresentation are not limited to exaggerating one's capability or resolve. Sometimes, a state may try to project the opposite image in order to foster a sense of complacency on the part of a potential adversary or to deflect hostility from itself. Thus, Japan chose to disguise its true fighting capability prior to its war with Russia in 1904. An underestimation of Japan's strength caused Russia to be over-confident and contributed to its defeat in that conflict. Misrepresentation can also involve attempts to signal that one does not pose a threat to another country, thereby seeking to avoid or postpone a conflict with the latter until a more propitious time. Prior to being attacked by Nazi Germany, the USSR pursued this policy and concluded a non-aggression treaty with Berlin. Significantly, however, such strategies tend to be adopted by the ascending, even though still weaker, powers.[11] These states have an incentive to conceal their true strength and to bide their time lest a premature confrontation interrupts their rising growth trajectory. Conversely and as already noted, an existing hegemon typically has the opposite incentive: to exaggerate its wideranging interests abroad and its capability and determination to defend these interests. Precisely because this dominant state has more power assets than the other states, it is better situated to succeed in bluffing – that is, to gain concessions from others by pretending to be disposed to fight them. Yet this tendency can get it into trouble because these bluffs may turn into ill-conceived and self-perpetuating commitments.[12] A hegemon may initially issue a threat in the hope that this threat is enough to get an opponent to yield. When this hope is dashed, however, the hegemon may feel that it has to actually implement its threat because, in the absence of such action, its reputation will be harmed.[13] There may be an interaction effect such that as a dominant power suffers relative decline it is more inclined to bluff and, when its bluff is called, it is more likely to revert to an assertive policy in order to preserve its sagging reputation.

How can a dominant power try to protect its wide-ranging interests from being challenged? As James Fearon has noted, there can be two generic approaches to deterrence.[14] The approach of "sinking costs" involves making preparations prior to a challenge in the hope of discouraging such a challenge in the first place. These efforts can entail stationing troops on an ally's soil (or in a contested territory) and building military bases there, stockpiling war materiel, and forming joint command and communication structures in preparation for a coordinated defense if a challenger launches an attack. The other approach involves "tying hands," for example by making repeated and public pledges to take a certain course of action should a stipulated contingency come to pass. By deliberately committing one's political prestige and credibility to these declarations, one is trying to signal the seriousness of one's announcements. If one fails to subsequently stand by these announcements, one would suffer serious embarrassment and a loss of legitimacy in the eyes of both domestic and foreign constituencies. Because "tying one's hands" by verbal declaration does not entail any front-end costs, this approach is tempting to would-be bluffers. One pays a price for bluffing only if one is shown to be insincere when presented with a challenge; that is, to be unwilling to back up one's commitment after a challenge has actually been mounted. Successful bluffs, by definition, are cheap victories because they do not require the tedious and heavy investment entailed by the "sunk costs" approach.

So what? In the context of an ongoing power transition, the dominant power is experiencing relative decline. Given this relative decline and in view of the foreign commitments it is likely to have accumulated over time, its resources are stretched thin and probably inadequate for meeting multiple real and imagined challenges abroad. This state is therefore likely to resort increasingly to "tying its hands" as the preferred approach to defend its perceived interests.[15] This dynamic corresponds with Britain's declared support for Czechoslovakia before World War II, when it really did not have either the ability or the will to make good its pledge. After the Munich Conference, Adolf Hitler thought that the British and the French were also bluffing when they said they would defend Poland. This phenomenon, reflecting the known tendency for states to engage in misrepresentation and for their counterparts to discount public declarations, describes a part of the dynamic leading to war. The increasing tendency for a declining hegemon to resort to "tied hands" rather than "sunk costs" in trying to defend its interests constitutes another important part of this dynamic.[16] With its dwindling resources, a declining hegemon is hard pressed to adopt "sunk costs" in order to deter potential challenges on multiple fronts, and it is attracted increasingly to the alternative of "tying its hands," since this latter approach does not involve the actual expenditure of tangible resources. Yet as a deterrence approach, "tying hands" has the distinct disadvantage of "throwing away the steering wheel." As in the game of chicken, this stance in effect says that if a confrontation is to be avoided, the other side must yield. By committing one's own and, indirectly, one's opponent's prestige and credibility in an escalating dispute, "tying hands" can lock the two sides into a collision course.

Besides private information and misrepresentation, rationalist accounts point to another reason for wars to occur despite their known inefficiency. The so-called *commitment problem* suggests that it is difficult to enforce binding agreements.[17] If a declining power makes concessions today, it can hardly persuade the rising power that it will not make any more concessions tomorrow. Similarly, regardless of the promises made by the rising power today about its limited aims, there is nothing to prevent it from insisting on further concessions from the declining power in the future. Naturally, the seriousness of this commitment problem depends in part on whether the process causing the ongoing power shift turns out to be transient and reversible, or whether it is seen to be permanent and inevitable. In addition, if the latter should be the case, the declining power's response to its predicament would be influenced by its judgment of its likely status under alternative international regimes in the future, a topic that will be addressed in the next chapter. For now, the implication raised by the commitment problem can be stated more starkly from the rising power's perspective. Far from wanting to instigate a confrontation or precipitate a crisis, this state would want to reassure the declining hegemon of its reasonable and limited goals, so that the latter would be less inclined to mount a preventive war against it. That is, from a rationalist perspective, it does not make sense for the rising power to antagonize or provoke the declining power to lash out against it when the balance of power is still operating to its disadvantage. Any rash behavior by the rising power would only make concerns about the commitment problem even more acute for the declining power.

To summarize our discussion of the rationalist perspective thus far, situations involving potential power transitions present great uncertainty to officials. These are times when leaders have more difficulty in making an accurate assessment of relative national power. These are also times when private information, such as that pertaining to technological breakthrough and strategic innovations in military affairs, should matter more. Therefore, situations of potential power transition are more likely to create international tension even without the additional danger caused by the aggressive ambitions of rising powers or panic on the part of declining powers. A state that has previously enjoyed a dominant position in international relations is more likely to engage in misrepresentation to exaggerate its resolve and capability as it tries to defend overseas interests accumulated over the years. Conversely, being a latecomer, the rising power has fewer vested interests to defend and is less likely to engage in this type of misrepresentation. Rather, the latecomer should be motivated to hide its true strength and prolong the period of transition so that it can be given more time to develop its strength. If accurate, these expectations contradict the view that a cocky and reckless latecomer is largely responsible for starting disputes aimed at displacing the hegemon from its dominant position. To the contrary, an awareness of the commitment problem should incline a latecomer to avoid provoking the still dominant hegemon to enter a premature showdown. Conversely, as its relative decline runs its course, the hegemon may be expected to rely more on "tying hands," and less on "sinking costs," in trying to deter challenges to its interests. The significance of this change in deterrence emphasis is not difficult to understand. A state's commitment is more believable when it is perceived to have the necessary capability to carry out this commitment. Significantly, a declining hegemon's increasing resort to "tying hands" happens in the context of its declining capability – that is, precisely when it is increasingly strapped for resources to meet multiple demands. It is therefore paradoxical that when the hegemon is powerful and when it has plenty of resources to make sunk investments, such expenditures are less necessary (and hence the hegemon's verbal declarations are more likely to be sufficient for successful deterrence). With the onset of severe decline, however, the hegemon faces serious resource constraints. These constraints, known to the hegemon's opponents, in turn compel this state to deploy its more limited resources in deterrence investments in order to demonstrate that its commitments are credible.

Verbal declarations absent "sunk costs" are easy and cheap to undertake. This being the case, one may expect states that are sincere about upholding their commitments as well as those that are insincere to both engage in "tying hands" as a deterrence strategy.[18] That the insincere states will try to masquerade as the sincere ones in turn invites others to question the hegemon's commitments, especially if its resources have already been strained due to precipitous decline and if it has a prior reputation for abandoning its commitments.[19] This discussion suggests that a rising latecomer is not necessarily the instigator of international conflict. International conflict can also result from the failure of a declining hegemon to "downsize" adequately its foreign policy role and to reduce its existing commitments in correspondence with its shrinking resource base. Paul Kennedy has aptly described this phenomenon as imperial overstretch.[20] A failure to undertake appropriate and timely economic and political adjustment also exacerbates the hegemon's relative and even absolute decline.

Not all people agree with the premise of rationalist theory. Prospect theory challenges the axiom that people decide on the basis of expected utilities and disutilities.[21] Yet, significantly, despite this serious disagreement with rationalist theory, prospect theory also suggests behavioral profiles for the declining hegemon and for the ascending latecomer that do not accord with the standard characterization given by the power-transition theory. For our purposes, the major insight of prospect theory is that people have an aversion to losses and that they are willing to take more risk in order to prevent a loss than to pursue a gain. Thus, when people are in the domain of gain – such as when their stocks have risen in value – they tend to become conservative and play "not to lose." As a result, a common mistake made by investors is that they sell their winning stocks too soon. The investors try to "lock in" their profit even though their stocks have the potential to appreciate even more in value. Conversely, people tend to hold on to their losing investments for too long. They appear to be psychologically disinclined to sell those stocks whose values have fallen because they are unwilling to accept losses. One manifestation of people's loss aversion is that the volume of stock trades tends to be higher when the market as a whole is rising in value, whereas this trading volume tends to be lower during the "down days."

Results from many experimental studies have confirmed people's general willingness to accept greater risk in order to avoid losses and, conversely, their reluctance to take on risk when pursuing gains. When offered a choice in the domain of gain, people would typically want to have a "sure thing" compared to a lottery offering the same or even greater expected value. Thus, they tend to prefer a certain pay-off of $50 to, say, a coin toss promising a 50 percent chance of $100 and a 50 percent chance of no monetary reward. This popular preference is striking because, according to the rationalist expectation, these choices should be a matter of indifference. When put in a domain of prospective loss, people display the opposite tendency of a willingness to accept greater risk. Accordingly, when faced with a choice of losing $50 for certain, and the alternative of a coin toss with a 50 percent chance of losing $100 and a 50 percent chance of not losing any money, most will take the latter option. These experimental results suggest strongly that people are more inclined to gamble in order to avoid a possible loss than in a comparable situation dealing with a prospective gain.

Prospect theory offers another insight that is pertinent to our discussion. Labeled as the "endowment effect," this insight suggests that people tend to attach higher value to something already in their possession than they are willing to pay for that same item bought from others. Thus, for instance, home owners typically demand a higher price for their house than the existing market conditions would warrant, and investors set the sale price of their stock at a level at which they themselves would not want to buy the same stock. In negotiations, one finds a comparable phenomenon such that each side believes that its concessions are more valuable than those made by the other side.

In addition, one would infer from prospect theory that leaders often fail to revise their failed policies but tend instead to escalate their commitment to and investment in such policies in an attempt to recover their sunk costs.[22] They are also prone to take large risks and to make heavy investments in order to avert relatively small losses. Finally, they tend to outweigh those outcomes deemed to be certain compared to others that appear to be only highly probable. Imperial Germany's behavior before World War I, such as during the 1905 Morocco crisis, the 1908 Bosnia crisis, the 1911 Agadir crisis, and the 1912 Balkan war, exemplified the first two tendencies. Berlin's bellicosity in these cases provoked and rallied the other states to oppose it, even though it was not quite prepared to go to war. As for the third tendency, a willingness to pay a premium for the certain rather than settling for the highly probable was perhaps part of the Bush administration's calculation leading to its decision to invade Iraq in order to ensure that Baghdad did not come to possess weapons of mass destruction.

It is not difficult to grasp some obvious implications that follow from prospect theory for our discussion on international tension arising from any real or imagined power transition. Due to people's general aversion to losses, it is more difficult for the leaders of a declining hegemon to accept the reality or prospect of their country's diminished influence and status. As a result of the endowment effect, these officials would not be able to adjust fully and quickly the accustomed role for their country in order to reflect its reduced capabilities. Instead, they are likely to hold on to outdated concepts and unrealistic commitments because a policy of retrenchment is likely to be psychologically traumatic as well as politically challenging. Given people's general inclination to gamble in an effort to stave off losses, these officials are more likely to engage in risky policies that can escalate into war. One possibility is to launch a preventive war against a rising power that is perceived to present a serious threat in the future. In contrast to the declining hegemon, a latecomer on the ascendant would be reluctant to gamble. Prospect theory suggests that this latecomer would be more interested in securing and consolidating its recent gains rather than in mounting an audacious campaign in search of further gains. Whereas the power-transition theory tends to depict the latecomer as an ambitious and over-confident upstart anxious for a showdown with the hegemon, our discussion based on both rationalist and prospect theories points to a different portrait. Far from being eager to initiate a confrontation, the latecomer should be risk-averse and cautious in its policies lest it provoke the hegemon into launching a preventive war against it. Being still stronger now but saddled with a process of gradual decline, the hegemon has the incentive and the capability to instigate a confrontation before the latecomer becomes too strong. The danger of war is more likely to come from the policies of this country than those of the latecomer. Imperial overstretch – an excessive role in view of the available resources – turns out to be not only a contributing cause behind the hegemon's likely decline,[23] but also a key source of rising international tension. The logic of this chapter leads one to expect the U.S. as a hyperpower to be involved in many more armed conflicts than China, which as a rising latecomer should be interested in maintaining a stable environment in order to continue its growth.

5 Preventive war and alternative responses to decline

Why would Germany start a war against the U.K. if its relative position could be expected to improve over time? And, if Germany had already overtaken the U.K. on the eve of World War I and, again, prior to World War II, why did it lose both conflicts? We have previously raised these puzzling questions, and it is now time to attempt an answer.

The standard characterization given by the power-transition theory depicts the two World Wars as a bid by Germany to displace the U.K. as the global hegemon. This depiction emphasizes the Anglo-German rivalry as the central motive and main dynamic that produced these conflicts. It explains the outcomes of both conflicts in terms of the relative strength of the opposing alliances, and not just the two leading antagonists. Germany lost both World Wars because the U.K. had more powerful allies.[1] The French, the Russians, and the Americans rallied to support the British, and thereby helped to tip the balance against the German-led coalition on both occasions. According to the authors of *The War Ledger*,

> while it is true that the challenger overtakes the dominant nation and that at the outset it is the challenger who is the stronger, it is equally true in the two cases [the two World Wars] tested that the coalition with the dominant nation is stronger than the coalition shaped by the challenger to unseat the leader and recast the international order.[2]

The histories of World War I and World War II, however, lend themselves to an alternative interpretation.[3] Although one could surely point to instances of tension and rivalry between Berlin and London prior to both conflicts, it seems a stretch to argue that Germany deliberately sought a showdown with the U.K. The available historical evidence points rather more strongly in the opposite direction, suggesting that in the case of World War I German leaders had wanted to neutralize the British. They wanted to avoid British intervention in a possible continental war. That the U.K. eventually joined a conflict which had originated from a quarrel between Serbia and Austria-Hungary reflected a failure of German diplomacy to keep the British on the sidelines. Far from an implied motive of trying to use the Balkan crisis to entice and entrap the British into a confrontation, Berlin had wanted to contain this crisis from engulfing London. In addition, instead of the view that the French and the Russians rallied to the British cause, it was the British who came to the rescue of the French and the Russians who would have otherwise lost the war to the Germans. Thus, rather than saying that the British prevailed because the French and the Russians had come to support them, it would be more reasonable to argue that the French and the Russians were spared complete defeat at the hands of the Germans due to British – and especially American – intervention. Indeed, as we will emphasize again later, it is not so much that the British side had more allies or more powerful allies. In the end, only one country mattered in determining the outcome of both World Wars, and that country was the U.S. Yet, as already remarked, the power-transition theory did not even accord the U.S. the status of a central contender in the international system despite the decisive influence exercised by the U.S. in these conflicts.

The U.K. fought in World War I not because Germany had wanted to fight the U.K. but rather because it was unable to prevent the U.K. from joining the war. Prior to World War II, Adolf Hitler sought a coalition with the U.K. He was, however, rebuffed by London, for example when he proposed a naval agreement in 1933. He was exasperated that London did not see "an Anglo-German combination [made] the most natural of alliances."[4] The failure of the British and the French to resist prior German moves to remilitarize the Rhineland, to expand armed forces, to establish *Anschluss* with Austria, and to demand the secession of Sudetenland from Czechoslovakia persuaded Adolf Hitler that they lacked the capabilities and the resolve to resist Germany effectively. He attacked Poland in September 1939 despite the fact that London and Paris had declared their intention to intervene on behalf of the Poles. Germany's invasion of Poland did of course force a showdown with the British and the French in the sense that the latter had to choose between war with Germany or peace on German terms. Hitler's reminiscences suggested that he did not wish to avoid a confrontation and that he would rather have a war with the U.K. and France earlier than later.[5] Still, actual combat on the western front was delayed for months after Germany's attack on Poland. Germany did not launch its invasion of France until May 1940. In part due to Hitler's decision to concentrate German forces on the seizure of Paris, the British expeditionary force managed to escape at Dunkirk. As late as 1941, there were attempts made to avoid a drawn-out struggle between Germany and the U.K.[6]

If Anglo-German rivalry cannot quite capture the motivations setting off World War I and World War II, what can account for the outbreak of these conflicts? Dale Copeland argued persuasively that these were preventive wars waged by Germany against Russia/the USSR.[7] Having already overtaken the U.K., Germany's primary interest was not to wrestle international supremacy from London but was, as already remarked, to prevent the British from joining the forthcoming fray on the side of Germany's principal enemy. Berlin was rather more concerned about the emergence of Russia/the USSR as a formidable challenger to Germany in the future. In Copeland's words, "both conflicts [World Wars] were rooted in a common cause: the German fear of the rise of Russia, a state with three times Germany's population and forty times its land mass."[8]

Although Germany continued to make absolute gains in its national power, in relative terms its power had already peaked shortly before both World Wars. Germany's growth trajectory had begun to decelerate whereas Russia/the USSR's development had taken off and started to accelerate at an increasing tempo.[9] The prospect of falling eventually behind the Russian colossus motivated the German leaders to initiate a preventive war. Significantly, the logic of preventive war is based on leaders' anticipation of future developments. Moreover, the primary motivation for waging this type of war is not an acquisitive desire to make gains but rather a defensive motive to avoid losses. That a state which is currently much stronger than its adversary but anticipates relative decline in the future chooses to wage a preventive war also points to the acuteness of the commitment problem. If officials see an inexorable trend that will eventually put their country at a relative disadvantage and if they have serious concerns about the rising power's future intentions, fighting a preventive war now may appear to be a more prudent course of action than postponing the inevitable confrontation until tomorrow.[10]

Copeland's careful historical analysis showed that the German leaders deliberately sought war in July 1914. Rather than the popular view of blundering into a war they had tried to avoid, the top officials in Berlin contrived to force a confrontation with Russia. None of the German leaders thought that St. Petersburg wanted war; all in fact agreed that Russia desired peace.[11] During the last days of the crisis, the German leaders' primary concern was not that war might break out but rather that peace might be kept. They manipulated both Russia and Austria-Hungary to commit their reputation to a course of action that all but made a pull-back from war impossible. In Copeland's words, they "systematically sought to draw the Russians into the war and then to preclude any possibility of Russia escaping the trap by capitulating to Austrian demands."[12] Thus, significantly, Berlin wanted to ensure that there would be no last-minute concessions by St. Petersburg to avert a war. This deliberate and determined attempt to seek war reflected the view that Germany's advantage would be eroded by a delay. War had to be initiated in 1914 at a moment most favorable to Germany, when its relative power had just peaked. German leaders preferred to have a continental war without the U.K. but were willing to accept the risk of British involvement. This characterization, however, is not the same as suggesting that they actively sought a confrontation with the U.K. with the aim of displacing the latter from its position of pre-eminence.

As noted above, Adolf Hitler was frustrated that his overtures to the U.K. were rebuffed. In a moment of exasperation he blamed London for not realizing that Russia was "now the greatest power factor in the whole of Europe."[13] In August 1939, he was quoted as saying, "everything I undertake is directed against the Russians; if the West is too stupid and blind to grasp this, then I shall be compelled to come to an agreement with the Russians, beat the West, and then after their defeat turn against the Soviet Union with all my forces."[14] Only after having failed again to keep the U.K. neutral,[15] Hitler turned to Stalin for the signing of the German–Soviet non-aggression pact, which was followed in short order by their joint invasion of Poland. This treaty, however, did not prevent the Nazis from invading the USSR in June 1941.

The depiction of both World Wars as resulting from Germany's preventive motivation against Russia/the USSR enables one to resolve an apparent enigma mentioned earlier. If Germany had already overtaken the U.K., why could it not wait a little longer so that, to paraphrase Paul Kennedy, Berlin's ambition for mastery over Europe could be duly realized within a short time? Why should Berlin be seemingly in such a hurry to instigate a confrontation with London in a premature bid for supremacy? The answer to these questions is that the U.K. was not the real concern for Germany, and that time was not perceived to be working in Germany's favor. Instead of competing with a once-dominant power already well on a course of relative decline, German leaders were far more anxious about an emergent Russia/the USSR whose rapid growth was eroding their country's advantage. With the passage of time, Germany's lead could be expected to shrink.[16] Thus, like the officials of other states, German leaders tried to be anticipatory.

This account underscores the point that by the time of World War I – not to mention World War II – the U.K. had already lost its hegemonic status. As Karen A. Rasler and William R. Thompson pointed out, "World War I did not bring the British leadership down. It only capped a process of competitive decline that was first discernible in the mid-nineteenth century and perhaps even a little earlier."[17] In the European theater, Germany had supplanted the U.K.[18] Having already become the dominant power in this region, Germany fought these wars in order to defeat a prospective challenger. How did Russia/the USSR behave, being aware of both its own growth potential and Germany's security concerns? It behaved in the manner predicted in our earlier discussion. St. Petersburg had exercised restraint in several Balkan crises prior to 1914, urging its Serbian ally to compromise. Indeed, even in the 1914 crisis Czar Nicholas's government had wanted to defuse the crisis. It was Germany that had sought a confrontation, bringing about the dynamic of chain-ganging (i.e., the contagion of conflict due to alliance ties) that turned a local conflict into World War I.[19] Significantly, the perception that Russia had suffered humiliating setbacks in previous crisis encounters caused St. Petersburg to be more reluctant to make further concessions at the expense of its own reputation and the interests of its ally (Serbia). The main point, however, is that far from promoting a showdown, Russia as an ascending state preferred a tranquil environment for its power to develop further.

Josef Stalin behaved also as we would have expected of the leader of a rising but still weaker power. He went so far as to collaborate with Germany in the division of Poland. The non-aggression pact he signed with Germany in August 1939 was another part of Stalin's reassurance game to convince Hitler that he did not pose a threat. Far from seeking to provoke German hostility, Soviet statecraft sought deliberately to deflect and contain it. Even though Winston Churchill and Franklin Roosevelt had warned Stalin about an impending Nazi invasion, the latter had steadfastly refused to be "goaded" into a conflict with Hitler. He dismissed obvious signs of German preparation for Operation Barbarossa,[20] and ordered his military to avoid any incident that might appear to be provocative and thus give Berlin a pretext to attack. In short, as an ascending latecomer, the USSR did not behave as a cocky upstart looking for a confrontation. It instead pursued appeasement and accommodation with the Nazis.

Of course, Stalin's policy did not work and the USSR was invaded. It is important, however, to recognize that although the German invasion turned the USSR into a British ally, it is far from an instance of another country coming to the defense of an existing hegemon or an existing international order. The fact of the matter is that German actions forced the Soviets to fight when the latter would rather have preferred not to be dragged into a war between Germany and the Western powers. That is, Germany's audacity and recklessness caused the USSR to fight on the Allies' side. Certainly the Allies' cause was stronger because the USSR joined this coalition. But as already noted, it would be a mistake to imply that the USSR had voluntarily joined the Western powers in a fight against the Nazis. To say that even though Germany was stronger than the U.K. it still lost both World Wars because the U.K. had more powerful friends is true enough but it omits important details.

In the end, only one country mattered in determining the eventual outcomes of World War I and World War II. Whether Burma, Bulgaria, Brazil, or Bolivia chose to fight on the side of the Allies or of the Axis powers, or to stay neutral, really would not make any difference. Even the involvement of France, Italy, or Japan would not have been decisive. The participation of these belligerents perhaps influenced how protracted these wars were, but not their ultimate outcome. As the world's most powerful state, intervention by the U.S. made all the difference in these global conflicts. Germany lost both World Wars because it was only the second most powerful country in the world. Germany's opponents won because the most powerful country fought on their side. Thus, American contributions were responsible for tipping the balance of forces in both World Wars. Without these American contributions, it is not difficult to imagine that Germany would have emerged victorious in these conflicts.

What motivated the U.S. to intervene? In both World Wars, the U.S. intervention came after the fighting had been going on for some time. It was not until April 1917 that the U.S. finally entered World War I. By then, France, the U.K., and Russia were practically exhausted. By November of that year, the Czar was overthrown. The new Bolshevik government subsequently concluded the Brest-Litovsk Treaty with Germany, taking the USSR out of the conflict. The U.S. entry to World War II came in 1942 after France was defeated and both the U.K. and the USSR were reeling from German assault. China had been at war with Japan for an even longer period of time, dating back to at least the Manchurian Incident in September 1931. Had it not been for the Japanese attack on Pearl Harbor in December 1941, U.S. intervention would have come even later.

Parenthetically, just as in the case of Germany's aggression in 1914 and 1939, Japan's invasion of China in the 1930s followed the logic of preventive war. Being larger and more populous than Japan, China's reunification and rejuvenation after the Nationalists' successful Northern Expedition in 1927 augured the prospect of a rising latecomer that could eventually displace Japan from its position as the pre-eminent Asian power. Japan's leaders were obsessed with their resource insecurity, a lesson supposedly learned from Germany's experience in World War I. In 1941, they faced heavy pressure to initiate armed hostilities against the U.S. as a part of the strategy of Southward Advance to make up for the resource shortfall. This resource shortfall was compounded by Japan's military quagmire in China, and Washington's decision to impose a strategic embargo against Japan and to freeze its assets in the U.S. With its heavy dependence on U.S. oil and scrap iron, Japan's military and economy were in danger of grinding to a halt within about eighteen months. Loss aversion, as predicted by prospect theory, inclined officials in Tokyo to take the fateful gamble of attacking Pearl Harbor. The U.S. embargo meant that with the passage of time, Japan would become ever weaker while "the United States was building an incomparably larger fleet."[21] Significantly in this instance, a weaker and declining state decided to lash out against a superior foe in order to forestall a further deterioration in its strategic position. A severe sense of insecurity rather than overconfidence was the impetus behind Japan's military planning.

Although world domination was possibly beyond Berlin's reach, Germany would have probably been able to secure regional hegemony in Europe in the absence of U.S. intervention. Perhaps Japan would also have been able to establish its hegemony in the Asia Pacific. As John Mearsheimer has argued,[22] after claiming for itself regional hegemony in the Western Hemisphere, a cardinal goal of U.S. foreign policy has always been to deny another state the same mastery over another region. In both World Wars, U.S. intervention came after the other belligerents had already been severely exhausted by years of fighting and when Germany and Japan threatened to create their respective regional spheres of influence. Should the latter countries be allowed to succeed in their plan of conquest, the U.S. would have been presented with two much more formidable rivals potentially capable of challenging its status as the world's premier power.[23] Consequently, U.S. intervention in both World Wars could be seen as instances where the logic of preventive war would also apply.

Yet the timing and circumstances of U.S. interventions were such that they again call attention to the folly of German and Japanese policies. A series of missteps on their part made U.S. intervention all but inevitable,[24] thereby turning their eventual defeat into a virtual certainty. By invading Russia/the USSR and by attacking the U.S., Germany and Japan were their own worst enemies. In the context of the power-transition theory, the dynamic of both World Wars was not quite that of the allies of the U.K. and Germany taking up their respective causes in a struggle to defend or overthrow the existing international order. Rather, as in the case of Napoleon's France,[25] Germany and, in World War II, Japan also struck repeatedly against other states which would have remained neutral or perhaps even bandwagoned with them.[26] By attacking or alienating states that would have liked to be left alone, their own actions created an overwhelming opposition against them. Thus, that London had more powerful friends than Berlin in the two World Wars was not necessarily because its cause was more popular.[27] Rather, the proximate cause for at least some major states becoming British allies had more to do with their fighting back after being attacked by Germany (or Japan).[28]

To say that the two World Wars can be more reasonably explained by Germany's preventive motivation against Russia/the USSR does not imply that preventive wars are either common or easy. Wars have been undertaken by weaker states against stronger ones out of a sense of desperation or opportunism.[29] Wars have also been fought when the stronger states feel that they can conquer or coerce the weaker states. Thus, not all – or even most – wars are necessarily started by a declining, but still stronger, power against a latecomer that is perceived as a source of future threat. A state would only launch a preventive war if its officials were convinced that its long-term growth prospects were extremely unfavorable, that its relative decline could not be arrested or reversed by political and economic reform, and that its adversary's hostile intentions would not change in the future.[30] Thus, a state that experiences a short-term military disadvantage would not be expected to launch a preventive war so long as it possesses a competitive economic base to catch up militarily.[31] Moreover, these officials must be persuaded that their country would suffer a severe penalty under a prospective new international regime controlled by their adversary. Even when these conditions are met, a preventive war would still present a daunting challenge to any state contemplating such an undertaking. As Kenneth Organski and Jacek Kugler have shown, wars tend to cause only a temporary pause in a defeated country's growth trajectory.[32] This country may be expected to resume its prewar growth pattern within a relatively short period of time. Thus, short of a policy of complete annihilation or a successful campaign to assert physical conquest and direct control,[33] a preventive war cannot ensure that the vanquished will not be able to recover eventually and become strong enough to mount another challenge. Naturally, precisely because a potential challenger tends to be a large country with diverse resources and cultural resilience, it is hard for a would-be conqueror to control or absorb it. Thus, even if Nazi Germany had defeated the USSR and Japan had militarily prevailed over China, their attempt at preventing the rise of a powerful neighbor would still probably fail in the long run.

Given these considerations, preventive war is not the only or even the most likely policy that a state suffering relative decline would reach out for. There are other possibilities, including appeasement, bandwagoning, retrenchment, and even a passive descent to decrepitude. The Ottoman Empire, imperial Spain, and Qin China suffered from the latter fate, and Austria-Hungary disappeared as a political entity after losing World War I. In contrast, the U.K. was adroit in its efforts to accommodate the U.S. while balancing against Germany. More recently, the USSR under Mikhail Gorbachev undertook a campaign of retrenchment and reform that, however, contributed to the collapse of the USSR and a sharp contraction of the Russian economy. Moscow made major unrequited concessions to the West, and these concessions in turn made it possible for the Cold War to end on basically Western terms. What can account for the different British and Soviet responses to their relative decline? Why, unlike the Germans, was preventive war not a serious option for them?[34]

Both the U.K. and the USSR maintained a large presence abroad. They therefore had the option of pulling back from their imperial possessions in order to retrench. For the U.K., this meant coming to terms with the U.S. regional hegemony in the Western Hemisphere. Settling the Canadian border with the Americans, conceding to the construction of the Panama Canal (a development which would further favor U.S. naval strength), and withdrawing the remaining British naval squadron from the North Atlantic went a long way toward accommodating U.S. interests. The U.K. also reduced its navy in the Asia Pacific and made a pact with Japan, a country that was just beginning to flex its muscles by the early twentieth century.[35] All these moves contributed to a larger strategic plan to concentrate British forces closer to home in order to defend against Germany's gathering strength. British policies of appeasement and accommodation toward the U.S. and Japan, respectively, were unsurprising in that, in a multi-polar environment, a declining great power had to guard against fighting several opponents simultaneously or being exhausted by a series of costly bilateral conflicts.

As for the USSR, although it did not have a traditional colonial empire as did the U.K., Moscow had dominated Eastern Europe and had subsidized client states elsewhere in its competition with the U.S. during the Cold War days. The decisions to recall the Red Army from Eastern Europe and to terminate Moscow's aid to its junior partners in the Third World were feasible moves in implementing an overall plan of retrenchment. Significantly, the value of the East European allies as a buffer zone against foreign aggression had diminished with the advent of nuclear deterrence. Given Moscow's second-strike capability, an important strategic rationale for holding on to Eastern Europe became obsolescent.

In contrast to the British and Soviet situations, imperial and Nazi Germany did not have an overseas empire from which to withdraw. Nor did this country have any substantial foreign possessions that could be used as payment to appease or accommodate would-be challengers. The geographic location of Germany was such that it had little room for maneuver. The option exercised by the British and the Soviets – pulling back from imperial outposts or even the "near abroad" – was not available to the Germans. In contrast to the British and Soviet leaders who faced the imperative of trimming foreign commitments in order to redirect much-needed resources for homeland defense or domestic reform, the German officials were challenged by the opposite predicament of searching for opportunities abroad in order to satisfy rising domestic demand.[36] Thus, the policy dilemma faced by Berlin was quite different from those confronting London and, more recently, Moscow. Moreover, Germany was still growing in absolute terms on the eve of both World Wars, even though it had already begun to experience relative decline. This situation again tends to set it apart from the U.K. which was suffering from a case of imperial overstretch by the late 1800s and early 1900s. As for the USSR, by the time Mikhail Gorbachev came to power, its economy had suffered stagnation since at least the 1970s and was about to enter a period of absolute, not just relative, decline.[37] Although the Soviet leaders had earlier attempted to use the Berlin crises and the Cuban Missile Crisis to reverse or at least stem their military disadvantage, this approach became infeasible by the 1980s as the gap separating the U.S. and Soviet power widened.[38]

There is another huge difference in the structural condition facing Germany, the U.K., and the USSR. This difference in systemic polarity in turn helps to account for their different responses to the onset of decline. The USSR was the main contestant against the U.S. in a bipolar world. The U.S. side consisted of the other major powers and the largest and most dynamic economies. With its defense burden already consuming nearly one-fifth of its national product, the USSR simply could not continue its political contest and arms race against the U.S., not to mention the entire Western coalition.[39] As Gorbachev had remarked, the USSR faced competition not only from the U.S., but also from Germany and Japan. It was falling further and further behind these rivals in the area of science and technology.[40] The bilateral nature of the contest in which the USSR was losing very badly meant that Moscow had little choice but to seek accommodation and retrenchment. The existing alignment did not allow the USSR to deflect pressure from itself by engaging in buck-passing.[41] There was no place for the USSR to hide, and no prospect of allying with another great power to stave off decline or to gain a much-needed breathing space.

In contrast, the world was multi-polar when the U.K. and Germany faced the onset of their relative decline. This multi-polarity opened up possibilities for diplomatic maneuvers.[42] British officials sought to accommodate the U.S., recruit Japan as a junior partner, and deter Germany (and Russia, which was threatening British India from the north) as a grand strategy. Prior to World War I, German officials in turn tried to isolate France, deter Russia, and neutralize the U.K. They also worked to bolster their junior partner, Austria-Hungary. In addition, as already noted, the U.K. and the USSR each tried to deflect Nazi Germany's hostility in the hope that the other would bear the brunt of Hitler's ambitions. Moreover, the U.S. could afford an isolationist stance. Therefore, states have many more options in a multi-polar world than in a bipolar world. Hiding, shirking, bandwagoning (i.e., making an alliance with a rising power in the hope of profiting from this relationship), chain-ganging (i.e., making an irrevocable commitment to an ally), and buck-passing (i.e., shifting to another state the primary burden of defending against an emergent threat) are more likely to be on the policy menu.[43] These options present a wide range of possible permutations for war and peace. Thus, on the one hand, multi-polarity enabled the U.K. to conciliate and even to cooperate with some rising powers (the U.S. and Japan), and to contain and confront some other rising powers (Germany and Russia). On the other hand, this same multi-polarity encouraged Germany into believing that buck-passing among its potential adversaries would enable it to isolate and conquer its victims sequentially. Accordingly, the same buck-passing tendency may make accommodation possible (e.g., when London hoped that Japan might relieve some of Britain's burden in the Far East) or war more likely (e.g., when the failure of the Western powers and the USSR to join forces emboldened Hitler). In short, then, the options facing a declining power tend to be more constrained in a bipolar system than in a multi-polar system.

The above discussion is related to an ongoing debate about how a system's polarity can influence the probability of war. Kenneth Waltz and John Mearsheimer are two leading theorists suggesting that bipolarity is more peaceful than multi-polarity.[44] Others are more agnostic, and present theoretical reasons and historical evidence to show that international peace can be facilitated and sustained in multi-polar systems under given conditions.[45] Dale Copeland has recently advanced this debate by showing that in the pre-nuclear age, bipolar systems were not more stable.[46] Sparta and Athens, and Carthage and Rome in ancient times, and France and Habsburg Spain in the early modern era were engulfed by war despite the bipolar nature of the then-prevailing international system. Even though it was no stronger and might actually be weaker, the declining state in these dyads risked a preventive war. In contrast, the preventive impulse would more likely be held in check in a multi-polar context because, by definition, none of the poles held a predominant position against a combination of all others, and because a war initiator would naturally be fearful of being exhausted and eventually defeated in a series of bilateral conflicts. The experience of the USSR, however, suggests that when the power gap separating the two contestants in a bipolar system becomes quite substantial, the declining state will eschew preventive war in favor of accommodation and even capitulation. Thus, relative decline in a bipolar system does not have to end in war. There may be a critical period during which preventive war presents itself as a viable option to the declining power. When, however, the gap separating the strong and the weak sides widens further, this option becomes increasingly less attractive.

This discussion brings us to a critical difference between contemporary international relations and the world of a century ago. It is important to recognize a third major factor influencing the relationship between the experience of decline and the outbreak of war, one that distinguishes the Soviet predicament from the challenges faced by the British and Germans. The advent of the nuclear age made a war against another great power even less thinkable, and a policy of retrenchment more acceptable. Facing a process of relentless and seemingly irreversible decline, Moscow chose retrenchment in the late 1980s. Lashing out against its opponents in the form of a preventive war would be unacceptable given the suicidal consequences of launching a nuclear war. At the same time, Moscow's possession of nuclear weapons made retrenchment more palatable because this capability could at least be counted on to serve as an effective insurance policy against the possibility of any foreign power being foolish enough to repeat the mistakes of Napoleon and Hitler.[47] Thus, significantly, a second-strike nuclear capability offers reassurance to a great power caught in a downward spiral. In order for a preventive war to be considered a viable option, the relevant officials must believe that they can prevail over their adversary at a reasonable cost. When a potential target of preventive war has the wherewithal to strike back with nuclear weapons, the logic of preventive war breaks down. This observation suggests that the advent of thermonuclear weapons and intercontinental missiles had made preventive war highly implausible by the early 1960s. At the same time, it introduces a significant caveat that if successful, current U.S. efforts to develop a missile-defense system can have a reverse effect by making the U.S. invulnerable to a nuclear retaliation, and hence remove the restraining effect this prospective retaliation has on any state contemplating a preventive war.

Significantly, the prospect of additional countries acquiring nuclear weapons enhances the preventive motivation on the part of those that already have them. To ensure that Iraq would not develop or possess weapons of mass destruction was given by Washington as the leading justification for the U.S. invasion in 2003. Efforts to deny nuclear weapons to Iran and North Korea could yet involve the U.S. in armed conflicts with these countries. The current threat faced by these prospective nuclear states is not unfamiliar to Beijing, since both the U.S. and the USSR actively considered and planned for a preventive strike against China before it had a chance to fully develop its nuclear potential.[48] Thus, a preventive war against some fledgling nuclear states is quite possible and perhaps even probable. The above discussion on the deterrent effect of nuclear weapons is therefore based on the premise of a secure retaliatory force.

To conclude this chapter, I argue that the two World Wars depart in important respects from the standard characterization provided by the power-transition theory. Instead of stemming from an Anglo-German rivalry over global supremacy, these wars could be more reasonably understood as Germany's initiation of a preventive war aimed at Russia/the USSR. Similarly, U.S. interventions in both World Wars were motivated by a desire to deny – that is, prevent – Germany and, in World War II, Japan from gaining a dominant status in their respective regions. Germany lost both World Wars because its recklessness forced the other states to take up arms against it, and because it was after all not the world's most powerful country. As the world's most powerful country, the U.S. played a decisive role in determining the final outcomes of both World Wars.

To trace the origin of both World Wars to a preventive motivation on the part of Germany should not be interpreted to mean that preventive wars are common. Germany's then-current military advantage *and* its disadvantage in potential power for long-term growth created a deadly combination that inclined its leaders to consider this option.[49] Our brief review of the British and, more recently, the Soviet response to their respective decline shows that a preventive war is likely to be the last policy resort for a country suffering from irreversible decline and facing expected hostility from a rising challenger. There are other policy alternatives available to a declining power. Hiding, shirking, retrenchment, and appeasement are such possibilities. Significantly, a declining power's overseas possessions create both the policy and geographic "space" for it to overcome imperial overstretch, making a program of retrenchment more feasible. In the absence of such possessions, there is less room for this state to pull back. Nuclear weapons should also make the risky proposition of preventive war even less attractive.[50] These weapons should give the officials of the declining state a sense of invulnerability from at least foreign attempts at physical conquest or direct military assault, and they would make allies and buffer states more dispensable. As the weaker of the two superpowers that was getting even weaker, the USSR had little choice but to accept retrenchment and status demotion in a bipolar world that pitted it against all the other great powers. The evidence introduced in the earlier chapters suggests that we are at a "unipolar moment," with the U.S. enjoying unrivaled power in the international system. America's predominance is far greater today than that achieved by the U.K. at even the peak of its power.[51] In this crucial respect, the accounts we have given about how Germany, the U.K., and the USSR had responded to the onset of their respective decline are not applicable to the U.S. Even if the U.S. lead over the other countries shrinks, it will continue to be the dominant power in the foreseeable future. Unlike the other great powers just mentioned, it is not in any danger of being displaced from its pre-eminent position in the international system.

Power transitions are not an infrequent phenomenon in history.[52] Prior to World War I, the U.K. had lost its pre-eminent position not only to the U.S. but also to Germany. In an earlier era, the Spanish empire lost its primacy to the U.K., and France was eclipsed by Germany after the Franco-Prussian War of 1870. More recently, although the USSR never threatened to overtake the U.S. during the Cold War, it was itself surpassed by Germany, Japan, and China at least in terms of these countries' relative economic output. As shown by these examples, although some power transitions were accompanied or followed by war, others ended peacefully. Whether the regime being overtaken was democratic or authoritarian does not appear to discriminate the peaceful power transitions from the violent ones.[53] Even though the USSR had an authoritarian government, albeit one that was in the process of liberalization, it did not resort to war in order to prevent Germany, Japan, and China from overtaking it.[54] Conversely, even though a democratic regime is not expected to start a war when facing foreign challenge, the U.S. justified its 2003 invasion of Iraq by explicit recourse to the logic of preventive war. Consequently, authoritarian regimes do not necessarily resort to war when presented with the prospect or reality of being overtaken, and democracies can attack their adversaries even in the absence of any ongoing or pending power transition.[55]

The power-transition theory tends to see a growing latecomer as the instigator of international conflict and a source of instability. It overlooks those historical circumstances that motivated a dominant power to consider or even actually wage a preventive war in the hope of sustaining its primacy and forestalling decline. The decision logic presented in this chapter offers a contrasting perspective, suggesting that a rising China is more likely to accommodate than challenge the international system. Unlike the usual analyses of China's rise, the discussion thus far treats this phenomenon in a historical context, drawing comparisons from past occasions when other states faced changes in their international position. Moreover, as should be evident by now, this discussion contends that China's rise cannot be analyzed as a case in isolation, without considering concurrent changes involving the other great powers and their reaction to China's relative gain. Therefore, China's rise is not *just* about China. The power-transition theory is specifically concerned about the differential rates of national growth and the national ambitions and phobias accompanying these changes, and it calls attention to the effects of these interacting factors on global peace. Precisely because China is not a unique case in the history of the rise and decline of nations, and precisely because a common tendency among many Sinologists is to study China alone, the discussion thus far has tried to introduce decision logic and historical precedents that consider how other great powers have acted or are likely to act when experiencing upward or downward mobility.

6 Appeasement and the distribution of benefits

The major insight and logic of the power-transition theory is that when a dissatisfied country gains sufficient power, it may be expected to challenge the existing dominant state. But why does the increased power of a rising state not make it less dissatisfied? Why does it remain dissatisfied despite its upward mobility in the international system? Presumably, as the title of a recent article suggested,[1] this is because power is not satisfaction. This proposition indicates in turn that there is something which the rising state wants that it cannot get even with its increased power. Moreover, it is possible that there is something that the already dominant power (whether or not it is in the process of decline) still wants to have or to have more of. What could be that something that a country which is gaining power and, for that matter, a country which already has a preponderance of power would want?

The power-transition theory acknowledges forthrightly that the rules of the international system are rigged to favor the dominant state, which benefits disproportionately from the existing arrangement.[2] It is supposed that latecomers are disadvantaged by this existing arrangement. When a latecomer acquires sufficient power, it may be expected to challenge the status quo. When this challenge is resisted by the dominant state, war ensues. The two sides desire to contest the status quo presumably because it confers uneven benefits on them, and because the existing distribution of benefits no longer reflects their changing power relationship. Since Kenneth Organski's original formulation, discourse on the power-transition theory has generally not given much thought to the relative amount of benefits accorded by the existing international order to states. By bringing back the idea that states draw different amounts of benefit from the status quo, one achieves four things. First, states are seen to pursue power not as an end in itself, but rather as a means to achieve other desiderata. Second, a state's satisfaction or dissatisfaction is no longer treated as if it is a matter of its inherent character or psychological outlook but rather becomes grounded in the amount of benefits it may expect to receive from the existing international order. Third, it points to failures to adjust the distribution of benefits quickly and fully in accord with the changing distribution of power as the main reason why states have disputes and conflicts. And fourth, and in contradiction to the standard expectation, my argument is that wars can happen not just because a rising power wants to increase its current benefits. Wars can also happen because the already dominant power wants also to increase its current (and already large) benefits. When the demand from either party encounters resistance, conflict is likely to ensue. Thus, significantly, the logic of the reasoning that gaining more power does not necessarily make a rising state more satisfied should also be equally applicable to a dominant power. Having already more power than the other great powers does not necessarily make this latter state want to cease claiming even more benefits for itself.

The power-transition theory shares with the status-discrepancy theory the idea that there are essentially two types of states.[3] Those that receive more than their fair share of benefits under the current system are satisfied. Others that are under-compensated are dissatisfied, and these frustrated states are likely to become a source of international instability when they make a claim for a larger share of the system's resources. Thus, there are states that run a "surplus" in the sense that they receive more than their fair share of status recognition or material benefits from the existing order, which was by and large constructed by them. Conversely, there are "deficit" states that are aggrieved because they receive less than their fair share of tangible and intangible pay-off. Frictions between the surplus states wanting to keep what they already have and the deficit states demanding additional allocation are a source of international conflict. This source is recognized by others working outside the tradition of power-transition and status-discrepancy theories. Thus, according to one prominent theorist, "the fact that the existing distribution of power and the hierarchy of prestige can sometimes be in conflict with one another is an important factor in international political change."[4] Robert Gilpin pointed furthermore to the natural tendency for states to grow at different rates, and the attendant consequence of inconsistencies being constantly produced between the existing distribution of international benefits and the evolving distribution of national power.[5]

Naturally, what constitutes a just or fair share of the system's benefits is subjective and contentious. Moreover, as I will explain below, these benefits are by their very nature not easily captured by quantitative indicators based on readily available aggregate data. Still, it seems that there is more to the story than the standard portrait that wars happen because a rising dissatisfied state wants to have a larger share of the system's benefits, and because a declining satiated state wants to hold on to what it already has. Provided that the pay-offs in question are divisible resources and barring other impediments to reaching a settlement as discussed in Chapter 4, the rationalist perspective suggests that it should be in the self-interest of the prospective contestants to work out a new distribution of benefits so that war may be averted.[6]

Although seemingly innocuous, the last remark alludes to several oft-overlooked issues. First, it suggests that there is nothing normatively sacrosanct about the existing distribution of benefits that, as already mentioned, was designed by the powerful countries to benefit themselves at the expense of others. Thus, this view rejects the idea that the current international hierarchy and the existing distribution of resources are necessarily natural or just.[7] Second, if war should occur, the blame goes not just to the latecomer that is often depicted as the instigator of conflict. If the dominant power resists the downsizing of its traditional role in view of its relative decline and insists on continuing to receive a disproportionate share of benefits, it is also partly responsible for the predicted conflict. Third, this observation in turn directs attention to those political and psychological rigidities that prevent a declining power from undertaking timely and appropriate adjustment of its role and its sense of entitlement. Moreover, this line of reasoning raises the possibility that appeasement – that is, a dominant state's concessions that increase the rising latecomer's benefit share – can offer a viable policy to avert war. Appeasement loses its negative connotation as an attempt to humor or bribe an aggressor state with unreasonable and even insatiable ambitions. Finally, and perhaps most importantly, the rationalist perspective argues that in view of the known inefficiency of war discussed in Chapter 4, a would-be challenger would not be inclined to launch an attack against the dominant power unless it has reason to believe that the ensuing conflict would produce an outcome that is superior to its current position. That is, a latecomer does not have an incentive to start a war unless it expects to improve its benefits over the default option of continuing with the status quo.

To further elaborate the last point, the larger the perceived deficit a latecomer feels it has been subjected to in terms of the gap between its share of power in the international system and its share of benefits received from this system, the more inclined it would be to undertake a war. The smaller this deficit, the less a latecomer would be motivated to start a war. Indeed, a state cannot credibly threaten war if it is already receiving as much benefit from the system as warranted by its relative power.[8] This is so because this state cannot hope to obtain more favorable terms by going to war. A prospective war would not make it better off, but would actually make it worse off. This prospective belligerent would have to incur all the costs and risks that come associated with fighting a war without being in the end able to bring about any improvement in its current position. Robert Powell has put the crux of the matter succinctly. He emphasized that:

> if the distribution of benefits mirrors the distribution of power, no state can credibly threaten to use force to change the status quo and the risk of war is smallest. If, however, there is a sufficiently large disparity between the distribution of power and benefits, the status quo may be threatened regardless of what the underlying distribution of power is.[9]

This view accords with the original argument of power-transition theory, stating: "only if the great powers think that the changing system challenges their positions, or if they no longer like the way benefits are divided, should the [power] shifts be deemed dangerous."[10] Current discussion on power-transition theory, however, overlooks this important point, which calls attention not just to the changes in the pertinent states' relative power, but also to the changes (or the lack thereof) in the relative benefits they draw from the international system. According to this perspective, wars happen not because a surging new power is overtaking a declining old power, but rather because there is a systemic failure to adjust the distribution of international benefits to reflect the evolving power balance.

What is true for the latecomer also holds for the dominant power. The latter cannot hope to do better in a bilateral war against the former than is determined by the objective distribution of power between them. With the onset of its relative decline and as one with a surplus of benefits from the system, the dominant power can try to appease the latecomer in an effort to persuade the latter that war is an unpromising proposition. Specifically, the dominant power would want to calibrate its concessions such that this pay-off to the latecomer would just outweigh any prospective gain that the latter can hope to achieve by going to war. These concessions are therefore deliberately set to make the option of going to war unattractive for the latecomer. Why should the dominant power make such concessions? It stands to gain from making these concessions because it would be worse off if it fought a war. Why? Because by averting war, the dominant power spares itself the costs and risks that would be entailed by war. These savings represent the net gains for the dominant power, an improvement over the deal that it would have to settle anyway at the end of a prospective armed conflict. As a state that probably has a surplus in benefits compared to its power, a dominant power would prefer appeasement to waging a preventive war unless it anticipates that the ongoing power shifts would work seriously to its disadvantage in the future (so that its current benefit surplus would turn into a serious benefit deficit with the passage of time).

Why should a latecomer accept the dominant power's concessions, which are likely to be less than its full entitlement? That is, why should a latecomer put up with small, incremental adjustments in the provision of additional international benefits accorded to it? The reason is that with its expectation of continued growth, the latecomer hopes to further improve its position subsequently. Thus, the prospect of future growth encourages the latecomer to postpone demanding that the allocation of benefits be brought fully and immediately in line with the new distribution of power.[11] As long as it is gaining on the dominant power, the latecomer should be willing to put up with gradual increases in its benefit share in the hope that additional adjustments will be forthcoming in the future. However, once the latecomer's growth decelerates or even reverses, there is little incentive for it to further defer its gratification. It may be expected to demand that its share of benefits be fully and immediately adjusted to reflect its relative power. There is no reason for the latecomer to wait any longer because its bargaining position will not improve further in the future. Its position may even begin to deteriorate because others – the late-latecomers – may be catching up fast.

The above proposition receives support and clarification from Robert Powell's formal game theoretic model, which shows that as a latecomer's power growth tapers off, it requires a large, lump-sum payment in order to secure peace.[12] If true, this proposition suggests that a surging China would be less troublesome for the U.S. than a China whose power has already peaked. This view argues that when a latecomer's growth is stalled and when its hope of catching up with the dominant power fades, it is more likely to gamble in an effort to close the gap separating it and the dominant power.[13] Moscow may have been thus motivated to place missiles in Cuba in 1962. Incidentally, the hypothesis presented above differs from the proposition that if a latecomer catches up with the dominant power at a slow speed, the danger of war between the two is diminished.[14]

The above discussion would also lead one to expect appeasement to be a quite common practice undertaken by states when facing a foreign threat. I have already discussed some of these episodes in Chapter 5. In the late 1800s, the U.K. made unilateral concessions to the U.S. without any expectation that these gestures would be reciprocated. Similarly, in the 1980s and 1990s the USSR/Russia undertook a series of unrequited moves, including the withdrawal of the Red Army from Eastern Europe, sharp reductions in Soviet armament, the dissolution of the Warsaw Pact, and even the voluntary breakup of the Soviet Union.[15] Although they were no longer the dominant powers even in their region, the U.K. and France tried to appease Nazi Germany in the late 1930s, most famously at the Munich Conference.[16] The USSR also engaged in the same policy in the hope of diverting Hitler's hostility. As these examples show, the practice of appeasement is not restricted to only a dominant power in decline. It may also be pursued by the lesser great powers whose peak had occurred quite some time ago, and also by others whose power surge was just beginning to take off.

Appeasement is cheap initially but becomes more expensive over time. For reasons already given, the initial concessions made to a rising latecomer tend to be modest and delayed. These concessions do not accord all the benefits that the latecomer's relative power would entitle it to. However, over time these concessions contribute to the latecomer's accumulation of more power, and this increased power in turn enables it to claim additional benefits. The tendency for the price of appeasement to escalate over time helps to explain in part why states may reverse their appeasement policy. After they had succumbed to German demands on several previous occasions, the U.K. and France finally committed themselves to war should Hitler invade Poland.

The conventional wisdom argues that the British and French acquired a reputation for being irresolute, and this reputation in turn increased Hitler's appetite for more concessions.[17] Several other case histories, however, suggest the opposite implication. If the preventive motivation attributed to the German leaders before World Wars I and II is reasonably accurate, these officials presumably acted in accordance with the injunction to avoid appeasing a rising Russia/the USSR. Germany struck militarily in the hope that it would not have to respond to Russian/Soviet demands in the future. On both occasions, the ensuing war ended badly for Germany. As already mentioned, in the late 1800s the U.K. decided to accommodate U.S. power in the Western Hemisphere. British officials, however, apparently did not believe that their concessions would be perceived by the Americans or by other foreigners as a sign of weak resolve.[18] Thus, they did not worry that these concessions would encourage further challenges to British interests elsewhere.

In their deliberations leading up to the Pearl Harbor attack, the Japanese leaders were convinced that the U.S. was resolved to oppose Tokyo's plan to conquer the European colonies in Southeast Asia and its intent to hold on to its conquest in China.[19] They did not doubt the credibility of the U.S. threat to intervene against Japan or the overwhelming U.S. power that could be brought to bear on Japan in the event of a war between these two countries. Far from engaging in appeasement, Washington practiced deterrence. Because they believed that an attack on Southeast Asia would inevitably bring about U.S. intervention, the Japanese leaders decided to seize the strategic initiative by taking war to the U.S. under circumstances most favorable to them.

These historical examples suggest that appeasement does not necessarily have an effect of abetting war, nor does the opposite approach of credible deterrence present a sure recipe for avoiding war. Daniel Treisman's analysis of British and Spanish policies during their respective period of historical decline confirms this observation.[20] The U.K. pursued selective appeasement, seeking to contain some potential adversaries while concentrating its scarce resources on other, more threatening foes. Its policy was sensitive to the pitfall that by indiscriminately fighting all perceived threats, the consequent dissipation of resources would make a country more vulnerable to enemies waiting in the wings. In contrast, Spain pursued an aggressive policy of confronting all challengers in the belief that its resultant reputation for bellicosity would deter future challenges. Instead of this hoped-for effect, however, Madrid's approach exacerbated its decline. Its battles against one foe made it vulnerable to attack from other quarters. By spreading its limited resources on several fronts, Spain put itself in a weaker position to deter and, when deterrence failed, to fight its enemies in future wars. Pushed to its logical extreme, the injunction against appeasement can be perverted into an argument in favor of launching a preventive war.

This presentation introduces another important question. Why did some of the historical cases end peacefully, whereas others escalated into violence? The discussion in Chapter 5 offered some hypotheses. I introduce an additional proposition specifically tied to the focus of this chapter on the discrepancy between a state's power share and its benefit share. When a state in relative decline expects that it will continue to enjoy a surplus of benefits in a new international regime under another hegemon, it will attempt appeasement or accommodation rather than preventive war. By backward logic, one may infer that the British leaders pursued the former approach because they had this reasonable expectation – specifically, they would continue to fare well, relative to their declining power, in a new international regime under U.S. control. Conversely, Germany's resort to preventive war implies that its leaders were worried about suffering a deficit in a prospective regime dominated by Russia/the USSR. Accordingly, whether a country anticipates a premium or discount in its future allocation of benefits from the international system should offer a clue about its likely response to an ongoing or prospective power transition.

In order to estimate whether a state is overpaid or short-changed in the amount of benefits it receives from the international system, one would want to have valid and reliable indicators. This is not easy because the concept of benefits and the concept of power tend to be conflated.[21] Thus, for example, a large number of diplomatic missions sent to a country may be indicative of its international prestige and stature, but this indicator can also point to this country's influence in international relations. Similarly, that a large number of foreigners are studying one's language naturally confers the native speakers an important advantage (or benefit) in the world of international business and travel. At the same time, the popularity of a language also speaks to the soft power (the cultural appeal) exercised by the pertinent country (or countries, when a language, such as English, French, or Spanish, is spoken in more than one country).[22] As another example, the veto provision for the permanent members of the Security Council is a form of special benefit for them but also a source of their special power. Recent discussions to reform the Security Council by increasing the number of veto-holders call attention to our intuitive understanding about the relationship between benefit and power. The U.K. and France appear to be the beneficiaries of a legacy that accords poorly with their relative power today, whereas the same privilege has been withheld from other, more deserving latecomers such as India, Brazil, Germany, and Japan.

In discussing a related topic on the provision of public goods by hegemons, Bruce Russett offers some examples that point to the subtle but important difference between power and benefits.[23] A state's ability to mount offshore defense and to undertake extended deterrence demonstrates its power. That this country is as a result spared the burden of having to fight a foreign enemy on its soil is a benefit. Similarly, the dismantlement of trade barriers after World War II, achieved largely due to U.S. efforts, may be seen as Washington's provision of a public good and a sign of U.S. influence. That as a consequence of this trade liberalization, former British and French colonies became accessible to highly competitive American firms extended private benefits to the U.S. As a third example, when a state's currency is accepted as the global medium for settling commercial accounts, this acceptance shows its financial power and again its contribution to the public good of facilitating global commerce. However, to the extent that this state derives a seigniorage privilege from its financial power, it receives an important benefit.[24] American banks, for example, are the usual beneficiaries of recycled petrodollars; that is, oil revenues which the exporting countries wish to deposit in overseas accounts.

Table 6.1 presents some plausible indicators pertaining to the relative amount of benefits each of the leading states drew from the international system. Fossil fuel is a scarce, depletable, and expensive resource. The price of energy, however, varies across the leading states, and some of them consume more energy than others even after adjusting for the differences in the size and development of their economy. Different reasons may be given for why the American people have been able to consume more oil and natural gas at a cheaper price than the citizens of other industrialized states, but the dominance of U.S. power, especially in the Middle East, could be counted as one of these reasons.[25] The key point of interest to us, however, is not that Americans consume more energy, but rather whether there exists any discrepancy between their level of energy consumption (which is treated here as a benefit drawn from the international system) and their country's relative power share (which is for this purpose to be indicated by the U.S. gross domestic product).

Table 6.1 Oil consumption and foreign direct investment as indicators of "benefits"

Country	Gross domestic product in PPP $ (trillions)	Gross domestic product in current $ (trillions)	Daily oil consumption (millions of bbl)	Net direct investment $ (billions)
U.S.	$11,750 (30.5)	$10,949[a] (39.9)	19.65[c] (40.1)	−133.9[a]
China	$7,262 (18.9)	$1,591 (5.8)	4.96[b] (10.1)	47.2[a]
Japan	$3,745 (9.7)	$4,301 (15.7)	5.29[c] (10.8)	−22.5[a]
India	$3,319 (8.6)	$663 (2.4)	2.13[c] (4.3)	3.2[b]
Germany	$2,362 (6.1)	$2,403[a] (8.8)	2.89[a] (5.9)	9.7[a]
U.K.	$1,782 (4.6)	$1,795[a] (6.5)	1.69[a] (3.5)	−30.5[a]
France	$1,737 (4.5)	$1,757[a] (6.4)	2.03[c] (4.1)	−9.7[a]
Italy	$1,609 (4.2)	$1,468[a] (5.4)	1.87[c] (3.8)	7.6[a]
Brazil	$1,492 (3.9)	$470 (1.7)	2.20[c] (4.5)	9.9[a]
Russia	$1,408 (3.7)	$553 (2.0)	2.31[a] (4.7)	−1.8[a]
Canada	$1,023 (2.7)	$857[a] (3.1)	1.75 (3.6)	−16.0[a]
Mexico	$1,006 (2.6)	$626[a] (2.3)	2.20[a] (4.5)	9.0[a]

Sources: www.cia.gov/cia/publications/factbook and devdata.worldbank.org/dataonline. FDI data are from World Development Indicators online.

Notes
a 2003; b 2002; c 2001.
The figures for gross domestic product and foreign direct investment are in current U.S. dollars. The numbers in parentheses are each country's percentage of the group's total. Unless otherwise noted, the data reported refer to 2004.

Any economic transaction, including foreign trade and foreign direct investment, would presumably benefit both sides of an exchange. Dependency theorists, however, have long argued that the relative terms of international exchange tend to favor the "core" countries at the expense of the "periphery" countries. There is a difference, for instance, between exporting bananas and jetliners. Moreover, the capital exporters typically enjoy stronger bargaining power in negotiating with the capital importers. The advent of globalization of commerce and production has enabled capital to gain an advantage over labor, because the former is more mobile and can cross national boundaries more easily than the latter. Therefore, a country's net amount of foreign direct investment may be taken as an indicator of its companies' ability to profit from direct sales in foreign markets and from offshore production platforms of goods for re-export to the home market.[26] This amount also indicates its relative position in controlling foreign assets. Whether investment or trade follows the flag,[27] one would expect that there should be a general correspondence between the two dimensions. Thus, it would be unsurprising to find that the more powerful countries procure more commercial benefits for themselves than the less powerful countries are able to. The pertinent question, however, is again whether, compared to their relative power, some leading countries derive more than their share of commercial benefits as indicated by their level of foreign direct investment.[28]

I report the level of oil consumption and the net flow of foreign direct investment, juxtaposing these figures with each leading state's gross domestic product.

In Chapter 2, I showed that whether one uses the purchasing-power parity to adjust a country's gross domestic product makes a rather significant difference in China's relative power standing. Without adjusting for differences in purchasing-power parity (PPP), the U.S. economy was about 690 percent larger than China's economy in 2004. After taking into account these differences, however, the U.S. economy is estimated to be only about 160 percent larger than China's economy. Thus, even though the PPP estimates still put the U.S. ahead of China, this U.S. lead becomes much smaller.

In seeking to judge the extent of discrepancy between a country's power share and its benefit share, whether the PPP figures are used again makes a rather big difference. By making China's economy appear bigger, the PPP-adjusted figure leads one to conclude that China actually consumes much less oil than it "deserves." Whereas China's economy constituted about 18.9 percent of the collective output of the twelve largest economies reported in Table 6.1, it was responsible for "only" 10.1 percent of the total amount of oil consumed by this group. To the extent that oil consumption is taken as a benefit which a state draws from the international system, China's share has been substantially below its relative power (as indicated by its gross domestic product after adjusting for purchasing-power parity). If, however, one does not adjust gross domestic product by purchasing-power parity, China consumed more than its "fair" share of oil. This country was responsible for 10.1 percent of the group's oil consumption while accounting for only 5.8 percent of its collective economic output unadjusted for purchasing-power parity.

Naturally, whether one uses purchasing-power parity as an adjustment has the opposite effect on the U.S. This country appears to have consumed its "fair" share of oil if no adjustment for purchasing-power parity is made. Making this adjustment, however, makes the U.S. economy appear smaller. Because the size of a country's economy is used to gauge whether it has over- or under-consumed its share of oil, this analytic move makes the U.S. appear as an over-consumer of oil.

The implication of using alternative economic figures can be rather profound. Adjusted for purchasing-power parity, China's economy appears to be behind the U.S. economy by a much shorter distance, and the gap between its relative power and its relative benefit becomes rather acute as a consequence. This adjustment therefore presents a much more ominous situation from the perspective discussed in this chapter. Conversely, if one uses the traditional estimates for gross domestic product without attempting adjustment for purchasing-power parity, a huge gap separates the American and Chinese economies, and China appears as a satisfied state because its share of oil consumption is higher than its power share as indicated by its relative economic size. In short, the adjustment for purchasing-power parity makes the case for a Sino-American power transition and the case for a dissatisfied China more plausible, whereas without this adjustment both propositions appear much less plausible.[29]

One reaches the same general conclusion when looking at the pertinent data for the U.S. Unadjusted for purchasing-power parity, the U.S. economy dwarfed China's economy and it used up no more oil than should be expected from its relative size. When figures adjusted for purchasing-power parity are accepted, the U.S. lead over the other economies (including China) appears to be smaller. At the same time, the U.S. appears to have drawn more benefits from the international system (in this case oil consumption) in comparison to its power share.[30] Parenthetically, if the unadjusted figures are used, Japan – and not China – would be the second largest economy and, as a significant under-consumer of oil relative to its economic size, Tokyo would appear to be a candidate for dissatisfaction stemming from the gap between its power share and its benefit share.

Table 6.1 also reports the size of net capital flow in foreign direct investment. Naturally, a country can be simultaneously an exporter and importer of capital.[31] As noted above, a state is supposed to reap more benefits from global commerce to the extent that it is a sender rather than a receiver of foreign direct investment (this distinction is signified by a minus sign and an implied plus sign, respectively, in Table 6.1). Dependency theory has drawn attention to this proposition, emphasizing that the operations of foreign-owned companies tend to benefit these companies' host country less than their home country.[32] Whether one agrees with this assertion, it still bears noting that China's economy has been far more open to foreign direct investment than has Japan's or, for that matter, America's, as the ratio between the stock of foreign direct investment and gross domestic product was 35 percent for China, 2 percent for Japan, and 13 percent for the U.S in 2002.[33]

It is immediately clear from Table 6.1 that China was the largest capital importer and the U.S. was the largest capital exporter. China's recent economic growth has surely been assisted in an important way by the infusion of foreign capital, technology, and managerial skill. Recognition of these foreign contributions to its growth, however, also suggests that it is at least to some extent beholden to the foreign providers of these resources. China's status as a net recipient of foreign direct investment is unremarkable except for the size of this capital. At $47.2 billion (in 2003), this amount was much bigger than that for the other developing countries such as India ($3.2 billion), Brazil ($9.9 billion), and Mexico ($9.0 billion).[34]

The size of capital exported by the leading states offers some idea about the global presence and, by extension, the profitability of their companies. By this measure, multinational corporations based in the U.S. had, by their investment decisions, made the greatest advance in extending their global reach. In 2003, the U.S. had the largest net flow to foreign destinations. Standing at $133.9 billion, this amount was much greater than that for Japan. Whereas the U.S. gross domestic product was about three times as large as Japan's gross domestic product (after adjusting for purchasing-power parity), the additional amount made to their existing overseas investment stock in 2003 was roughly six times larger for the U.S. than for Japan. Interestingly, even though the U.K. had a much smaller economy than Japan, it had a substantially larger investment outflow as befitting a country that was previously the dominant power in the world's political economy. This observation in turn reinforces a point made earlier that the great powers of a bygone era tend to continue to draw more than their proportionate share of benefits from the international system, whose rules and principles they had shaped and even constructed. Such states do not for understandable reasons relish the idea of system reform that would or could threaten their advantageous position.[35] That these states can continue to benefit disproportionately from their earlier power positions also points to the rather lengthy lag in bringing the benefit shares of these once dominant states in closer correspondence with their current power shares.

The above discussion shows that a seemingly innocuous decision on whether to present the relative size of a national economy in current unadjusted dollars or in purchasing-power parity can make a significant difference to the substantive conclusions one reaches. Given different measures, one will see different realities. Whereas China's economy appears much bigger when it is counted in terms of purchasing-power parity, this adjustment would also make China's benefit share look proportionately much smaller. At the same time, by making the U.S. economy appear smaller relative to the other economies, this move would also show that the U.S. has made a rather disproportionate claim on the available international benefits. By the PPP measure, the U.S. appears to be consuming more than its "fair" share of oil. The implication is that if such PPP-adjusted data are used to show an ongoing power transition between the U.S. and China, one is also compelled to conclude that the benefits received by the U.S. will have to be trimmed in order to reflect the changing power distribution. Conversely, if an adjustment is not made for purchasing-power parity, the U.S. economy appears much larger and seems so far ahead of China that there is no reasonable prospect for a power transition to occur in the foreseeable future. This accounting would also make the U.S.'s share of benefits, as indicated by its oil consumption, appear to be quite reasonable.

That sharply different conclusions may be drawn from Table 6.1 is underscored when one realizes that on the basis of gross domestic product unadjusted for purchasing-power parity, Japan and not China should be recognized as the second most powerful country.[36] Moreover, judged by this measure and the data on oil consumption, it should be Japan and not China that is being under-allocated its share of benefits. That one candidate country rather than another is given more serious recognition as a possible latecomer challenger in the discourse of power-transition theory returns us to an earlier observation.[37]

In the late 1800s, there were several countries whose development was on an upward trajectory. Besides the U.S., Germany, Russia, and Japan were all rising powers. The U.K. turned its attention to concentrate on Germany, located nearby, rather than the potential threats coming from the more distant countries. It has been suggested that the peaceful transition between the U.S. and the U.K. showed the entrepreneurial acumen of opinion leaders in both countries who emphasized their countries' political and cultural affinity.[38] As discussed in Chapter 3, traditional Anglo-American friendship or mutual acceptance does not offer a very satisfactory explanation for the peaceful transition between these two countries. After all, their relationship was often acrimonious and competitive before London made its final decision to accommodate rising U.S. power in the Western Hemisphere, and it was the U.K. (not Germany) that fought the U.S. in 1812. Moreover, political and cultural affinity would have predicted that London would choose Germany rather than Russia and Japan as an ally in World War I.

Nevertheless, social construction has surely played a major role in the belated recognition of and suggested response to a power transition. Not all power transitions are seen as such. For example, not many Americans were alarmed by the USSR being overtaken by rising powers that happened to be U.S. allies during the Cold War, or felt compelled to explain the absence of war occasioned by these power transitions. As already argued in Chapter 3, the attribution of some states as allegedly revisionist and others as ostensibly status-quo oriented does not quite correspond to the actual behavior of these powers in the nineteenth century. All the ascending countries were in fact expansionist, seeking aggrandizement at their neighbors' expense.[39] As mentioned earlier, Japan undertook systematic adoption of Western institutions and tried to project the image of a modern "civilized" state by following Western practices and conventions. While Japan sought to play by the then prevailing rules of imperialism, the U.S. actually attempted to create its own rules by fostering the Monroe Doctrine.[40] The attributed American amity and animosity toward the U.K. and Germany, respectively, were as much the consequences of evolving government policies and official relations as their antecedents. Therefore, the identification of a potential challenger and the characterization of revisionism and anti-status-quo orientation are not without a considerable amount of ideational construction and historical reinterpretation.

This chapter has also tried to stress that wars do not result from changes in national capabilities per se or even specifically from a dissatisfied power's being able to gain more capabilities that puts it in a situation of greater parity with the ostensibly satiated states. Rather, wars tend to occur due to national benefits not being matched by national capabilities. As indicated by the quotation from Powell introduced earlier in this chapter, when national benefits match national capabilities, the danger of war is the smallest. Conversely, the danger of war rises when the discrepancy between these two variables becomes larger for each contestant, regardless of the balance of power between them. This perspective therefore argues that in order to explain the outbreak of war, one should be concerned not only with relative power shifts, but also with the ease and timeliness with which adjustments are made to the existing distribution of benefits in order to reflect the new power reality. To the extent that what is commonly described as appeasement attends to this adjustment, international peace and stability should more likely be preserved than undermined as a result of pursuing this policy.

7 Conundra of containment and engagement

The argument made in the last chapter – that wars happen because there are discrepancies between states' power shares and their benefit shares – is surely different from the standard conclusion reached by American scholars on international relations in general and on China in particular. This argument is likely to be controversial. It calls attention to the reason why a rising state may be dissatisfied, namely that the benefits it receives from the international system are not fully in accord with its relative power. This motivation to wage war, however, does not have to apply only to this rising power. A dominant power may be equally motivated to fight in order to keep the benefits to which it has become accustomed or even to pursue policies that are intended to further increase its benefits. When the international distribution of benefits is not fully or quickly adjusted to reflect the new international distribution of power, this disequilibrium becomes a source for war. If countries receive their "fair" share of benefits in proportion to their power share, there is no incentive for them to go to war because they cannot hope to improve their position by threatening war. Any such threat would not be credible.

The argument advanced above emphasizes that it takes at least two sides to fight a war. This perspective takes issue with the view that systemic wars are caused by a cocky, aggressive upstart seeking to take over the world. The existing international order was designed by the powerful states that had shaped it, and it was designed to work to their advantage. Thus, this discussion does not take the existing distribution of benefits or, for that matter, the existing distribution of power to be somehow natural, legitimate, or fixed. One would expect that the distribution of benefits at any given time does not reflect accurately the changing distribution of power. Those states that are favored by the current system may be expected to resist adjustments that reduce their benefits and international role. Others that are disadvantaged by it may be expected to challenge their benefit allocation.

By emphasizing the need to change the distribution of benefits in accordance with the evolving distribution of power, my presentation offers a radically different approach from those currently being promoted by American conservatives and liberals alike. It is unsurprising that these two camps tend to focus, respectively, on the two dimensions of power and satisfaction highlighted in the standard discourse on power transition. Participants in the American policy debate about how to address China are inclined to propose steps designed either to constrain China's power growth or to influence its outlook.[1] The conservatives have little confidence in the benign intentions of latecomers such as China.[2] They would accordingly advocate containment of Beijing's power. In their view, Washington should try to limit the prospects for China's growth and its power projection, even if these moves would antagonize the Chinese and thereby increase Sino-American tension. The liberals would recommend engagement. By engagement, they mean increasing trade with and investment in China, and promoting cultural and political contact with the Chinese in order to bring about domestic change inside China. That is, their objective is to transform Chinese society and government so that the latter would become more congenial to U.S. values and interests. Both the conservatives and liberals are quite forthright in stating their policy prescriptions. Neither group, however, will endear itself to the Chinese because its explicit aim is either to block China's ascent or to undermine the current Chinese system.

What are the prognoses for the blocking and the conversion attempts, respectively? I have remarked earlier on the Phoenix phenomenon whereby a defeated state manages to resume its prewar growth trajectory within a relatively short period of time after the hostilities have ended. In a matter of about two decades, its economy reaches a level that one would have expected if war had not taken place.[3] The recovery of Germany, Japan, and Italy following World War II points to these countries' resilience. Today we find all three among the ten largest economies in the world. The Phoenix phenomenon calls attention to the challenge faced by a would-be aggressor contemplating preventive war. Even if this country is able to prevail militarily in the ensuing conflict, its target cannot be prevented from regaining its prewar strength or status. Physical occupation and foreign administration of a defeated country in the face of popular opposition offer a very unpalatable prospect in today's world.[4] Significantly, if the Phoenix factor refers to the economic recovery of countries defeated in a war, the victorious ones are also likely to resume their prewar paths of economic growth. Karen A. Rasler and William R. Thompson concluded from their statistical analysis that "the economic impact of global war, for both the winners and losers, invaded and noninvaded, is of relatively temporary duration."[5] Thus, wars – even World Wars – do not appear to affect the longer-term growth trajectories of the belligerents.

If war is an unpromising proposition for the purpose of stopping a latecomer's growth,[6] does a policy of economic blockade offer more appealing prospects? The power-transition theory is quite emphatic on the point that a state's growth is determined by its domestic conditions, especially the size, productivity, and mobilization potential of its people. In the words of the authors of *The War Ledger*, "the major source of power for a nation is its own socioeconomic and political development."[7] They were skeptical that states' growth trajectories can be affected by outside influences, including a resort to war in view of the Phoenix factor discussed above. In their view, "[the] fundamental evolution of power distribution is set and cannot be manipulated."[8] While taking on a much more evolutionary than deterministic perspective, the long-cycle formulation of global leadership also emphasizes a state's domestic capability to pioneer technological innovations as the key driver for its power.[9]

Attempts at economic coercion have not been known for their success in recent applications against the Serbian and Iraqi governments, even though their civilian populations paid a heavy price. Although the Cuban and North Korean economies would surely have been better off had they not been subjected to decades of U.S. economic embargo, they have thus far limped along and avoided collapse since they both lost their main source of economic and political support during the Cold War. There is, however, an important paradox suggested by the experience of these two countries. A policy of economic coercion is difficult to apply if the target country has little ongoing commercial relations with the outside world, relations that could otherwise be used as a bargaining lever. One cannot threaten to take away something when there is nothing to be taken away.

Significantly, threats to deny or disrupt significant economic intercourse can have a boomerang effect. The target of these threats faces a stark choice between being subjugated as a commercial dependent and making an audacious bid for economic autarky. Indeed, as Dale Copeland has shown,[10] when powerful states become heavily dependent on external sources of raw materials and foodstuffs for their domestic needs, they are likely to respond with belligerence rather than capitulation if confronted with the prospect of having their access to these sources blocked. Germany before both World Wars and Japan in the 1930s faced this challenge, and chose war to secure this access. Indeed, in both cases, a drive to achieve self-sufficiency motivated an expansionist policy to seek regional hegemony. Japan's efforts to build an "East Asian Co-Prosperity Sphere" stemmed from its leaders' concerns about their country's severe economic vulnerability. This very vulnerability made the U.S. strategic embargo all the more threatening. Ironically, Washington's embargo had the effect of finally uniting the Japanese Army and Navy, which had until late 1941 been torn apart by inter-service rivalry and sharp disagreements about the so-called northern and southern strategies (aimed, respectively, at the USSR and Southeast Asia with the U.S. as a possible target). They came to an agreement to launch a risky war against the U.S. rather than trimming their imperial ambitions only weeks before the Pearl Harbor attack. Once the militarists agreed to this path, however, "no civilian could have pried them apart."[11] When faced with a devastating strategic embargo, a vulnerable target will choose its policy on the basis of comparing the economic costs of the embargo and the political costs of making the necessary concessions to lift this embargo, and its search for other alternative means to make up for the shortfall brought about by this embargo. If concessions are unacceptable because they impinge on higher national goals and if other alternatives are unavailable (including "playing for time"), it may choose war with unfavorable odds.

Japan's experience suggests that instead of deterring an adversary, an economic embargo can have the reverse effect of provoking it to attack. The effects of the embargo can influence the power and motivation of an opposing country's domestic factions, especially with respect to its military establishment. As a consequence, Edward Mansfield and Jack Snyder argued, "it is especially important for the international community to maintain a supportive economic and security environment during the most precarious stages of a democratic transition," and concluded that "one implication is that the United States should avoid disrupting trade relations with China while it is in the midst of a future transition to democracy."[12]

In a re-examination of the well-known dataset by Gary Hufbauer, Jeffrey Schott, and Kimberly Elliott,[13] Robert Pape concluded that sanctions worked in only 5 percent of the cases.[14] He hypothesized that sanctions would change a target state's behavior only if the latter is a relatively small country whose trade is highly dependent on the sanctioning state and if the sanctioning state's demands involve relatively minor issues that "do not affect the target country's territory, security, wealth, or the regime's domestic security."[15]

Whether a strategy of economic denial would work depends on a number of other factors. Two seem particularly pertinent. To what extent does the target economy depend on the outside world for its economic well-being? Larger, more self-sufficient economies are less vulnerable to external attempts at coercion. This remark in turn directs attention to the extent that China's current and prospective economic growth is driven by access to foreign markets and assisted by the import of foreign capital and technology. If China's domestic resources have become a more important source of its growth, there is less that foreigners can do to apply pressure. Significantly, if such pressure is attempted, the resulting repercussions in disrupting ongoing commercial relations would ripple beyond China. Those doing business with the Chinese, including Americans and third-country nationals (such as those in Southeast Asia), would also be hurt.[16] The extent to which any such economic hardship translates into political difficulties for the respective governments is in turn an important consideration. After all, a threat to impose trade or investment sanctions is tantamount to a public declaration and challenge by the sender (i.e., the initiating state) that it is more willing to accept the ensuing economic deprivation and political pressure than the target.

Whether attempts at economic denial will succeed also depends on whether there are other prospective sellers or buyers standing ready to replace the boycotting state. The greater the number of states joining a sanction effort, the more likely this project will succeed.[17] Conversely, the easier it is for the target state to turn to alternative sources to replace any shortfalls caused by the sanction, the more likely it is that this project will fail. Efforts to sanction Italy and Japan in the 1930s for their aggression against Abyssinia (Ethiopia) and China and, more recently, against the USSR for the Polish communist government's crackdown on the labor union Solidarity encountered this difficulty. In these cases, sanctions did not make a substantial material impact on the economy of the sanctioned. As noted previously, however, the U.S. embargo of strategic material against Japan prior to the Pearl Harbor attack did have an effect in convincing the officials in Tokyo that Washington would oppose Japan's encroachment on the European colonies in Southeast Asia. Thus, sanctions can have an effect in addition to just the intended material deprivation; they serve also to signal the sender states' future intentions.

Economic blockade or sanction deliberately contrives economic scarcity for political gain. This resulting scarcity, however, increases the incentive for profiteers to cheat. Moreover, the more collaborators required for this undertaking, the greater the danger for defection according to the logic of collective action.[18] Napoleon's Continental System, aimed at blockading the U.K., encountered these difficulties, and attempts seeking to impose a grain or oil embargo in recent years also ran into the same challenge.[19] In contrast to Napoleon's project, the latter attempts were aimed at changing the target states' incentives rather than their capabilities. In the grain and oil embargoes, international suppliers rearranged their sales distribution such that the intended targets continued to receive these imports from alternative sources, albeit at a higher price.

An example focused more specifically on limiting an adversary's current capabilities and its potential for future growth may be found in the experience of the Coordinating Committee for Multilateral Strategic Export Control (COCOM) which assumed the overall responsibility for the Western states' export of technology to the USSR and the other communist states in the 1950s and 1960s.[20] Compared to the Europeans and the Japanese, the Americans pushed for a more restrictive policy. During much of COCOM's existence, the U.S. did not face a strong domestic lobby with a vested interest in continuing and expanding existing business ties with the communist world for the simple reason that U.S. companies did not at that time have these commercial ties with the USSR and its allies. As one would expect from prospect theory, because the U.S. did not encounter this resistance to loss aversion by American firms, Washington was in a position to insist on more stringent export controls. This situation is apt to change after intense trade ties have been established. These ties create stakeholders who can be hurt should the existing commercial relations with a country such as China be disrupted. Thus, economic interdependence (by definition) cuts both ways. As already mentioned, such disruption may cause financial hardship and political pressure on both sides of a sanction relationship. Important domestic constituents may therefore be expected to mobilize (or be mobilized) in support of or opposition to attempts at economic coercion.[21]

Attempts to hamper a potential adversary's capabilities can be focused on weapons acquisition rather than a general economic blockade. In spring 2005 the European Union was poised to lift its arms embargo against China until heavy U.S. lobbying forced it to reconsider. The requirement that a prospective change of E.U. policy must be approved unanimously by all its member states slowed down the momentum toward lifting the embargo despite vocal French and German advocacy to the contrary. This general episode is suggestive of the strong influence that Washington commands in negotiations with other states.[22]

Two points follow from the above discussion. First, it is easier to continue a course of economic denial in the absence of any ongoing exchange. Conversely, it is more difficult to discontinue exchanges after they have begun and have therefore created stakeholders on both sides of a relationship. It is reasonable to expect that economic disruption – or alternatively, continuation or even expansion of the existing economic ties – will benefit some groups while hurting others. Therefore, the extent to which a state can credibly threaten to implement or resist a deliberate attempt to disrupt trade or investment depends critically on the political access and influence of those groups that stand to gain or lose from the proposed policy. In line with the perspective of two-level games, both states in a prospective embargo or sanction relationship will have to deal with not only their respective foreign counterpart but also their respective domestic constituents.[23] A state will have a more difficult time in pursuing such a policy when corporate interests have traditionally enjoyed access to and influence in its policy process. The more an incumbent government depends on the political and financial support of groups with a vested interest in continuing and even expanding the existing economic relationship,[24] the more difficult it is for this government to threaten its disruption.

A containment policy can involve simultaneous attempts to limit an adversary's capacity for internal growth and to construct external alliances to block its projection of power abroad. The U.S. of course already has formal alliances with South Korea and Japan, and a quasi-protective relationship with Taiwan under the doctrine of "strategic ambiguity." Notwithstanding these countries' traditional political and military ties with the U.S., they have increasingly gravitated economically to China's growing market. China has replaced the U.S. as the largest trade partner for these and other countries. A long-standing debate in the international relations literature concerns how the neighbors of a rising power may be expected to behave. Do they coalesce in a coalition to oppose this rising power, as traditional realists would lead us to expect?[25] Do they engage in buck-passing in the hope that someone else will take on the burden of defending against this emergent threat? Or do they accommodate and appease the rising power, and even join it in a partnership?

Contrary to the expectation that states always balance against a neighbor that is gaining relative power, some have practiced bandwagoning – that is, joining forces with the ascending power.[26] These states are often motivated by the desire to be part of an anticipated winning coalition, and therefore to partake in the spoils of war or profitable commercial relations. When faced with the prospect of a regional hegemon, other states have sometimes tried "hiding" and buck-passing. Still others have sought to "transcend" their security situation by proposing new ideas or institutions to address changes in power relations.[27] The historical evidence seems to suggest that the situation predicted by traditional realists – namely, a collective effort by the rising state's neighbors to contain its power – tends to be the least likely outcome.[28]

This does not mean that a situation of balance of power has rarely existed historically. Such a situation has not generally stemmed from a collective effort by several countries to block or contain a rising neighbor. It has rather tended to result from the rising power's own actions that had the effect of forcing others to rally against it. British diplomacy was never very successful in organizing a coalition to fight against Napoleonic France. This coalition came into being rather because

Napoleonic France struck repeatedly against its neighbors. In doing so, it frustrated attempts by Austria-Hungary, Russia, Prussia, and Spain to appease France or to hide from French aggression. Therefore, the eventual alliance that defeated France came about because France left its members with no alternative but to fight it. This alliance was due more to France's behavior than to any collective desire by its neighbors to block its ascent.

The same general phenomenon was repeated prior to World War I. There was no concerted European intervention in the Western Hemisphere with the avowed purpose of preventing the U.S. from achieving regional hegemony there. Conversely, the U.S. did not join an anti-German coalition until World War I was well underway. Even in 1914, London's intention was in substantial doubt until Germany's invasion of Belgium decided the issue of whether the U.K. would fight.[29] Italy vacillated. It bandwagoned initially, but pulled back subsequently when Germany's prospects appeared unpromising. As for Russia, it fit the description of an incipient power in ascendance better than Germany. Even though Germany was more powerful, the peak of its relative power had already been reached prior to 1914. To the extent that German power presented a threat and therefore a strong motivation for its neighbors to engage in balancing behavior, France's diplomacy (especially in pursuing a Franco-Russian alliance reached in 1894) came closest to this characterization.

As already described in Chapter 4, the U.K., France, the USSR, and the U.S. engaged in buck-passing when dealing with Nazi Germany. The former three countries also tried appeasement and, in the case of the USSR, even bandwagoning (which also characterized Benito Mussolini's motivation). When eventually an anti-Axis alliance did come into being, it again came about as a result of the recklessness of Germany and its ally, Japan. By attacking their neighbors again and again, they forced countries that would have preferred to be left alone to join instead in a collective fight for survival. This coalition did not develop to deter German or Japanese aggression, but only emerged to prevent Germany's and Japan's victory after these countries had already launched their attack. It was not a coalition that had tried to balance against the Axis powers before the onset of armed conflict, but rather a vastly superior force that sought the latter countries' defeat after being attacked by them.

These historical episodes suggest that one would not expect China's neighbors to somehow of their own accord start a coalition to contain Beijing's increasing power. Indeed, as David Kang has noted,[30] there is thus far scant evidence of China's neighbors joining an alliance to block its power ascent. In his words, "other nations will accommodate China's central position in East Asia, rather than balance against it."[31] The critical variable that has brought about such a combination, as noted above in connection with Robert Powell's research, is a hegemonic aspirant's demonstrable territorial and political ambition as evidenced by its repeated attacks on its neighbors.[32] These attacks more than anything else gave the aggressor's victims no other option but to fight back, and they exacerbated so seriously the other states' security concerns that these states were finally energized to organize themselves for collective defense.[33] In short, absent a pattern of behavior that alarms, alienates, and antagonizes its neighbors, a rising power is not expected to encounter a blocking coalition. Furthermore, in Kang's view,

> U.S. attempts to form a balancing coalition against China may be counterproductive. As countries in Northeast and Southeast Asia increasingly orient their economic and political focus toward China, Asian nations, if forced to choose between the United States and China, may not make the choice that many Westerners assume they will.[34]

In a somewhat similar vein, David Shambaugh remarked,

> China's interests and regional preferences may well coincide with those of its neighbors and the United States, providing opportunities for collaboration. The nascent tendency of some Asian states to bandwagon with Beijing is likely to become more manifest over time.[35]

There is certainly little sign that China's neighbors are taking part in traditional forms of balance of power. They have not organized, nor even started discussions about, formal alliances to contain a rising China. They have also not undertaken any action that may be construed as ramping up their defense programs in an effort to deter China. Nor have there been any concerted diplomatic efforts to oppose China on those issues of critical concern to it, such as Taiwan's status and stability on the Korean peninsula. Washington has of course had formal defense pacts or close military collaboration (even if tacit or informal in the case of Taiwan) with Japan, South Korea, Thailand, Singapore, and the Philippines. Yet all these countries have experienced a huge expansion in their trade and investment relations with China, and the trajectories of their commercial relations continue to be upward. Remarkably, even in the case of Taiwan, China has assumed the role of this island's leading trade partner and investment destination. And, even in Taiwan, the procurement of expensive U.S. arms has been blocked by a reluctant legislature. Even when states such as Japan and Singapore initiate or expand their military ties with the U.S. and thus may be construed to be engaging in hedging behavior (for example cooperating with Washington in maritime- and missile-defense projects), such actions are not necessarily efforts aimed immediately at China. One needs to consider alternative explanations for these actions, such as a motivation to counter a threat from another source (e.g., North Korea, Islamic insurgents), to seek economic rent or technology transfer, to appease domestic political constituents and public opinion, or to create bargaining leverage for extracting concessions from parties other than Beijing and on issues other than military security.[36]

In this context, Beijing's sovereignty claims over Taiwan and in the South China Sea may arouse its neighbors' security concerns. The ripple effects from a possible invasion attempt on Taiwan or from armed clashes with the other rival claimants in the South China Sea could do more to bring about a coalition aimed at blocking Beijing's expansion than Washington's sponsorship can achieve without such a development. Moreover, in view of the financial influence of the overseas Chinese communities, the dynamic of domestic ethnic politics in several Southeast Asian countries is more likely to shape their policy toward China than the latter's emergent power per se.[37]

Turning our attention from containment to engagement, two ideas appear often to motivate discussions about the latter approach. The first refers to molding attitudes and shaping values as a consequence of increased contact. The hope is that the Chinese people and government will evolve to adopt an outlook more congenial to American interests and values. Contact therefore serves an instrumental purpose in promoting the conversion of the Chinese people or at least their socialization into norms befitting a responsible member of the international community.[38] Although not always acknowledged explicitly, advocacy of this policy course is about the promotion of ideas in the manner of Gramscian hegemony.[39] It is about a campaign of cultural imperialism with the aim that values such as individualism, consumerism, capitalism, competitive politics, globalization, and those embodied by McWorld be accepted and internalized by non-Americans as natural and legitimate.[40] There is a huge literature on both the nature of "soft power" to shape others' ideals, interests, and even identity, and the deleterious effects that such foreign influences can sometimes have in the developing world.[41] Although the French film producer Marin Karmitz was speaking about the U.S. movie industry, his observation extended beyond the influence of Hollywood when he remarked:

> The U.S. movie industry is a big business, but behind the industrial aspect, there is also an ideological one. Sound and pictures have always been used for propaganda, and the real battle at the moment is over who is going to be allowed to control the world's images, and so sell a certain lifestyle, a certain culture, certain products and certain ideas.[42]

These critical remarks do not deny that among the proponents of engagement are also those who hope that increased communication and interaction may improve mutual understanding, and even enhance mutual responsiveness over time. The conversion motive is missing in the work of those who write in the tradition of Karl Deutsch's security community.[43] The emphasis in this genre of engagement is on generalized reciprocity, equal partnership, and mutual adjustment. Attention goes to the building of common institutions and shared expectations, with the use of military threats becoming an unacceptable means for settling differences.[44] The latter threats have certainly not been banished from China's external relations even though its engagement with the outside world, such as in the form of increased commercial transactions and participation in multilateral institutions, has risen enormously over the past three or so decades.

Yet, as reported in Chapter 3, China is generally seen to have played a constructive role in international relations. It has settled most of its territorial disputes, ratified a large number of international treaties, and cooperated in international efforts to combat terrorism and curb nuclear proliferation (most notably with respect to North Korea). If one is to judge the extent of a country's international socialization by these indicators and others such as the frequency of its resort to arms abroad, Beijing's conduct does not compare unfavorably with the other major states.[45]

One would want to be cautious in attributing Beijing's generally cooperative and peaceful conduct to a policy of engagement by the U.S. or any other country. Selection effect would be a consideration. For instance, rather than participation in international organizations causing the member states to become more cooperative and peaceful, the more cooperative and peaceful states are disposed to join these institutions in the first place.[46] Therefore, a change in Beijing's behavior may be explained by its decision to be more cooperative with the outside world (such as joining more international organizations and taking part in foreign trade), thus reversing the imputed causal flow from engagement to cooperation.

Furthermore, China's receptivity to be engaged and the other states' willingness to engage it may indeed presage more cordial relations and closer cooperation – but one based on strategic calculation rather than normative socialization. Thus, it was not entirely coincidental that Sino-American diplomatic thawing and China's return to the United Nations occurred in the context of these countries' joining forces to oppose the USSR. Accordingly, rather than closer cooperation being explained by greater engagement, both of these variables are themselves to be accounted for by a higher-order explanatory factor. The intent of engagement in this instance is not so much to promote adherence to global norms as to facilitate collaboration for partisan objectives. This observation implies in turn that the dynamics in question should be studied as a matter of bargaining or mutual partisan adjustment rather than as a question of socializing rogue states to accept international standards.[47]

The second idea often found in liberal discourse refers to the creation of stakeholders.[48] The standard argument is that increased commerce will give important domestic constituents in China an incentive to continue and expand their access to U.S. capital, technology, and the consumer market. These Chinese stakeholders would then be self-motivated to lobby Beijing for policies that would not jeopardize the ongoing commercial ties. The implicit assumption in this reasoning is that the management and enhancement of these relations would become central to Beijing's policy agenda, so that other, less important objectives would be increasingly dominated by this core interest. Another implicit assumption is that should the existing ties be interrupted, China would incur more costly consequences than the U.S.

Both assumptions are subject to question. There is evidence suggesting that pairs of states with high trade volume are less likely to be engulfed by militarized disputes than other dyads with low trade volume.[49] This pattern may be due to the fact that states with a rewarding commercial relationship are reluctant to jeopardize their trade, or because friendly states are more likely to trade with each other in the first place.[50] It is, however, doubtful that the absolute size of a state's overall trade volume or the amount of its trade with a specific partner should be indicative of the relative importance of international commerce in its hierarchy of interests.[51]

After all, the largest trading states – both in the sense of their overall trade volume and in terms of the volume of their bilateral trade – have gone to war against each other. The main belligerents in both World Wars were among the most active trading states and each other's leading commercial partners.

As already implied earlier, the extent to which a disruption in trade (or investment) will turn out to be costly to one or the other party depends in part on the ease of replacement and the price to be paid for this replacement. The more easily replacement buyers or sellers can be found and the less the price differential from the existing arrangement, the less costly a threatened disruption would be. When one country threatens another with trade or investment disruption, it is attempting linkage politics. It is using trade or investment as a lever to bargain for a concession in another area. In order for this demand to succeed, the replacement costs for the commercial interruption must be perceived to be higher for the target elite than the price of concessions being demanded by the sender state.

By definition, a threat of sanction is an attempt to manipulate economics for political purpose. Whenever the possibility of this action is raised publicly, one is in effect suggesting that one cares about a political desideratum (such as human rights, nuclear non-proliferation) more than the continuation of commercial exchanges. It may or may not be true that China's export reliance on the U.S. market makes a potential trade disruption more costly to it than to the U.S. As already suggested, this question depends in part on the extra cost each party will have to incur in dealing with alternative sellers and buyers. The more pertinent question for a prospective sanction to succeed, however, is whether Beijing cares more about the political concessions being demanded by Washington than the economic costs of the threatened loss of trade with the U.S. Although the party being sanctioned wants ideally to avoid suffering the costs of trade denial, it may be even more concerned about paying a price in its other goals (such as national sovereignty, regime survival, domestic popularity and legitimacy) as a condition for lifting a sanction against it. Thus, whether trade disruption (or investment disruption) is more costly to one party than the other is really not the critical determinant of whether a prospective sanction will succeed. The critical determinant is whether the target cares more about the forgone trade (or investment) or about some other value(s) it has been asked to give up for the sake of avoiding the sanction. Thus, for instance, does Beijing put a higher value on reunification with Taiwan or lost trade with the U.S.?

When would one expect an effort to link politics to economics to succeed? Why, for example, should the parties undertake a joint negotiation over U.S. grain sales to China and U.S. arms sales to Taiwan, instead of treating these transactions separately?[52] The parties would do so only if both can benefit by joining these transactions. By not pressing to the full extent what it can reasonably be entitled to in the first deal (thus in effect granting a concession to the other side), one party can seek compensation from the other in the second deal (thus, in effect, asking the other side to return its favor). The forgone advantage in the first instance becomes a basis for demanding an offset in the second instance. Thus, to illustrate, whether China offers to buy U.S. wheat at a price above the world market or whether the U.S. offers to sell this wheat at a price below that offered by the competing suppliers would in turn create a claim for reciprocal concession in the matter of U.S. weapons sales to Taiwan. Significantly, in the absence of concessions granted in the first instance, there is no basis for demanding concessions in the second instance.

A revealing example about the connection described above comes from Albert Hirschman's classic study on the relationship between national power and foreign trade. Nazi Germany deliberately overpaid for the commodities it imported from the Balkans, thereby fostering this region's export dependency on Germany and also gaining a favorable access for Germany's manufactured goods to this region.[53] Asymmetric trade that favored the Balkan countries created the basis for Berlin's political influence. Americans tend naturally to see China's access to the U.S. market and its huge bilateral trade surplus as proof of an advantage over and even a favor to Beijing. The Chinese are conversely inclined to put the best light on their massive purchase of U.S. debt instruments and the opening up of their domestic market for U.S. investment.[54] Of course, neither side's behavior is driven by altruism. Whether one or the other party enjoys a bargaining advantage depends on whether it has achieved a better deal from the other than that which may be had with other potential partners, and whether it cares more about losing this deal than some other desiderata that it has to sacrifice in order to keep this deal.[55]

The preceding discussion contends that in order for one state to succeed in using trade, investment, or monetary policies to pressure another state to agree to a political concession, it must have eschewed some advantage in their economic relationship so that this forgone benefit may be used as a bargaining chip for reciprocal favor. This formulation in turn raises the question: Why did the state attempting this economic statecraft decide not to maximize its full economic advantage in the first place? What would make it or its firms refrain from going after the best economic deal they could have achieved? Presumably, absent assurances of sufficient offsetting side-payments (such as state subsidies), it would be difficult to persuade most private companies to accept this arrangement. By implication, the exercise of such economic statecraft would be easier for authoritarian states to implement than for a democracy where private enterprise has a strong, independent voice in the political process.

There is still another implication from the above discussion. Assuming that over time one state has become more dependent on its economic relations with another, would the latter country stand a better chance of getting the former to meet its demands for political concession? As mentioned above, the answer depends in part on whether the state demanding political concession has deliberately settled for an economic deal that is less favorable to it than it could have achieved elsewhere. It also depends on whether this state has escalated its demands with its perception of rising economic interdependence and the heavier damages that the other side will suffer should the ongoing relationship be disrupted. That is to say, there is no reason to assume that the demands from the state asking for political concessions will remain fixed if it is perceived to have gained additional bargaining leverage from mounting economic exchanges. What appears to this state to present a source of its strength must conversely mean in its eyes a source of weakness for the other side. One would expect this state therefore to raise its demands in order to get its counterpart to concede even more. As a consequence, one would not necessarily expect mounting economic intercourse or even increased asymmetry in bargaining power to enhance the prospect of successful economic coercion.

Some colleagues have suggested that the opportunity costs of disrupting an ongoing economic relationship are in themselves unlikely to produce a peaceful settlement of dispute. Rather, they have argued that the existence of a significant ongoing economic relationship enables both parties to engage in more credible communication when caught in a dispute.[56] By threatening to disrupt this relationship at significant cost to itself, each party has a means to demonstrate its resolve. Thus, states with heavy trade, large investment stake, and close monetary coordination with each other have this means to signal their intentions that is unavailable to those other states without these ties. Economic threats then can substitute for military threats. As discussed in Chapter 4, even though both belligerents realize that war is an inefficient way to settle their differences, they nevertheless resort to arms in order to overcome the problem of private information. In other words, performance on the battlefield offers a way to disclose each side's "true" intentions and capabilities, information that would otherwise be discounted by one's opponent as "cheap talk" when announced in peacetime diplomatic communication. The existence of ongoing trade, investment, and monetary transactions, however, provides an alternative to military combat to signal a state's serious concern and high resolve. The greater the financial costs this state shows it is willing to incur by terminating or limiting the ongoing economic ties, the more credible would be its signal. Naturally, the credibility of a state's resolve would also be greater if its political, military, and economic signals are coordinated to convey the same message.

Before concluding this chapter, it should be emphasized again that not all liberal writings show an instrumental interest in using cultural or commercial contact for the purpose of converting the Chinese government and society or for creating levers for extracting concessions. There is a large and deservedly influential body of literature in international relations that points to such contact as a way to promote mutual responsiveness, shared interests, and reciprocal trust and respect. The emphasis of this literature is on discovering common grounds and building joint institutions. I have already mentioned the pioneering work of Karl Deutsch and his colleagues, pointing to communication as a basis for developing empathy, mutual adjustment, and even eventually common identification as evidenced by the realization of a "security community." More recently, there has been a revival of scholarly interest in Immanuel Kant's famous treatise,[57] in which this classic liberal emphasized a "tripod" – consisting of a republican form of government, a cosmopolitan outlook, and an expanding federation of like-minded states – that provides a path to "perpetual peace." Those who follow this liberal tradition put a premium on voluntarism, reciprocity, equal partnership, and multilateralism. Their work lacks the undertone of unilateral and even ethnocentric assertiveness that characterizes the conversion and extraction motivations among some advocates of "engagement."

Significantly, Kantian peace and the Deutschean security community require the existence of a "political market," where the actors involved have built up their reputation for reliability and cooperation over an extended period of time. Their exchanges are governed by what may be described as self-enforcing agreements such that the expected future benefits of a relationship serve as an effective deterrent against defection and cheating by all parties.[58] These exchanges evolve from and are secured by established social conventions, strong political institutions, and dense networks of interdependence that foster trust, promote transparency, and discourage opportunism. These conditions obviously do not currently exist in Sino-American relations as evidenced by the prevailing discourse on both sides of this relationship.

This chapter takes one to the logical implications of the power-transition thesis. If a revisionist latecomer with accumulating power is the main source of danger to international peace, then this peace can only be assured by either blocking this state's further power ascent or by changing its regime or society. The main tendencies in U.S. discourse on the rise of China reflect these approaches. They fall either toward the containment end, or toward the engagement end with a view to converting the Chinese to accept values and interests that are more congenial to the Americans. Because the containment advocates are likely to be self-acknowledged realists, they have little confidence in the ability of international law, intergovernmental organizations, or transnational economic ties to restrain Beijing. The engagement proponents naturally have more faith in the power of international contact and exchanges to restrain and even reform Beijing. They often, however, give the impression that the international institutions, norms, and exchanges being suggested to socialize Beijing would operate in only one direction. That is, somehow Washington would not or should not be subjected to the same purported influence stemming from participating in intergovernmental organizations or engaging in international commerce. There is consequently often surprise and even dismay when Beijing engages institutions of multilateral diplomacy (such as the United Nations and the World Trade Organization) to check U.S. strategic initiatives or when interest groups inside the U.S. lobby for policies perceived to be favorable to China. When international institutions take positions that Washington dislikes, they are bypassed or even boycotted.[59] Because the standard discourse focuses on either power containment or regime change, it overlooks the timely and appropriate adjustment of proportionate benefits as a critical determinant of international peace. Moreover, for various reasons explained in this chapter, both the containment and engagement approaches make important assumptions whose validity requires critical historical and empirical scrutiny. Containment naturally requires one to deny oneself the benefits of exchange for the sake of denying such benefits to the other side, whereas engagement entails acceptance of mutual accessibility and reciprocal influence. In other words, both approaches are double-edged. Both sides of a relationship can resort to them, even though, as will be seen in the next chapter, the Chinese are likely to introduce different emphases and nuances in their effort to manage U.S. preponderance.

8 Managing the hegemon
In lieu of frontal confrontation

How does one expect a rising latecomer to behave? Our earlier discussion of the rationalist perspective suggests that this state should be a status-quo power. It would try to maintain the current state of affairs lest the continuation of its growth trajectory be interrupted or flattened. It would avoid provoking the declining but still stronger power. Recognizing that time is on its side, this latecomer would try to minimize the danger of any premature confrontation. Its general aversion to taking risks conforms to the expectation of prospect theory, which postulates that this latecomer would be more interested in consolidating its recent gains than in precipitating a showdown that would jeopardize these gains. This remark does not suggest that such a country will refrain from taking any risky action. Indeed, when it perceives that its recent gains are being threatened, it may be expected to accept great risks in an effort to fend off such losses.

These attributions are in general accord with conclusions reached by colleagues who specialize in China's foreign relations and whose logic of inquiry and source of evidence tend to differ from those who study international relations. According to Michael D. Swaine and Ashley J. Tellis, China's grand strategy amounts to "the acquisition of comprehensive national power deriving from a continued reform of the economy without the impediments and distractions of security competition."[1] In a similar vein, Avery Goldstein attributed to Beijing a grand strategy aimed at "[increasing] the country's international clout without triggering a counterbalancing reaction."[2] The two tracks of this grand strategy are to enhance China's value as an attractive and even indispensable partner on issues critical to other states, and to cultivate its reputation as a responsible member of the international community. This characterization points to a posture designed to stabilize China's foreign relations and to reassure other states of its growing influence. This posture seeks to project an image of moderation and cooperation, and contradicts the image of a revisionist upstart determined to upset the existing international order.

Significantly, the strategic posture attributed to contemporary China is not unique to that country, and appears to be generic to rising latecomers in general. When Prussia/Germany was an ascending but still weaker power in Europe, Bismarckian diplomacy was generally cautious and aimed at preserving the regional order.[3] Similarly, neither the U.S. nor the USSR as latecomers sought

a military conflict with the U.K. and Germany, both of which were experiencing relative decline. Although generally described as a case of isolationism, Washington's policy prior to World War I could be more accurately characterized as a program designed to secure its regional hegemony in the Western Hemisphere. The U.S. was surely neither passive nor inactive in this region; its isolationist posture applied only to its interactions with Europe.[4] Similar tendencies of risk aversion and a preference for being left alone may be discerned for the USSR prior to World War II. Rather than wanting to confront Germany, Moscow tried to accommodate and even collaborate with Berlin in the hope of diverting Nazi hostility to other targets.

These observations do not deny that these latecomers can be opportunistic, such that they can make offensive moves when circumstances are propitious. The Austro-Prussian War, the Franco-Prussian War, the Spanish–American War, and the Soviet Union's attack on Finland and Poland offer major examples in this regard. Recognizing that such offensive moves are possible, however, does not alter the fact that these wars were initiated and fought under circumstances that heavily favored the latecomers. In addition, these wars were also waged under circumstances with a low risk of escalation and contagion. The latecomers fought weak and isolated opponents, in situations promising their easy victory and involving a low probability of third parties becoming involved in opposition to their cause. While they were undoubtedly the instigators (or, in the case of the USSR's invasion of Poland, a co-conspirator) of these conflicts, these latecomers did not choose the dominant power as the target of their aggression as the power-transition theory would predict. Parenthetically, past military clashes involving China had been similarly initiated by Beijing under circumstances with a limited danger of escalation and contagion.[5]

Several conclusions follow from this account. First, latecomers tend to be cautious powers. Second, they are more likely to clash militarily with secondary powers than with the leading hegemon. Third, when these latecomers are faced with actual or prospective losses, they may be expected to fight back vigorously. The USSR found itself in this situation after being attacked by Germany in 1941. A direct assault, however, is not necessary in order to make a latecomer feel that it is already in or is about to be put in a domain of loss. Thus, paradoxically, the Japanese decision to attack Pearl Harbor was a gamble undertaken out of desperation.[6] The U.S. intervention in the Korean War shortly after the Communist Party came to power in Beijing offers another case in point.[7] The march of U.S. and South Korean forces toward the Yalu, in the context of Douglas MacArthur's thinly veiled threats about "rolling back" communism, gave impetus to the Chinese counter-intervention. Beijing did not shirk from accepting the risk of fighting the superior forces of the U.S. and its allies. Thus, obviously, risk avoidance is a situational rather than a dispositional trait. While it may be more interested in consolidating its recent gains, a latecomer may still be expected to fight a stronger foe when it feels that these gains are threatened.[8]

Significantly, as implied above, prospective losses for a regime are not limited to external relations. Domestic conditions can also compromise a regime's political control and legitimacy, thus presenting a cause for its vulnerability to trigger such a setback. In this light, it becomes more understandable that some Sinologists have observed a tendency for domestic turmoil or leadership instability to encourage a more strident foreign policy posture. Beijing's precipitation of the 1958 Taiwan Strait crisis and its 1969 military clashes with the USSR coincided with the Great Leap Forward Campaign and the Cultural Revolution, respectively.[9] One need not resort to uniquely Chinese factors or even invoke the diversionary theory of war in order to account for this tendency.[10] Prospect theory predicts greater risk-taking behavior when people are faced with an actual or possible loss.

Significantly, this discussion underscores a point made earlier. The source of foreign belligerence is more likely to come from a declining rather than a rising power. A latecomer in ascendance may be expected to eschew risks, whereas one whose power trajectory has stalled or even reversed will be a more tenacious and even reckless adversary. The Cuban Missile Crisis offers an especially revealing example. Nikita Khrushchev's daring move to introduce median- and intermediate-range missiles to Cuba – in face of the known U.S. opposition to such a gamble – is a sign of desperation for a country that no longer expected to catch up with the dominant power, and not an expression of confidence by a latecomer poised to overtake the dominant power. For reasons given by both prospect theory and its rationalist counterpart, a growing China will in fact be a more accommodating China. When China's growth slips, however, Beijing will no longer be willing to further postpone demands that have heretofore been deferred. So long as China's growth continues, Beijing would not want to precipitate a showdown with the U.S. such as the one started by the USSR in 1962. If anything, one would expect Beijing to play a game of reassurance, seeking to signal to the U.S. and China's neighbors that it is a status-quo power committed to the existing order.[11]

The above discussion suggests another significant point. If a regime's prospective losses must take into account its domestic standing, then ongoing trends in China would make Beijing's domestic considerations a more salient factor in influencing its foreign policy. Beijing's decision process is today more pluralistic and less dominated by a few leading personalities, and public opinion has more influence in this process. Competition among rival factions will increasingly incline leaders to turn to popular nationalism as a source of legitimacy.[12] This development is especially pertinent to the potential for a Sino-American confrontation over the status of Taiwan. A decision by Taiwan's leaders to declare *de jure* independence is significant not so much from the perspective of any material deprivation for Beijing, since the two sides have existed in *de facto* separation for over half a century. Rather, should this event come to pass, the most severe loss for the Chinese leaders would be on the domestic front. In the absence of effective counter-moves, these leaders would suffer serious damage to their nationalist credentials and their political legitimacy. Significantly, and seemingly unrecognized by some liberal advocates in the U.S., a process leading to greater democratic opening, elite competition, and popular voice will only increase – not decrease – this penalty that Beijing's leaders will have to pay domestically if they are to accept Taiwan's *de jure* independence. Thus, contrary to the view that democratization would make China more accommodating in its foreign relations, the opposite is actually more likely to be the case so far as Taiwan is concerned.[13] The Chinese people can and do have many misgivings about their government, but reunification with Taiwan is such a universally popular and politically sensitive issue that it would be a mistake to assume Beijing's quiescence in this matter. There is a long theoretical tradition and mounting empirical evidence showing that mass partici- pation in the absence of robust political institutions tends to produce instability in a newly democratizing country's domestic politics and foreign relations.[14] An "insecure elite" and "energized masses" create a combustible mixture that has historically increased the danger that emergent democracies will go to war.[15]

Several logical and empirical implications follow from the ongoing trends. China has become Taiwan's main trade partner, and Taiwan has become an important investor in China. In 2005, 70 percent of Taiwan's foreign direct invest- ment and 40 percent of its exports went to China (including Hong Kong).[16] Bilateral tourist exchanges have been on the rise, and direct, regularly scheduled shipping and air travel between the two sides are likely to be established in the near future. It has been reported that almost 1 million Taiwanese businesspeople and their families have taken up residence on the Mainland. For all practical purposes, there has been an ongoing process of economic and cultural integration despite continued political separation. If the current trends continue, there will be *de facto* unification. Thus, Beijing has time on its side. Accordingly, it should have little incentive to alter the current processes that would further enhance its bargaining position over time. Conversely, the pro-independence advocates on Taiwan are faced with the challenge of working against these processes. This perspective in turn implies that any challenge to the status quo is more likely to come from Taipei than from Beijing.[17]

Only one country can reverse the asymmetric cross-Strait relation working in Beijing's favor. For obvious reasons, Beijing wants to neutralize the U.S. influence. Thus, another implication from this discussion is that far from desiring a confrontation with Washington, Beijing has every incentive to avoid this possibility. Should a Sino-American confrontation take place over Taiwan, it would not be because Beijing wants to have such a showdown, but rather because it has been unable to persuade Washington to refrain from intervening.[18] If, as some have suggested, one can draw a historical lesson from Anglo-German relations in 1914, it would be that the U.K. joined the anti-German coalition not because Berlin had sought to involve London in a fight but rather because it had failed in its effort to prevent London from becoming involved.

Yet a third implication from this discussion is that a Sino-American conflict over the Taiwan Strait is possible regardless of whether there is an ongoing power transition between the two countries. If China was willing to fight the U.S. in 1950 when it was in a much weaker position, the existence of a power asymme- try obviously did not play a decisive role in Beijing's calculations. War between the two countries is possible even without China managing to catch up with the U.S.[19] As one observer has warned, "from time to time, Beijing makes it clear that it will declare war if Taiwan moves toward independence, regardless of the costs. And it would be dangerous to ignore this reality."[20]

As discussed already, whether a state is inclined to take on a stronger adversary depends in large part on its perceptions of prospective losses. The greater the anticipated damage to a regime's core values and interests, the more inclined it is to accept risky actions to forestall it. This does not necessarily imply that the actions being considered or undertaken are seen to promise a good chance of success. On the contrary, these actions may be perceived to offer only a low probability of success, but they are still preferred to the alternatives of inaction or succumbing to the opponent's demands. The Japanese gamble in attacking the U.S. Pacific Fleet stationed at Pearl Harbor illustrates this point. Similarly, Saddam Hussein's response to U.S. pressure offers another example.

Standard discussion in U.S. scholarship on international relations, especially in the realist tradition, sees two primary ways in which states seek to enhance their security. They can engage in either "internal balancing" or "external balancing."[21] That is, states can either devote a larger portion of their domestic product to military expenditures or join other states in an alliance to increase their collective power. It seems natural to expect an ambitious, rising latecomer to spend more on armament. This armament is supposed to cause a "security dilemma," whereby other states feel threatened and thus motivated to undertake counter-armament programs. The result is an arms race such as the Anglo-German naval competition prior to World War I. As for "external balancing," neighbors of a rising latecomer are expected to join forces to contain it. This containment effort, however, has been hypothesized to cause a sense of encirclement that in turn inclines the latecomer to seek allies of its own. The resulting alliance commitments tend to exacerbate mutual insecurity and make it less possible for leaders, such as those prior to World War I, to pull back from a collision course for fear of letting down their allies or causing the distribution of power to turn to their disadvantage.

One would not, however, expect Beijing to follow these behavioral patterns of internal or external balancing. Even though its economy has been expanding, China has not ramped up its military program. As seen in Chapter 2, Chinese defense spending falls substantially behind the U.S. level, both in absolute and relative terms. It stands to reason that Beijing would be reluctant to enter any arms race with the U.S. holding a huge lead and comparative advantage. Beijing cannot hope to win such an arms race, which can only increase Washington's misgivings about Chinese intentions. In the meantime, a diversion of scarce resources from civilian production to military consumption can only come at a heavy opportunity cost to China's economic growth.[22] Indeed, there is little evidence that China's defense spending has sought to "balance" against the U.S., thus repeating the mistake made by Moscow whose crushing defense burden eventually bankrupted the Soviet economy. In the words of one leading Chinese scholar of international relations, "it would be foolhardy . . . for Beijing to challenge directly the international order and the institutions favored by the Western world – and indeed, such a challenge is unlikely."[23]

Nor would one expect Beijing to search for foreign allies and clients in an attempt aimed at external balancing. This observation does not imply that Beijing would eschew the cultivation of transnational networks, such as those based on its rising commercial ties with countries in Western Europe and Southeast Asia, that could advance its interests and shield them from unwanted developments. This is, however, a very different undertaking from the "pactomania" that characterized the competition between the U.S. and the USSR during the Cold War. One would not expect Beijing to take up the active and oppositional profile implied by a program of external balancing. There is little indication in Beijing's current behavior to point to such a propensity.

Rather, as befitting the role of a rising latecomer suggested by our previous discussion, one would expect Beijing to pursue a strategic course that is the very opposite of internal and external balancing. This strategic course consists of important elements of what has been described as "soft balancing," although it also contains aspects that are not captured by this latter concept. Soft balancing refers to "actions that do not directly challenge U.S. military preponderance but that use nonmilitary tools to deny, frustrate, and undermine aggressive unilateral U.S. military policies."[24] According to Robert Pape, international institutions, economic statecraft, and diplomatic coordination have been prominent tools in attempts by other states to soft balance the U.S. after its invasion of Iraq in 2003.[25]

My characterization of Chinese strategy conforms to the injunctions of traditional Chinese statecraft better than the standard U.S. expectations on hard balancing. These injunctions emphasize the conservation of one's energy, the dissipation of an enemy's resources, and the exploitation of an adversary's predispositions rather than confronting its strong points. As Sun Tzu famously enjoined, "attaining one hundred victories in one hundred battles is not the highest achievement; subjugating the enemy without having to fight is the true pinnacle of excellence."[26] Thus, the emphasis of statecraft goes to the application of political acumen rather than the contest of physical prowess. In Sun Tzu's words, "the highest realization of warfare is to attack the enemy's plans, the next is to attack its alliances, the next is to attack its army, and the lowest is to attack its fortifications."[27]

Like other countries, China's statecraft is multidimensional and involves opposing injunctions or bimodal reasoning (e.g., to be bold *and* cautious, to bluff strength *and* to feign weakness, to be patient *and* to be opportunistic). As a matter of comparison with standard U.S. strategic thinking, however, it is less likely to assume that a state's power trajectory will be characterized by a linear progression.[28] Instead, the Chinese are more likely to take a dialectic or cyclical view of the waning and waxing of national power. Moreover, they tend to attribute a state's own internal conditions rather than external pressure as the principal source for constraining and modifying its behavior and as the main cause for its eventual rise or decline. Finally, challenges to a dominant power are viewed less in terms of a contest of raw power and more as an attempt aimed at influencing its incentives and calculations. The highest achievement in statecraft is not to prevail in a physical struggle but rather to subjugate an adversary without having to resort to arms. Intangibles in the form of strategy, morale, leadership, perseverance, and timing and location would trump tangibles such as weaponry and money. These ideas contrast with the typical U.S. emphasis on internal or external balancing as the principal means of containing or defeating a foreign rival. They point to ways of "going around" and delaying U.S. goals in a deeper sense.[29]

Although the power-transition logic would imply that the rising and declining states are caught in a competitive dynamic, this discussion instead suggests that Beijing would avoid challenging Washington directly. Rather than opposing the U.S. on every major issue of concern to Washington, one would rather expect Beijing to express verbal support on matters such as combating international terrorism, preventing nuclear proliferation, stabilizing currency values, and resisting trade protection. Whether such verbal support is backed by tangible action, however, is a different matter. To the extent that Washington really cares about these issues, it can be left to do the heavy lifting, with others, including Beijing, possibly benefiting from the fruits of these U.S. efforts. To the extent that Beijing's cooperation is sought, it gains leverage for demanding concessions in other areas. This cooperation may take the form of either action or inaction (such as putting pressure on North Korea to give up its nuclear program or refraining from exporting missile technology to Iran or Pakistan, or devaluing the *renminbi* during the Asian financial crisis of the late 1990s).

That Beijing may be expected to join rather than oppose the U.S. on many issues suggests more than just an implied incentive to free-ride on Washington's efforts or a desire to extract offsetting compensation for its cooperation. Significantly, this behavior also focuses attention on an important distinction between the current preferences of American officials and the basic U.S. national interests. Current official preferences are not taken to be necessarily the equivalent to fundamental and enduring national interests. Thus, a strategy to indulge and even abet current U.S. preferences may be justified as a way to circumvent and even defeat the realization of more important, longer-term U.S. interests.[30]

"Standing aside" presents another option for a rising latecomer such as China.[31] In this case, Beijing may be expected to issue verbal criticism without putting up active resistance. China's reaction to the U.S. attack on Serbia and Iraq follows this path. There is little that China could do to stop or hamper U.S. actions in these cases, and others (such as France and Russia) could be counted on to assume a leading role in opposing the U.S. initiative. To the extent that these U.S. actions distract Washington's attention or disperse its forces, they relieve pressure on China. Over-extension by the U.S. then works to China's advantage. According to Sun Tzu, "if the enemy must prepare to defend many positions, then its forces facing us will be few."[32] Thus, a dominant power's hubris and over-confidence may be turned to its disadvantage.[33] One does not need to out-muscle a stronger opponent, but one can try to exhaust it by sapping its energy. Far from trying to check the opponent's hegemonic impulses, one accommodates and even encourages it so that it becomes entangled on many fronts. After all, a supremely self-confident hegemon would not be inclined to wage a preventive war – nor would a seriously overstretched hegemon be in a position to undertake such a project.

Engagement may also be expected in Beijing's management of its relations with Washington. It is hardly surprising that intergovernmental organizations and commercial interdependence present the opportunity for reciprocal influence. Thus, Beijing has increasingly resorted to multilateral fora, such as the

United Nations, ASEAN Plus Three,[34] and the Shanghai Cooperation Organization,[35] to restrain Washington's unilateralism. Similarly, domestic groups in the U.S., such as the U.S.–China Business Council, may be expected to self-mobilize to lobby for more accommodating policies toward Beijing. With China's increasing participation in intergovernmental organizations and its mounting commercial exchanges with U.S. firms, these points of contact provide another avenue for managing bilateral relations. Beijing's resort to these engagement approaches reflects classic Chinese thought which enjoins one to apply the other's spear against its own shield.[36] One emulates the other and adopts its strategic advice and tools to contain threats emanating from it.

Significantly, the views discussed above imply that deterrence efforts need not rely solely on one's own retaliatory or defensive capability, or even on the active assistance of allies and partners. To the extent that the dominant power's domestic politics are characterized by fragmented interests, divided visions, and a tendency for policy cycling, one may expect its internal forces to present a powerful restraint against the current incumbent's policies whatever these policies may be. The possibility for external leverage, however, is the greatest in matters where the dominant power's elite and public are internally conflicted due to competing interests and avowed principles. "Free trade" offers an example of such a wedge issue. Access to the Chinese market is important to many large U.S. corporations, which tend to historically support conservative Republican candidates. To the extent that U.S. business groups are self-motivated to continue and expand commercial ties with China, they become the best advocates Beijing can hope to have for a friendly U.S. posture. Similarly, to the extent that liberal Democrats have historically favored a large role for international organizations, the norms and rules of existing regimes may be used to argue against unilateral U.S. actions whether in trade protection or armed intervention.

Restraining influence can also come from those states that are important U.S. allies or clients. To the extent that unwanted events will have negative ripple effects for significant third parties that the U.S. cares about, it will restrain itself from playing its stronger hand. For instance, Washington would be wary of taking a more forceful stand if Sino-American tension were to dampen economic activities or exacerbate political problems in friendly Southeast and Northeast Asian countries. Deterrence in such situations does not require the active mobilization of a defensive alliance; rather, it can rely on the self-mobilization of those groups or entities whose economic vitality and/or regime legitimacy are important to Washington and whose well-being is intertwined with the evolution of Sino-American relations. Given their respective political and economic ties with China, Pakistan and South Korea are prominent examples of countries in this position. The former is crucial for the U.S. campaign against international terrorism, and the latter is important to Washington's concern for a stable and nuclear-free Korean peninsula.

The key elements of China's approach to managing the hegemon place a premium on feigning weakness and conserving energy, eschewing competition in the other's strong suit, abetting the opposition's excesses, diverting the latter's attention to alternative targets, leveraging domestic divisions in the other's political economy, and projecting an image of being too big to swallow and too tough to mess with. In short, this approach accords with Sun Tzu's observation that "being unconquerable lies with oneself whereas being conquerable lies with the enemy; one who excels in strategy succeeds in making oneself unconquerable even though it is not within his control to make the enemy necessarily conquerable." By implication, fatal strategic setbacks are more likely to be due to one's own mistakes than to the opponent's actions. Avoidance of such errors helps to put one in an unassailable position. Allowing one's opponent ample opportunity to commit these errors would conversely put it in a self-defeating position.

Although I have argued that my expectation and characterization of Beijing's strategic conduct find support in traditional Chinese thinking, it would be a mistake to infer from my remarks that the behavioral patterns and underlying rationale described are uniquely or distinctly Chinese. Despite the prediction of neorealists, it appears that balancing against a powerful state has not been the dominant behavioral modality in history. When faced with hegemonic threat, states have instead tended to appease, bandwagon, pass the buck, "hide," and "transcend" by offering institutional arrangements that go beyond resolving an immediate dispute.[37] Napoleon's France was defeated only because it insisted on attacking its allies and neutrals, thus thwarting their attempts to appease and bandwagon. By repeatedly lashing out against its neighbors, France finally produced by its own aggressive actions a coalition of opposing states that Britain's diplomacy had sought but failed to bring about. Similarly, Nazi Germany brought about its own downfall by not only fighting the U.K. and France, but also by declaring war on the USSR and the U.S. – the two world powers that only wanted to be left alone.[38] Therefore, a dominant state's recklessness and arrogance turned potential allies and neutrals into enemies. The impetus that fostered a coalition against the hegemon or would-be hegemon came from its own aggressive actions rather than from a natural instinct on the part of the weaker states to balance against its power. By implication, this state's demise can be traced to its own conduct. Abetting this state's aggressive tendencies, rather than necessarily opposing these tendencies all the time by resort to internal or external balancing, therefore presents itself as one approach to managing a hegemon.

It will not have escaped the reader's notice that the logic of hegemonic decline given by Chinese strategists accords in general outline with another well-known process described by Western historians. A tendency to "overreach" – to take on extensive foreign commitments beyond the domestic economy's capacity to sustain – has been an important part of the familiar story of imperial decline,[39] with the USSR being the latest empire to suffer from severe economic decay and political disintegration due to a crushing security burden.[40] That at some point military expenditures and overseas obligations would impose a severe opportunity cost in forgone domestic spending, whether in public or private consumption and investment (including investment in human capital), seems reasonably probable.[41] In assuming a tendency for a hegemon's excessive ambitions to eventually deplete its available resources and cause a domestic crisis of confidence, the Chinese views are again unexceptional.

If this analysis is correct, Beijing's strategy for managing a dominant power points to precisely the opposite modal behavior than that which is expected by the power-transition theory. The prevailing U.S. rendition of this theory hypothesizes a cocky and impatient challenger whose imprudence gets it into a premature and asymmetric fight that it is destined to lose. Instead, this discussion suggests that China may be expected to play for time, to avoid an inflated profile, to profess modesty in goals and capability, and to seek to expand and strengthen multilateral ties and institutions. The underlying strategic logic cautions against overplaying one's hand, and extends to the dominant power ample opportunity to overplay its hand. Self-restraint rather than just restraining the other then becomes a cardinal tenet for the successful management of the dominant power. At the same time, the dominant power's failure to exercise proper self-discipline causes its over-extension, contributes to its domestic hollowing and dissension, and arouses counter-mobilization abroad, developments that would in turn set it on a course of eventual decline. Classic Chinese military treatises are well known for their advice to feign weakness and bide time, to abet the other's arrogance and distract its attention, and to prevail over the other without having to fight.[42] This strategic perspective implies an extended time horizon and a certain confidence in being able to persevere through and recover from the inevitable occasional setback that interrupts a generally favorable long-term trend. Military instruments play an important but still secondary part in this conception of statecraft. They serve primarily to demonstrate minimum deterrence and a will for assured resistance and retaliation if attacked, rather than being intended to gain physical superiority on the battlefield (or what Americans call war-winning capabilities).[43]

In summary, this discussion suggests that one would not expect a rising China to pursue a strategy of active resistance or direct confrontation with the U.S. Neither a program of accelerated armament nor an active campaign to recruit alliance partners is likely. One would not expect Beijing to take part in a power rivalry with Washington such that we will witness a repetition of the competitive dynamic between the U.S. and the USSR during the Cold War. Beijing is likely to behave cautiously rather than rashly. Its policy repertoire will consist of engagement, entanglement, even evasion. It has more to lose than to gain by challenging Washington. This does not mean, however, that a clash between the two countries is impossible or even unlikely. As Joseph Nye remarked, "if the United States and China stumble into war or a cold war in East Asia, it will more likely be caused by inept policy related to Taiwan's independence rather than China's success as a global challenger."[44] The logic presented in this book would lead us to expect that should such a collision occur, it is likely because China finds itself in the domain of loss. Moreover, as Dale Copeland has remarked, "if destabilizing policies are to be initiated, the perpetrator will likely be a declining United States."[45] Beijing's strategic approach is aptly summarized by Deng Xiaoping's injunction to "observe calmly; secure our position; cope with affairs calmly; hide our capacities and bide our time; be good at manipulating a low profile; never claim leadership."[46] Such advice fits poorly with the portrait of an impatient and arrogant challenger, often presented with Imperial Germany in the Anglo-German rivalry of a century ago as a model. Chinese and American commentators alike have remarked about an emphasis on self-restraint in China's current foreign policy or, in Jonathan Pollack's words,[47] a deliberate attempt to limit Beijing's exposure to "America's strategic headlights" and to reassure China's neighbors about its "peaceful ascent."

9 Extended deterrence and the logic of selection

Systemic wars tend to originate from local conflicts that subsequently engulf the great powers. As James Morrow observed, "general wars typically begin small and then expand to encompass all the major powers."[1] Although these wars may eventually involve those leading states experiencing a power transition, they do not usually arise initially from a direct confrontation between them. The leading states often become involved only subsequently as a result of the contagious effects of alliance commitments.

The proximate cause for the outbreak of both World War I and World War II had to do with a failure in extended deterrence.[2] Extended deterrence refers to an attempt by a defender to discourage a challenger from attacking its protégé.[3] The defender tries to dissuade the challenger from attacking its protégé by threatening to intervene on the latter's behalf. When the challenger attacks the protégé despite the defender's warning, extended deterrence fails. Should the defender decide to honor its pledge to come to the protégé's assistance, war is likely to break out between the defender and the challenger.[4] This occurrence signifies the contagion of an initial bilateral conflict to involve other parties. In July 1914, St. Petersburg was motivated to prevent a humiliating defeat of its Serbian ally at the hands of Austria-Hungary. At the same time, Berlin was determined to support its ally Austria-Hungary in a showdown with Russia.[5] In September 1939, London and Paris committed themselves to the defense of Warsaw. Their attempt at extended deterrence failed when Adolf Hitler invaded Poland, causing the U.K. and France to declare war against Nazi Germany. In December 1941, Washington's attempt at extended deterrence against Japan also failed. Instead of preventing Japan from attacking the European colonies in Southeast Asia, this U.S. effort led to a decision by Tokyo to seize the strategic initiative by attacking Pearl Harbor.

Even if one were to accept that the Anglo-German rivalry was the chief dynamic responsible for producing World Wars I and II, the European episodes mentioned above suggest that the original spark setting off these conflicts came from a contest involving some other party or parties, which were Britain's or Germany's junior partners or protégés.[6] Thus, these global conflicts did not originate from a direct confrontation between Germany and the U.K. Rather, a failed attempt at extended deterrence was the reason behind the escalation and contagion processes that ultimately put Berlin and London on a collision course.[7] As suggested on several occasions already, if a militarized dispute and even armed conflict should occur between China and the U.S., the most likely cause would be a contest over the status of Taiwan.

Such a contest would follow the general outline of an extended deterrence, with the U.S. in the role of a defender and China in the role of a challenger.[8] In contrast to when a state tries to deter an attack against itself, extended deterrence represents an effort to protect another country. The latter effort is more difficult because, as Thomas Schelling has emphasized, "the difference between the national homeland and everything 'abroad' is the difference between threats that are inherently credible, even if unspoken, and threats that have to be made credible."[9] Although a challenger can reasonably expect that the target of its attack will fight back, it is more doubtful that a state will defend another state under attack.[10] After all, allies quite frequently abandon their friends in need. According to one estimate, states honor their defense commitments to allies in only 27 percent of cases.[11] Thus, it is perhaps understandable that Hitler was skeptical about Britain's pledge to defend Poland, remarking: "Why should Britain fight? You don't let yourself get killed for any ally."[12] Hitler doubted London's, and Paris's, resolve to fight for Poland, but he also questioned whether they were capable of rendering the necessary assistance to their ally even if they were resolved to do so. Neither Britain nor France had troops deployed where they could make a difference to the Nazi invasion of Poland. Thus, even if they had intended to come to Warsaw's aid, London and Paris could not do anything to contest Berlin's military action. Without their armed forces actually positioned to oppose the Nazi invasion, British and French pledges lacked credibility in Hitler's eyes.

Some colleagues are likely to challenge the characterization of the U.S. policy toward China and Taiwan as a case of extended deterrence. A major development in the recent literature on deterrence follows Robert Jervis's pioneering insights that were developed further by the thoughtful theoretical and empirical research undertaken by Timothy Crawford.[13] Instead of extended deterrence, the U.S. policy in the Taiwan Strait has been described as pivotal deterrence. According to the latter concept, the U.S. seeks *dual* deterrence so that neither side of the Taiwan Strait attempts to alter the status quo unilaterally. Thus, Washington tries to discourage Beijing from launching an armed attack against Taiwan and also tries simultaneously to discourage Taipei from declaring formal independence (an action which is likely to provoke Beijing to launch an armed attack). According to this formulation, Washington enjoys a pivotal position in the triangular relationship because it has the freedom to align with either Beijing or Taipei, but the latter two do not have the option of aligning with each other. This pivotal position gives the U.S. leverage to tip the balance between the two contending sides, enabling it to manipulate the two rivals by promising support to the more "reasonable" side and withholding support or even actively opposing the more "recalcitrant" side. The pivot's bargaining position is enhanced when the two rivals lack any alliance option and so cannot gain support from yet another outside party to neutralize the pivot's deterrence threat.

There is a fundamental difference between the Taiwan Strait situation and the other historical cases studied by Crawford.[14] The pivotal states in the other cases did not have a role in creating the status quo they were seeking to maintain. In contrast, the U.S. was directly responsible for the separation of Taiwan from China. Had it not been for Harry Truman's order for the Seventh Fleet to "neutralize" the Taiwan Strait in 1950, the Chinese Civil War would have ended with a successful communist invasion of the last bastion of Nationalist power on Taiwan.[15] In the current context, pivotal deterrence by the U.S. can accordingly be construed to have the effect or even the intent of perpetuating the separation of the two sides of the Taiwan Strait, a situation that Washington was responsible for bringing about in the first place. The condition that the pivotal state should have the option of aligning with either side of a dispute does not quite obtain in this case, as it does not seem likely that Washington will ever threaten alignment with Beijing in order to force Taipei to reunify with China. As one observer has remarked,

> Chinese leaders believe, with some justification, that the Taiwan issue has occasionally been used to pressure them. American leaders will argue that they are not responsible for the rise of Taiwanese political parties advocating independence and that they have not encouraged them. But the only reason pro-independence forces in Taiwan do not fear Chinese retaliation is because of the U.S. commitment to intervene.[16]

Moreover, as will be pointed out again later, the pivotal deterrence policy attributed to the U.S. is tantamount to asking Beijing to accept *de facto* independence by Taiwan in exchange for Washington's pressure on Taipei to eschew *de jure* independence. Why should Beijing find this quid pro quo attractive if it implies an acceptance of the permanent separation of Taiwan from China? Similarly, as will be raised again later, why should Taipei believe that its strategic importance to Washington should be any different if it declared independence than if it did not? Why should Washington care any less about its fate if it pursued *de jure* independence than if it just maintains its current *de facto* independence?

The crux of the matter appears not to be whether the U.S. prefers Taipei to continue its current status of *de facto* independence rather than make a declaration of *de jure* independence. Rather it is about what the U.S. would do if Taipei were to pursue that latter option. Assuming Taipei has declared *de jure* independence, would Washington stand by and let Beijing take over the island or would it intervene against such a takeover? For a policy of pivotal deterrence to be credible, Taipei must be made to believe that Washington does really intend to abandon it should it declare formal independence. But, as already mentioned, why should Taipei believe that its strategic importance to Washington would be affected by a mere legal formality such that in one case the U.S. would stand aside in face of a Chinese attack and, in the other, it would risk going to war against China?

As suggested above, should Taiwan declare *de jure* independence, the U.S. would have to decide whether to intervene on its behalf when faced with Chinese military action. Should the U.S. decide to protect Taiwan even after it has declared *de jure* independence, this choice would invalidate the proposition that Washington's policy heretofore has been one of pivotal deterrence. If, however, the U.S. decided to stand aside, this action would not necessarily confirm its practice of pivotal deterrence. This is because U.S. inaction in that event would be congruent with either the proposition that the U.S. has been practicing pivotal deterrence or the proposition that it has been pursuing extended deterrence but has chosen to back down in face of a Chinese challenge. Given that Taipei has chosen to declare *de jure* independence, a subsequent U.S. decision to refrain from intervening on its behalf would not in itself be able to tell us whether Washington has had a policy of pivotal deterrence or one of extended deterrence. It is, however, to be expected that Washington would have an incentive to claim that it has sought pivotal deterrence even if it has actually been practicing extended deterrence. Even though in reality pivotal deterrence is "an *imposition* [emphasis in the original] of order and peaceful change that, above all else, suits the pivot's interests,"[17] the pivot is motivated to project the image of an honest broker seeking to mediate the bilateral conflict between the adversaries and to prevent a war between them from coming to pass.

Parenthetically, should Taipei move to declare *de jure* independence, one might infer that its leaders must have private information suggesting that Washington really has a policy of extended deterrence, even though it may have publicly presented its policy as pivotal deterrence. The logic of this inference is of course that a decision to declare *de jure* independence implies that Taipei is reasonably sure that the U.S. will still come to its defense even after it has made this move. It would suggest that Taipei does not believe in Washington's threat of abandonment as implied by a U.S. policy of pivotal deterrence.

A professed policy of pivotal deterrence has the advantage of enabling Washington to pursue influence on both sides of the Taiwan Strait, something that extended deterrence cannot promise. The former approach moreover confers freedom of action and, given the greater ambiguity about future U.S. action implied by this approach, offers Washington more discretion in deciding whether and, if so, how to act in the event of a war between the adversaries. The decision facing the U.S. would inevitably be a subjective and political judgment since, as Timothy Crawford argued, "even in theory, it is often hard to determine 'objectively' just who is the aggressor – the one that attacks first, or the one that provoked it?" The pivotal state does not just consider the "facts" about the origination of a conflict but also takes into account its wider strategic interests beyond the immediate situation. "If in light of those factors, it is expedient for the pivot not to retaliate against one side, it may very well decide to blame the other side, regardless of who 'started it.'"[18]

Pivotal deterrence suggests a certain even-handedness as implied by the pivot's ambiguous posture,[19] yet Beijing is unlikely to agree with this characterization of the Taiwan situation. Rather, the Chinese leaders are likely to see the situation resembling an attempt by the U.S. at extended deterrence, albeit with important nuances and qualifications to be discussed later in this chapter. Whether characterized as pivotal deterrence or extended deterrence, Washington faces the challenge of not simply declaring that it has an interest or even an important interest in the development of cross-Strait relations, but that it has an interest which, after adjusting for capability disparities, should carry more weight than Beijing's interest and Taipei's interest. It is of course difficult to convince either Beijing or Taipei that Washington's inherent stake in their conflict is greater than theirs. Moreover, it is difficult to convince either Beijing or Taipei that Taiwan is inherently rather than derivatively important to Washington. That is, the status of Taiwan is important to the U.S. in and of itself rather than its being conditional on Washington's other higher policy goals, including how China may contribute to these other goals and how the U.S. may be able to impede China's power ascent. An important insight of Crawford's research pertains to the tendency that the more powerful a pivot is, the less likely its commitments will be credible in the eyes of the other states. The preponderance of U.S. power, paradoxically, makes it more difficult to convince Beijing or Taipei that Washington has a vital interest at stake in their relations. "Because [the U.S.] will remain preponderant and relatively secure regardless of who wins, it will be hard-pressed to convey to the adversaries the strength of its motivation to prevent war."[20] Another reason for this paradox is that preponderant power weakens credible commitments. A dominant power will face less serious consequences if it reneges on its commitments. It can break promises with relative impunity, especially if the other states involved have few or no alternative sources of support or protection.

There is, in addition to this motivational asymmetry, another important difference in the application of U.S. dual deterrence, a difference that applies to situations such as the Greek–Turkish and Indian–Pakistani disputes. Given the power asymmetry between China and Taiwan, an attempt at pivotal deterrence by the U.S. involves fundamentally different threats. To pressure Taipei, all Washington has to do is to threaten inaction. In the absence of an ally that can offset its more powerful rival, abandonment means that Taiwan will be militarily overwhelmed (just as Greece and Pakistan would be in a war against their more powerful rivals without intervention by another strong power such as the USSR or China). To pressure Beijing, however, involves a fundamentally different task for the U.S. Instead of just warning that it would step aside, Washington would have to threaten active intervention. If push comes to shove, it would itself have to do the actual "heavy lifting" to "beat" China as opposed to letting China "beat" Taiwan in the alternative scenario. This asymmetry of implied effort suggests in turn that one is closer to a situation of extended deterrence. Despite frequent public discussions about the U.S. selling weapons to Taiwan so that the latter can mount a more effective deterrence against China, the reality of the situation is that absent the threat of U.S. intervention, Taiwan would not be able to deter a Chinese attack by itself. Moreover, as shown in Operation Desert Storm when the U.S. asked the Saudis to leave the fighting to the U.S., Taiwan's military force would be a hindrance rather than help in conducting U.S. military campaigns against China.

These remarks point in turn to a departure from a necessary condition for pivotal deterrence, which requires that the rivals perceive each other to be more threatening than the pivot. Although Taipei may perceive Beijing to be more threatening than Washington,[21] it is questionable that Beijing similarly perceives Taipei to be more threatening than Washington. The U.S., not Taiwan, has the wherewithal to hurt China. Without U.S. backing, Taiwan would not be able to resist China's pressure. This observation again suggests that the U.S. role in the Taiwan Strait comes closer to extended deterrence than pivotal deterrence. The critical relationship is a bilateral one between Beijing and Washington rather than a triangular one including Taipei.

As suggested above, a posture of strategic ambiguity offers inherent opportunities for bluffing. Yet, when one is exposed as a bluffer, one pays a reputation price in that others will question one's commitments in the future. In the long run, states can benefit from being honest because their diplomatic communication would thus enable them to determine the relative importance of issues to one another: "All states can be better off over time if they are more likely to concede when issues are relatively unimportant to them and to resist on issues they consider relatively important. This process is a type of 'trade' of issues over time."[22] When would states decide to bluff rather than be honest?

Many factors are plausible but three come to mind as obvious leading candidates. Powerful states are more inclined to bluff. They expect that their bluffs are less likely to be called by their weaker opponents because the latter would be discouraged by the prospective costs of a mistaken challenge (that is, the prospect that the weaker opponents will have to pay a heavy price if it turns out that the powerful states in question are not bluffing). Moreover, for a really preponderant state, the consequences of being exposed as a bluffer in a specific situation are unlikely to be serious. Even if others may as a result have doubts about the reliability of its commitments, to whom else can they turn for assistance? What other alliance options do they have?

Second, as suggested previously, states whose power is suffering from relative decline may also be more inclined to bluff. These states are more willing to accept risks in order to prevent a loss of their existing assets or to forestall a revision of their policy aspirations. Their incentive to bluff is also reinforced by the expectation that there may be a lag in the other states' estimates of their capability or resolve in the context of ongoing changes (that is, declining states may hope to capitalize on their past reputation).

Third, states with a very high or a very low stake in an issue are unlikely to bluff. When a state has an obvious high stake in an issue (such as China in regard to the status of Taiwan), there is no need for it to bluff that its interests are engaged. Conversely, when a state has a low stake in an issue, an attempt to bluff its engagement will not be credible and will likely be challenged. In intermediate situations when a state's stake in an issue is not "evidently" clear, bluffing is most likely to be tried. The very act of announcing that it has an interest in an issue enhances the salience of this issue for the pronouncing state. This pronouncement contrives and, at the same time, creates a stake: "[The] temptation to bluff is strongest when the defender cares a middling amount about the issues."[23]

This discussion points to those factors that are likely to motivate the U.S. more than China to bluff about a dispute over the Taiwan Strait. How can the U.S. attempt to convince China that it is not bluffing? As discussed in Chapter 4, "sunk costs" and "tied hands" offer two ideal-type approaches to extended deterrence. The "sunk costs" approach stresses costly and tangible investments to prepare for a possible attack by a challenger on one's protégé. Although rarely presented in this light in the relevant U.S. literature, the 1962 decision by Nikita Khrushchev to introduce medium- and intermediate-range missiles to Cuba could be plausibly interpreted as an attempt to protect this Soviet ally from another attack by the U.S. after the Bay of Pigs episode.[24] The "tied hands" approach points to a declaratory emphasis seeking to engage the defender's reputation. This actor deliberately takes on "audience costs" so that it will suffer serious damage to its political standing or reputation should it renege on its promise to defend the protégé. Because, as explained before, officials assume that their counterparts will misrepresent their capabilities and intentions, they are likely to dismiss "cheap talk."[25] In order for a defender to be taken seriously, it must be willing to incur costs that a less determined actor would not be inclined to accept. That is, in order for a sincere defender to distinguish itself from one that is only bluffing, it must take on costs and run risks that an insincere defender would not be willing to accept.

There have already been several deterrence encounters between China and the U.S. over Taiwan and the offshore islands (Quemoy and Matsu), most recently when Washington sent two carrier battle groups to the Taiwan Strait in 1996.[26] The extent to which Washington is committed to the defense of Taiwan, however, is uncertain. The U.S. abrogated its mutual defense treaty with Taiwan and withdrew its military personnel from the island, when Washington and Beijing restored diplomatic relations on January 1, 1979. Moreover, American officials have on many occasions formally acknowledged the principle that there is only one China and that Taiwan is part of China.[27] At the same time, Washington has announced that it is against any unilateral effort by either side of the Taiwan Strait to alter the status quo. The Taiwan Relations Act declares that any attempt to alter this status quo by non-peaceful means would be a serious concern for the U.S. There is therefore an inherent contradiction suggested by, on the one hand, an acknowledgment of Chinese sovereignty over Taiwan and, on the other hand, an opposition to Beijing's prerogative to deal with this island as a matter of its domestic affairs.[28] The current U.S. policy may be described as "strategic ambiguity" because there has not been any clear and firm indication as to how Washington would react should there be a conflict between the two sides of the Taiwan Strait. Obviously, a posture of "strategic ambiguity" does not correspond with either the "sunk costs" or the "tied hands" approach to extended deterrence.

The *implied* U.S. policy is that Washington would discourage Taipei from declaring *de jure* independence but it would come to the island's defense should it become the target of an unprovoked attack by China. As already mentioned in the earlier discussion on pivotal deterrence, this implied policy suggests that there are at least two meanings attached to the status quo and two deterrence efforts being mounted by the U.S. Washington seeks to prevent an armed attempt by

Beijing to coerce Taipei, but it also wants simultaneously to discourage Taipei from changing its legal status by declaring formal independence. These two ostensible U.S. goals suggest that, depending on one's frame of reference, the notion of status quo can mean very different things. The meaning of status quo also depends on one's historical memory so that Beijing's attempt to prevent Taipei's secession may be interpreted as seeking to preserve the status quo, to alter the status quo, or to restore the status quo before the island's political separation from the Mainland due to the intervention of the U.S. Seventh Fleet in 1950.[29] Parenthetically, a state may entertain an ambition to revise the local status quo (such as incorporating or reincorporating Taiwan as a Chinese province) without, however, necessarily implying a challenge to or even discontent with the international status quo as represented by the rules and norms of the global order. Indeed, generic and dichotomous characterizations of states as either revisionist or status-quo oriented can be misleading because, as Timothy Crawford sensibly cautioned, "most states have a mixed bag of preferences: They play defense and offense at the same time, seeking to preserve the status quo in some situations and to upend it in others."[30]

Returning to Washington's policy of strategic ambiguity, this posture seems bizarre.[31] From the brief presentation given above on several case histories of extended deterrence, should one not expect to hear clear and consistent warnings from the U.S. in an effort to deter China from attacking Taiwan? James Fearon has noted that signaling deterrence threats involves "all or nothing." That is, when Beijing knows how a serious defender would have behaved (it would have declared, "we will fight you if you attack Taiwan"), anything less (such as "we *may* fight you if you attack Taiwan) is unlikely to be credible.[32] Moreover, Washington's proposition is tantamount to a promise to discourage Taipei from declaring *de jure* independence in exchange for Beijing's acceptance of a continuation of Taiwan's current *de facto* independence. Why would Beijing want to agree to this deal if it means a permanent postponement of its goal of national reunification?

The U.S. posture also seems puzzling because of its implied message to Taipei. Why would Taiwan's officials want to believe that Washington is serious about coming to its aid in the event of a Chinese invasion? After all, the Taiwan Relations Act is a unilateral declaration by the U.S., and it does not have the legal force of the mutual defense treaty that Washington had abrogated. In addition, it stretches one's credulity to argue that somehow Taiwan's intrinsic value to Washington would change according to whether the island makes a move to achieve *de jure* independence. If not, why should one believe that the U.S. will come to its defense if it suffers an unprovoked attack from China, but will stand aside and let China seize the island if Taipei declares independence? Moreover, if whether or not Taipei declares *de jure* independence is pivotal in deciding whether or not the U.S. would intervene, wouldn't Washington have turned over to its protégé this critical determination about whether or not it would intervene? It does not quite make sense for any country to turn over this decision to another country, least of all to a protégé (thereby creating a potential problem of the "tail wagging the dog").

How can one explain this puzzle? There are several possible explanations. The first is that Washington's strategic ambiguity is due to inadvertence or incompetence. This explanation is highly implausible but one may recall that, prior to its intervention in the Korean War, American officials such as Dean Acheson and Douglas MacArthur had implied in their public statements that the Korean peninsula was outside the U.S. defense perimeter.[33] Similarly, Britain's failure to communicate a serious commitment to the defense of the Falklands (or the Malvinas) could have given Buenos Aires the false impression that its attempt to seize these islands would not encounter any resistance from London. As a third example, prior to the first Gulf War in August 1990, the U.S. had apparently failed to warn Iraq sufficiently to deter its invasion of Kuwait. The U.S. ambassador to Baghdad, April Glaspie, had reportedly told Saddam Hussein that "we have no opinion on the Arab–Arab conflicts, like your border disagreement with Kuwait."[34] This attribution has led to speculation that Washington had deliberately "lured and tricked" Saddam Hussein to attack Kuwait,[35] so that the U.S. would in turn have a pretext to attack Iraq. This second possible explanation is again very implausible with respect to Washington's posture of "strategic ambiguity" as applied to the Taiwan case. Still, there has been speculation that Washington had even laid a trap for its ostensible allies, the U.K. and France, in the 1956 Suez Canal crisis. It did not try to stop the British and French from invading Egypt.[36] The Eisenhower administration only put heavy pressure on London and Paris after they had launched their invasion in a show of public diplomacy to force them to withdraw from Egypt. By imposing an embarrassing setback on these two countries that had previously been the dominant colonial powers in the region, the U.S. was supposedly able to exacerbate their declining influence and replace them as the premier foreign power in the Middle East.

If these attributions of inadvertence, incompetence, and entrapment appear far-fetched, then what else can account for the U.S. posture of strategic ambiguity with respect to Taiwan? Another possibility is that Washington is genuinely uncertain about how to react in case of a challenge by Beijing. There is a bureaucratic stalemate between important officials, policy institutions, and interest groups. Absent a consensus on how to deal with China, strategic ambiguity then is a matter of making a virtue out of necessity. It reflects an attempt to cover up internal policy differences, and to put off tough choices. This possible explanation points to bureaucratic politics in Washington rather than the state of affairs in the Taiwan Strait as the main influence shaping U.S. deterrence policy. Still another possible explanation is that the posture of strategic ambiguity reflects mutual partisan adjustment by not only Washington,[37] but also Beijing and Taipei. The basis for this interpretation is that although the three parties have competing agendas, they have also learned to adapt to each other's constraints and to even devise an interim arrangement that is at least acceptable if not optimal for each. Each side in this triangular relationship has been able to make realistic assessments of the others' situation, adopt flexible adjustments in its policy according to what is currently feasible and, at the same time, communicate effectively the limits of its tolerance.[38] The result is a willingness to refrain from forcing issues and to allow the ongoing processes to mature.

Washington's posture of strategic ambiguity becomes more understandable in this light. This posture has the virtue of not antagonizing Beijing, thereby avoiding compromising other security issues (e.g., Korea, terrorism) important to the U.S. or jeopardizing growing Sino-American commercial relations. Absent a definite commitment to Taiwan, Washington can continue to bargain for Beijing's cooperation in other matters. Ambiguity also defuses expected criticisms from domestic conservatives for failing to support Taiwan. But why would Beijing want to go along with this policy? As already argued, so long as its ongoing interactions with Taiwan are moving in the direction of strengthening its future position, China can afford to wait because the long-term prospects for national reunification are improving.[39] The economies on the two sides of the Taiwan Strait have become increasingly integrated, with 40 percent of Taiwan's exports and 70 percent of its foreign direct investment going to China in 2005. This economic integration in turn has had important domestic political consequences in Taiwan, with business interests promoting even closer commercial ties and the further removal of political barriers to these ties.[40] In the meantime, Beijing will have American assistance in restraining Taipei from declaring *de jure* independence. Which other third party would be more influential in discouraging Taipei from taking this step? But what is there for Taipei in this arrangement? It gains access to the Mainland market, while putting off an extremely divisive internal debate on reunification versus independence.[41] Moreover, its officials do not have to treat a decision on independence as a matter of "all or nothing," but can instead make incremental changes that move toward or back away from this prospect. Therefore, proposed changes in the laws governing referendum, the abolition of the National Assembly ostensibly representing constituencies on the Mainland, the elimination of provincial institutions on the island,[42] and the initiation of direct transport across the Taiwan Strait may be used to signal its intentions and to extract concessions from both Beijing and Washington. Ambiguity serves its purpose well because it would lose its bargaining lever and, worse, invite Beijing's retaliation and Washington's disapproval if it were to cross the line of formal declaration of independence. This bargaining lever derives from a threat to declare independence and not from actually doing so.

The above interpretation suggests that Washington, Beijing, and Taipei have tacitly agreed to refrain from introducing any political shocks to the ongoing economic and social integration occurring across the Taiwan Strait. All three have in effect accepted indeterminacy for now and agreed to play for time. I argued earlier that if a Sino-American clash occurs, it is most likely to be over the status of Taiwan. I have also suggested that even though China is weaker than the U.S., it cannot be expected to remain quiescent should Taipei declare *de jure* independence. The interpretation advanced here, however, is that all three parties understand the danger of an unwanted confrontation. Their current policies suggest partisan adjustment to contain this danger. The realization that they have a shared stake but lack unilateral control over the situation provides a basis for interim accommodation.[43] The larger point is that we have not thus far seen the escalation of tension that the power-transition theory warns about when a late-comer narrows the capability gap separating it from the dominant power.

Due to an inability to penetrate the decision processes of all three sides, one cannot of course be sure that the above interpretation is correct. Indeed, as emphasized in Chapter 4, private information and the tendency to engage in misrepresentation hamper attempts by even the relevant officials to grasp accurately the intentions and capabilities of their counterparts. Certainly, it would be unwarranted for scholars without access to classified information and confidential communication to claim any source of unique wisdom. Nevertheless, scholars can still try to determine whether the interpretation offered above conforms to general historical patterns of past deterrence encounters and whether major insights deduced from the rationalist perspective can shed additional light on this interpretation.

As should be evident from the previous discussion, the rationalist perspective does not claim that people are infallible in making judgments. Rather, it simply argues that people are strategic in the sense that they try to calibrate the relationship between means and ends and to adjust their behavior in anticipation of how others will react to their moves. History as we know it reflects the strategic choices exercised by people. When they decide not to act in a particular fashion – such as to challenge a defender's announced intention to protect a protégé – an event does not take place. History does not record these non-occurrences, and it presents a biased sample of only those actualized events out of a universe of all possible events. This sample represents those occasions when the relevant actors "selected" themselves into an encounter. That history represents these selection effects in turn gives scholars and officials an analytic lever to infer people's strategic motivation.[44]

For example, we know that most wars are bilateral rather than multilateral affairs. Why? One possibility is that potential aggressors anticipate the reactions of third parties, and they deliberately select targets without allies or with only unreliable allies. When others are likely to intervene on behalf of a prospective target, the potential aggressor will refrain from attacking – thereby causing a non-event. That aggressors consistently select isolated and vulnerable targets thus accounts for the fact that most wars have been bilateral contests. As another example of selection effect, many observers have noted that economic sanctions rarely achieve their goals. It is, however, likely that most international disputes are resolved before they escalate to the level requiring the actual imposition of sanctions. That is, only those cases involving the most resistant or recalcitrant targets will ever reach the point of investment boycott or trade embargo. The record of observed sanctions therefore over-represents these difficult cases, including those involving targets, such as Cuba, Iraq, and North Korea, which have been subjected to U.S. attempts at economic coercion. The low incidence of sanction successes can be in part accounted for by this selection effect.[45]

What do these examples and, more specifically, the logic of selection have to do with the discussion of extended deterrence and the danger of war with respect to the Taiwan Strait? We can derive some useful inferences from past patterns of extended deterrence and war, and judge whether they can offer clarification and perhaps even prognosis in the specific case of Sino-American relations pertaining to Taiwan's status. The following discussion also relates back to several factors – such as regime character, geographic distance, economic interdependence, audience costs, and the commitment problem – addressed in previous chapters.

One strong empirical generalization from quantitative research on international conflicts is that democracies tend to prevail over their opponents in wars, although this advantage tends to decrease if a war becomes protracted.[46] This pattern reflects only partially the fact that democracies tend to have stronger armed forces. The logic of selection argues that because democratic leaders are more liable to be sanctioned by their electorate for unsuccessful wars, they are more cautious – that is, selective – in choosing which wars to fight. Compared to their authoritarian counterparts, they have to be more confident of winning – and winning quickly and at relatively low cost – in order to enter a conflict. The authoritarian leaders can accept more risks when deciding to go to war, because they are less likely to jeopardize their political standing or control even if they suffer defeat.[47] Thus, democracies win more than their fair share of wars because their leaders demand a higher probability of victory before choosing belligerence. By implication, U.S. officials should have a higher threshold for "selecting" their country into a foreign conflict than Chinese leaders who are less constrained by the prospect of domestic political repercussions.[48] This implication accords with the rationale given earlier for Washington's strategic ambiguity, although it obviously does not prove it.

A second strong empirical pattern determined by quantitative international research is that, after controlling for pertinent factors such as national power and geographic contiguity, democracies tend to have more peaceful relations. Whether this generalization is limited to relations among democracies or whether it can be extended to democracies' relations with non-democracies is a matter of considerable debate.[49] The more pertinent point for our current discussion, however, is that the tendency for democracies to experience fewer disputes and the tendency for those disputes involving them to be less likely to escalate to armed conflict can again, at least in part, be accounted for by selection effect. Precisely because democracies' opponents realize that the democratic leaders are more cautious, as explained above, they are more likely to be persuaded that when a democratic leader does decide to engage in a dispute, he or she is more serious and confident about the cause. Consequently, before disputes reach a more intense stage, the authoritarian leaders are more likely to back off. That is, the authoritarian leaders are likely to take their democratic opponents more seriously than other authoritarian leaders.[50] The implication of this selection effect is that, other things being equal, the lower incidence of democracies' involvement in militarized disputes or extended deterrence encounters may be explained by a greater tendency for their opponents to back down – and is not due to the democracies' more peaceful disposition.[51] Comparatively speaking, the authoritarian opponents of democracies are generally less disposed to engage in retaliatory escalation, and this tendency helps in turn to prevent conflicts from taking a spiral course. In earlier crises over Taiwan, Beijing was the side that initiated de-escalation, thereby "selecting" itself "out" of a possible direct military clash with the U.S.

As discussed in Chapter 4, James Fearon presented two idealized approaches to deterrence: "tying hands" and "sinking costs."[52] The proposition presented above, that democratic leaders are more cautious about "selecting" themselves into a war out of a concern for being censured by their domestic constituents, introduces a corollary hypothesis. Because democratic leaders have to face more serious domestic repercussions when their policies fail, they are better able than their authoritarian counterparts to resort to "tying hands" by engaging their reputation. That is, democratic leaders can communicate more effectively their resolve (such as to protect a protégé) by deliberately incurring "audience costs."[53] They do so by issuing clear, consistent, and public warnings to a potential challenger, and by staking their own and their administration's reputation on a policy to resist any aggressive move by a potential challenger. These warnings gain credibility to the extent that a failure to implement the announced deterrence commitment will exact a heavy political cost for the democratic incumbents. The more willing these officials are to submit themselves to this possible sanction by their electorate, opposition parties, and independent media, the more believable their commitment becomes. Because, by definition, authoritarian leaders are less vulnerable to a domestic backlash for reneging on their promises, their declarations are inherently less believable. They are therefore forced to undertake more tangible investments ("sunk costs") in order to demonstrate that they are serious about their deterrence threats. In short, democratic leaders have an advantage over their authoritarian counterparts with respect to making credible deterrence threats. They can resort to domestic audience costs to enhance their deterrence credibility, whereas the authoritarian leaders face greater difficulty in this undertaking.

The democracies' advantage, however, is also a double-edged sword because when their leaders refrain from making explicit and even irrevocable pledges to come to the aid of a protégé under attack, their silence speaks volumes. Why would these officials expect that an ambiguous posture would deter a potential adversary, when their attempt at deterrence would be much more effective if it carried the message "we will fight you" rather than "we may fight you"?[54] The puzzle expressed earlier about Washington's deterrence posture with respect to Taiwan reflects its failure to tie its hands in order to lend credibility to its effort at extended deterrence. Because the democracies' potential adversaries realize the advantage offered by audience costs to democracies and because they expect the democracies to take advantage of this resort to audience costs, a failure to engage and publicize an incumbent administration's deterrence commitment will in turn be taken as a signal implying that the defender may not be completely committed to the protégé's defense.

Historical data offer another pattern that is pertinent to our discussion. Compared to autocracies, democracies are more likely to take part in defense pacts. Why?

The reason does not have to be that these states are status-quo powers and are therefore more interested in and committed to maintaining the international order. Nor does this greater disposition on the part of democracies to join defense pacts necessarily imply that they are more willing to stand by each other during times of need. By their very nature, democratic institutions provide contested elections that allow voters to choose among political candidates with different policy perspectives. Democratic politicians have short office tenure, and electoral cycles and changes in popular mandate may be expected to disrupt and upset policy arrangements. Foreign counterparts cannot count on future politicians in a democracy to honor the pledges made by their predecessors. The inherent uncertainty in democratic politics causes a concern for the enforceability of agreements or the continued validity of private understanding, especially when one can expect routine changes in those leaders in charge of foreign affairs. Therefore, although democratic officials have an inherent advantage in making credible commitments while they are in office, the alternation of office holders means that they have to overcome a commitment problem in the longer term because regular transfers of power between politicians and parties with different perspectives and agendas can be expected. Authoritarian leaders, with their long hold on power, do not face nearly the same predicament.

Because democracies face a more severe commitment problem, they encounter more pressure from their protégés to enter into formal defense treaties.[55] In addition to their value in signaling to potential foreign adversaries the democracies' future intentions in case of war, these treaties have the practical effect of tying the hands of the defender's future administrations. Thus, when a democracy signs a defense treaty, it is not just telling a potential challenger its intention to intervene on behalf of a protégé, but it is also reassuring this protégé that its future officials are legally bound to honor this commitment. Because there is a greater demand for democracies to demonstrate commitment credibility, these states "select" themselves into more treaty obligations to defend their partners. However, due to the instability inherent in democratic politics, these countries are also more likely to subsequently "select" themselves out of treaty obligations.[56] That is, democracies tend to be less reliable allies when the moment comes to actually honor the pledges made previously by another administration. This tendency implies that even when a democracy has made a treaty commitment and invested heavy "sunk costs," the depth of its support for a protégé may still be questioned by a challenger due not to any doubts about the democracy's military capability but rather to its shifting domestic politics. The U.S. experience in Indochina seems to be relevant here.

The commitment problem extends beyond a concern about how to bind a future administration to pledges made by the current administration. It also pertains to the matter of whether deals negotiated with a current administration can be enforced because this deal may be vetoed or otherwise invalidated by a skeptical legislature or hostile public opinion. Washington's official public acknowledgment about the principle of one China and the limits to be imposed on arms sales to Taiwan often encounters the reality of domestic politics. The proximate cause for the most recent crisis over the Taiwan Strait in 1995–96 had to do with a reversal of repeated assurances given by the highest officials in the U.S. executive branch that it would not issue a visa for Taiwan's president, Lee Teng-hui, to visit the U.S. This reversal came in the wake of heavy congressional pressure and within literally days of explicit assurances given to Beijing's officials. Similarly, the politics of presidential election apparently motivated George H. Bush to sell F-16 fighters to Taiwan despite earlier assurances to Beijing that the U.S. would scale back such sales over time.[57] Thus, divided government and domestic partisan politics complicate the commitment problem for democracies, even when it is about enforcing current deals rather than those whose implementation will not become due well into the future.[58]

It is not difficult to grasp the relevance of this discussion for the Taiwan Strait. Instead of continuing its treaty of mutual defense with Taiwan (as in the case of Japan and South Korea), the U.S. had abrogated it. It is also not hard to understand that promises are easier to make when one does not expect to have to keep them.[59] A prospective defender should have less difficulty pledging its support to a protégé when it does not expect the latter to come under attack. Conversely, such pledges are more challenging when the defender expects a high probability that it will actually have to honour them at a significant cost to itself. Naturally, a protégé would be most interested in acquiring the defender's commitment (preferably in a public, transparent, and legally binding form) precisely when it feels most vulnerable to an attack.[60] It also goes without saying that once a defender has committed itself formally to a protégé's defense by entering into a treaty with the latter, its bargaining leverage is diminished. That is, a protégé's uncertainty about whether a defender will come to its assistance gives the defender a way to extract concessions from it. Once this ambiguity is greatly reduced if not removed, one is more likely to encounter the phenomenon of the "tail wagging the dog."

We discussed earlier (Chapter 7) the possible effects of rising economic exchanges on Sino-American relations. Fearon has observed that the more costly a disruption in these exchanges will be to a potential challenger, the more likely it is to expect the defender to use these economic exchanges as a leverage to advance the latter's policy of extended deterrence. Significantly, this realization in turn leads the potential challenger to expect the defender to be more disposed to bluff its commitment to the protégé.[61] The defender has an incentive to pretend that it draws minimal benefits from the ongoing economic exchanges, and to exaggerate the benefits that the challenger draws from these exchanges. The more asymmetric are these benefits to the challenger's advantage in fact or in perception (in the eyes of either or both parties),[62] the greater the defender's temptation to misrepresent its support for the protégé. Paradoxically, this condition implies that the defender will be required to make *more* sunk investment in order to demonstrate that its commitment to the protégé is genuine and serious.

The phenomenon that intense bilateral trade tends to discourage conflict is not unrelated to selection effect. States that expect to be enemies in the next war are reluctant to become dependent on each other for their vital economic needs, and each would be wary of conferring the benefits of trade on the other lest it become stronger as a result. Conversely, states are less concerned about relative gains from trade if they do not expect to fight their trade partner.[63] This logic of selection therefore accounts for the relative peace between states with dense commercial relations. Thus, trade does not make states more peaceful; rather, states expecting to remain in peace are more likely to trade in the first place and to increase their trade subsequently. This hypothesis introduces an important consideration with respect to extended deterrence, one that is related to Fearon's point mentioned above. If a potential challenger believes that increasing economic exchanges with the defender have made it (the challenger) a more valuable partner for the defender, the defender will have to undertake more deterrence investments in order to show that the protégé's security is still more valuable to it (the defender) than continuing business as usual with the potential challenger. Thus, rather than making "sunk costs" less important, rising Sino-American commercial ties would require more such demonstration from Washington if it wants to effectively deter Beijing from attacking Taipei. To repeat and emphasize, rising Sino-American trade does not necessarily create a stronger basis for Washington to dissuade Beijing from invading Taiwan. If anything, it probably makes tangible and costly investments by Washington dedicated to the defense of Taiwan even more imperative. The former trend does not substitute for the latter necessity, and may in fact make the latter condition even more urgent.

Naturally, the more costly, the more sustained and the more specifically dedicated is the nature of the defender's security investments made for the sake of the protégé, the more likely the challenger will be inclined to believe the defender's threat of intervention. This remark implies, for instance, that the defender cannot allow its arms sales to the protégé to be misconstrued by the challenger as an attempt by the defender to improve its own trade balance rather than to serve the protégé's defense needs. When even some politicians in Taiwan claim that U.S. arms are too expensive and are being sold to advance Washington's commercial interests rather than Taipei's security needs, the credibility of the implied deterrence threat suffers.

One can discern another selection effect. A defender's attempt at extended deterrence depends on a potential challenger's perception of its (the defender's) inherent stake in the dispute between the challenger and the protégé. A defender can proclaim that its security interests are global, but research has shown that the geographic location of the defender's deterrence commitments makes a difference to whether they are likely to be challenged.[64] Commitments undertaken in the defender's home region are less likely to encounter opposition because others are more persuaded that the defender has a serious stake inclining it to intervene in case of an attack against a protégé located near to its home base. Conversely, the more distant a protégé is located from the defender, the more likely it is for the latter's deterrence attempt to meet a challenge. Geographic distance can of course point to a state's gradual loss of power, as it seeks to project its influence further away from its home base, an idea proposed by Kenneth Boulding some time ago,[65] but it also appears to represent an indicator of a defender's inherent stake in a dispute and therefore its resolve in opposing a possible challenge. The logic of selection suggests that one should see a distribution pattern such that there are fewer challenges to a defender's protection of nearby protégés than distant protégés. Potential challengers often opt not to mount a challenge in the defender's "near abroad," thus contributing to the more frequent deterrence encounters that happen further away from the defender's home. To the extent that physical distance serves as a proxy for the contesting parties' relative resolve, one would also expect that given a challenge to extended deterrence, the challenger is more likely to succeed when both it and the protégé are located far away from the defender's home region. Reversing the Taiwan situation, the U.S. had more inherent stake than the USSR which tried to protect Cuba following the Bay of Pigs invasion.

Analysts generally agree that the U.S. holds a conventional and nuclear capability vastly superior to China's military forces.[66] History, however, offers many examples of a weaker party accepting and even initiating a war against a stronger adversary.[67] The weaker side offsets its disadvantage in capability by its more focused attention on the issue being contested and by its greater determination to prevail in this contest. Therefore, even though the stronger side has more tangible assets, the weaker side is favored by an asymmetry in policy attention and resolve (a hegemon, after all, has multiple interests around the world and is constantly distracted to attend to the crisis *du jour*). Weaker states have at least sometimes done well in wars against stronger states, as in the Vietnam and Korean wars when the U.S. was defeated or fought to a draw. The communists in these conflicts did not have any delusion about U.S. capabilities and, in the case of Japan's attack on Pearl Harbor described earlier, officials of the self-acknowledged weaker side took war to a stronger opponent also without any illusions about the latter's resolve to intervene on behalf of the European colonial powers in Southeast Asia. Therefore, being convinced that the U.S. has superior capabilities and that Washington is determined to oppose its challenge is not enough to prevent Beijing from contesting the status of Taiwan, even at the risk of causing a military collision with the U.S.[68]

Beijing accords more policy priority to the status of Taiwan than Washington, which can do little about the difference in this issue's inherent stake for the two sides. Whatever Washington says and does cannot persuade others, least of all the Chinese leaders, that it cares as much about Taiwan as Beijing or even as much as those other policy items that rank even higher on Washington's agenda. Far more pertinent, however, is the perception and even the reality that Beijing itself cares deeply about Taiwan's status, and the relevant stake – in terms of this issue's positive and negative consequences – is much more salient to and significant for it in comparison to Washington. When faced with an unfavorable military balance and a determined defender, a challenger has a low probability of success in trying to coerce the protégé. This low probability, however, does not say anything about the challenger's expected pay-off, which of course combines the probability of an outcome with its utility to the challenger. Moreover, and in line with the previous discussion on risky behavior to avert losses, a low probability of success as indicated by an unfavorable balance of military forces does not necessarily prevent a weaker side from accepting war against a stronger side in order to prevent a serious setback in its other more important policy objectives.

This formulation implies that a defeat on the battlefield may not be perceived by the leaders of the weaker side as the greatest evil to be avoided, because they may care even more about other still more important objectives such as regime legitimacy, political control, and national integrity. Whether one agrees or disagrees with these leaders' motivations and values, one need again only recall China's decision to enter the Korean War, North Vietnam's decision to resist the U.S. in Indochina, and Japan's decision to attack Pearl Harbor in order to understand that a stronger and resolved defender cannot guarantee that there will not be any challenge to its effort at extended deterrence.[69] Whether this challenge will be forthcoming will depend on the challenger's resolve and its perceived stake – not only what it has to gain from a confrontation, but also what it has to lose if it lets things drift. By reasoning backward, one would infer that when weaker states "select" themselves into a deterrence encounter with an adversary known to be stronger and more determined, they must have compelling domestic reasons for taking this course of action. There is likely to be substantial political solidarity and policy agreement among the leaders of these weaker states in order for this policy to be adopted, and this policy is likely to enjoy substantial popular support from their citizens. The other plausible interpretation of why the leaders of weaker states (e.g., Manuel Noriega, Slobodan Milosevic, Saddam Hussein) knowingly confront a stronger and determined adversary is that these officials must have come to the conclusion that no matter how much they concede, their opponent will settle for nothing short of their political demise.[70] If the stronger power's ultimate goal is regime change and the physical incarceration of the opposing state's leaders, the latter have little to lose by choosing to resist the former.

The logic of selection suggests that should there be another Taiwan crisis, it will be more difficult for Washington to deter Beijing. Fearon introduced the basic insight for the rationale behind this hypothesis.[71] There are cases of general extended deterrence when a defender warns against any provocation against its protégé (or protégés) in the absence of any specific move by a potential aggressor to upset the status quo. Thus a generic pledge by the U.S. to defend its European allies against a Soviet invasion is an example of general extended deterrence. This general extended deterrence turns into a situation of immediate extended deterrence when the defender tries to head off a change in the status quo in response to tangible actions already undertaken by a challenger to threaten its protégé. Even though they did not involve a direct Soviet attack on a protégé, the Berlin crises of the 1960s approximated instances of immediate extended deterrence when Washington reacted to moves by Moscow and its ally, East Germany, to restrict the Western powers' access to that city. Beijing's warnings to Washington in response to the imminent defeat of the North Korean regime prior to China's intervention in the Korean War provides another, perhaps more relevant, example of immediate extended deterrence. Information on the defender's strong military assets deployed in the contested area, its command of nuclear weapons, its treaty commitment to the protégé, its commercial relations with the protégé, and the political support enjoyed by the protégé in the defender's legislature is available in the public domain. Such evidence should convince a challenger that there is a higher probability that a defender will come to the protégé's assistance than if such information had pointed in the other direction.

Therefore, a state should be less likely to mount a challenge given these indications of the defender's capability and its likely resolve. General extended deterrence should accordingly succeed more often in these situations. Significantly, if a challenger decides nevertheless to initiate a confrontation even knowing the defender's capability and its likely resolve, then the defender's effort at immediate extended deterrence is likely to fail. That is, if the challenger initiates a confrontation under these circumstances, it must mean that it has already considered the publicly available information and has discounted this information. From the rationalist perspective, discounting this public information can only mean that the challenger has private information which overrides the importance of the public information known, for example, to journalists and scholars who write about international relations.[72] The challenger must know something which inclines it to challenge a defender that it knows to be stronger and more resolved. The logic of selection therefore suggests that should a defender be forced to undertake immediate extended deterrence – that is, to take action against a challenge when the challenger should already have known the defender's announced commitment to the protégé and the impressive assets that the defender has at its disposal to carry out this commitment – this effort is more likely to fail. It is more likely to fail because the challenger must be comparatively stronger (at least in the eyes of its own leaders) and it must be highly resolved. This is so for the simple fact that a less strong or less resolved challenger would not have chosen to confront the defender in view of the generic indications pointing to the credibility of the latter's policy of general extended deterrence (such as when the defender has strong commercial ties and a defense treaty with the protégé, or has nuclear weapons and an impressive capability to project its naval and air forces).

The implication of these remarks should be straightforward for Sino-American relations with respect to Taiwan. If, as argued by most analysts, the U.S. possesses demonstrably stronger capabilities and a compelling interest and stake in the status of Taiwan, one would not expect China to make a move against Taiwan. The U.S. general extended deterrence should therefore succeed. If, however, China decides nevertheless to challenge Taiwan's status for whatever reason, it will then be much more difficult for Washington to resist this challenge. Accordingly, should Washington find itself in a situation of immediate extended deterrence with respect to Taiwan, its efforts are more likely to fail because only a stronger and more determined China would have selected itself into this situation. Why else would Beijing want to engage an adversary which is stronger and which has declared its intention to resist any unilateral attempt to change the status quo in the Taiwan Strait?

The same conclusion can be reached by resorting to another series of inferences. The U.S. and China have had several prior deterrence encounters. In each of these previous cases, China de-escalated in response to a strong U.S. reaction to defend Taiwan. The leaders in Beijing should have drawn a lesson from their experience. They should have concluded that American leaders were actually serious about defending Taiwan. They should also have realized that challenging a defender or even feigning such a challenge is not without a cost.[73] Because these deterrence encounters are public affairs, others (including one's own domestic constituents and political opposition) take notice of their outcomes. Failed challenges therefore exact at least a reputation cost at home and abroad, and sometimes produce even more severe political consequences.[74] If leaders learn from the past, one would expect that a failed challenge would not be followed by another attempt. Significantly, the logic of selection argues that should the challenger initiate yet another deterrence encounter after failing to change the status quo in its prior attempt, one should expect this challenger to be stronger and more determined in the subsequent round. Indeed, if this expectation makes sense, one should expect the probability of the challenger's success to improve over a series of repeated deterrence encounters. The reason behind this proposition is simply that given its previous setback, a challenger would not mount another challenge unless it believes that its odds of success have improved. Something must have changed in the interim between the timing of two consecutive deterrence encounters to warrant the challenger becoming more optimistic and trying again – knowing what it already knows about the defender's prior actions and the political costs associated with its own prior setback. Stated simply, the chances that Beijing would start another crisis over Taiwan are reduced by its prior experience. This expectation, however, does not mean that it will not start another crisis, possibly in the event of a formal declaration of independence by Taiwan. Moreover, should Beijing initiate another challenge, it must believe that it is in a better position to prevail this time than last time – or it must be convinced that it has more to lose if it remains inactive this time than last time or that it has more to gain by acting this time than last time. In other words, should another occasion for immediate extended deterrence arise over the Taiwan Strait, the U.S. will have a more difficult time deterring a stronger and more determined China for which the stakes have also become higher than before.

It has been hypothesized previously that a rising power has an incentive to perpetuate the ongoing trends so that it can continue to grow and develop. It has little to gain by taking rash actions that upset these trends. This proposition in turn relates to the question of opportunism. Officials and scholars alike are naturally interested in this question. Are states likely to act opportunistically to exploit situations that promise short-term gains even if their actions entail long-term opportunity costs? The logic of selection suggests that a rising state is unlikely to engage in such myopic behavior simply because any opportunistic behavior will cost it more in the long run than whatever short-term gains it can hope to achieve. This does not mean that the temptation to defect, as in the game of the prisoners' dilemma, is banished. Rather, this temptation is more likely to characterize a declining power than a rising power. After all, the hope that current trends will continue to provide and even increase its prospective gains tends to incline the leaders of a rising power to be more sensitive to the "shadow of the future."[75] Conversely, opportunistic behavior is more likely to come from a declining power because it is more anxious to reverse an unfavorable trend.

In conclusion, China as the rising power should not be anxious to precipitate a confrontation with the U.S. over Taiwan or over any other issue. It should want to secure a stable domestic and international environment to continue its growth. Moreover, the implication of Washington's strategic ambiguity points to the existence of a tacit acceptance by all three sides involved in the Taiwan Strait to allow ongoing processes to unfold and mature without any side taking provocative action. Therefore, the general prognosis offered here is that unlike episodes of failed extended deterrence that set off World Wars I and II, current trends favor an eventual settlement of Taiwan's status. This prognosis, however, does not rule out the possibility of a Sino-American confrontation over Taiwan. If a confrontation occurs, the precipitant is more likely to originate from some action taken by Washington or Taipei than Beijing. Any move by Taipei toward formal independence – which, in Beijing's view, is a unilateral change of the status quo – is likely to be highly provocative.[76]

This analysis has relied on historical generalizations and rationalist inferences to advance its propositions. It has not resorted to the citation of open source material (such as media reports) or interviews with officials to make its case. This latter approach has its proponents but it has been eschewed in this analysis out of concern for protecting private information and avoiding misrepresentation. Open-source material is in the public domain and is already known to officials and analysts alike. Leaders would have already incorporated such information in reaching their decisions, which reflect the more important influence exercised by the private information available to them. By definition, private information concerns state secrets so that one would not want to disclose them to others. Moreover, even when officials decide to disclose information about their decision processes and policy concerns, their audience takes such disclosure with "a grain of salt" because officials often have an incentive to put a "spin" on their story or to engage in outright misrepresentation. There is accordingly a persistent problem faced by analysts because when insiders know, they often will not tell; and when they tell, their story may not be entirely credible.

When conclusions or inferences reached by different research approaches converge, they presumably command a greater degree of confidence. It is therefore gratifying that the interpretation offered here corresponds generally with that based on documentary analysis and interviews. Robert Ross reached the conclusion that "the United States can be very confident that, absent a Taiwan declaration of independence, it can continue to deter the use of force by China against Taiwan."[77] Unlike Ross's analysis, however, I have not given U.S. military capability and the American retaliatory threats as much analytic weight in gauging the likely success of Washington's effort at extended deterrence. While agreeing with the assessment that the U.S. holds a vast advantage in conventional and nuclear forces, I am more agnostic about the credibility of America's declared resolve. More importantly, however, I argue that the success of deterrence efforts depends on the expected gain – or the expected loss – for a challenger. Even when the military balance operates to the challenger's disadvantage and even when the challenger is convinced of the defender's resolve, it can still mount a challenge because it perceives that it has more at stake. Asymmetric stakes for the challenger and the defender can incline the former to accept a relatively low probability of success (as implied by the unfavorable distribution of military forces) because it can hope for a much larger reward if its policy pays off or, as emphasized by prospect theory with respect to risky behavior to avert setback, if it anticipates much more severe losses absent decisive action. It is telling that in all those cases of wars and crises launched by a state poised to suffer a relative decline or one for which this process has already set in – such as Germany's initiation of World Wars I and II, Japan's attack on Pearl Harbor, and the USSR's precipitation of the Berlin and Cuban Missile crises – an urgent, even desperate, desire to forestall an imminent or ongoing deterioration in one's international position served as the primary motivation for bellicosity. Such risky behavior is more likely to come from the pro-independence factions in Taipei than Beijing, as current trends (reflecting China's growing power, Taiwan's rising economic dependence, and burgeoning cross-Strait cultural and political exchanges) favor the prospects for eventual reunification. The danger of a Sino-American confrontation is more likely to stem from the pro-independence initiatives of Chen Shui-Bian's administration, initiatives that could in turn put Beijing in the domain of loss especially with respect to its domestic popularity and legitimacy.

10 Conclusion

Theoretical and policy implications

What is this book's argument? I submit an epistemological and a substantive argument. With respect to epistemology, I have not treated China's rise as *the* analytic focus of discussion. The phenomenon of China's growing power cannot be studied in isolation – apart from the international positions of other states, especially the U.S., and their reaction to China's rise. Hence, I attempt to relate China's rise to Washington's continued preponderance in the international system. I decline to treat China's rise as an isolated or even special case in another sense. I present historical analogies and comparisons that place China's recent re-emergence as a major power and the implications of this re-emergence for other states in the broader context of the rise and decline experienced by its counterparts and predecessors. Therefore, I argue that one should analyze China's situation as a case or instance of a generic class. In this inquiry, I introduce recent advances in international relations scholarship – such as rationalist and prospect theories, theories of preventive war and democratic peace, and theories of extended and pivotal deterrence – in order to inform the study of China which has tended to be dominated by Sinologists. Some colleagues who are China specialists may be puzzled by the fact that parts of this book – for example when I discuss rationalist and prospect expectations of war, and the resort to appeasement and preventive war, in Chapters 4 and 5 respectively – seem to have downplayed China's rise. It should be obvious by now that this book is not *just* about China. Indeed, how can one talk about China's rise or its potential revisionist intentions without introducing empirical evidence and analytic standards that would enable one to assess China's capabilities and conduct in a comparative and historical context?

Substantively, my argument in this book takes issue with the power-transition theory as it has often been applied to China's rise. Briefly, I argue that despite the growth of China's economy in recent decades, the available evidence does not support any claim that China is overtaking or even approaching the U.S. as a contender for international primacy. This remark suggests that one of the scope conditions of the power-transition theory, which is concerned with the struggle for world domination by the hegemon and challenger (which is supposed to be at least 80 percent as strong as the hegemon), is not met. Even in a regional competition in the Asia Pacific, China is vastly outmatched by the U.S. in economic and especially military capabilities. Moreover, even its status as a regional hegemon in the Western Hemisphere and the world's largest and most dynamic economy did not qualify the U.S. as a contender for global leadership in the years prior to 1945.

I also question the standard attribution that China is a revisionist state and the U.S. is a status-quo state, and the proposition that an impatient and cocky latecomer is usually responsible for starting a systemic war. Moreover, I question whether the Anglo-German rivalry offers an appropriate historical illustration of the power-transition theory and the principal dynamic producing World Wars I and II. Instead, I point to German–Russian tension – especially Germany's preventive motivation – as the main cause of these conflicts. Therefore, I suggest a contrarian perspective, hypothesizing that systemic wars are more likely to be launched by a nervous declining power than by a latecomer that expects to become stronger in the future. My description of Chinese strategic predilections, interpretation of the historical conduct of Russia/the USSR in the face of Berlin's security concerns, and inferences from both rationalist and prospect theories of decision choice all lead to a picture of a risk-averse latecomer, the opposite of the power-transition theory's depiction. In contrast to the prevailing U.S. discourse on containing or engaging China, I call attention to a central but overlooked tenet of this theory – namely, a latecomer's dissatisfaction with its share of the tangible and intangible benefits accorded by the international system. A failure to adjust this allocation of benefits in response to power shifts is hypothesized to cause international tension. This tension is due both to the latecomer's sense of relative deprivation and the incumbent hegemon's reluctance to revise the existing allocation to its relative disadvantage. One can be dissatisfied with the distribution of benefits without being bent on challenging the world order.

I present yet another contrarian perspective in arguing that systemic wars are not the result of a direct confrontation between a rising latecomer and a declining hegemon. Rather than seeking to challenge the incumbent or previous hegemon, a rising latecomer has historically sought to avoid such a confrontation. War broke out not because the latecomer had wanted to fight the hegemon, but rather because it was unable to prevent it from becoming involved. This involvement resulted from a failure of extended deterrence mounted by either party. Consequently, systemic wars have been due to the contagion and escalation of disputes that initially involved the protégé of one or the other side. The historical role played by this third party draws attention to Taiwan as a possible source of Sino-American conflict. My discussion of extended deterrence and pivotal deterrence again offers a contrarian argument, suggesting that it is possible for a challenger to be completely convinced of the defender's superior power and its demonstrable resolve, but to be still willing to risk a military clash with it. This suggestion, however, is quite different from the characterization of an ambitious and bellicose latecomer bent upon revising the international order.

Some may wonder why this book has focused on a critique of the power-transition theory rather than striking out to formulate a separate new theory. There are three reasons. First, the power-transition theory offers a popular perspective for scholars and officials. It has great resonance in the U.S. and China. For Americans, it points to a source of worry, auguring a more dangerous world ahead. It conjures up a future world in which the pre-eminent position of the U.S., which many have grown accustomed to and may even have assumed to be only natural, is likely to come under challenge. Conversely, this theory offers a source of achievement and even pride for the Chinese. Yet this sense can coexist with a strong feeling of insecurity and even paranoia that others, especially the U.S., are seeking to block China's ascent and that they may very well succeed in this attempt.[1] Thus, paradoxically, both the supposed declining and ascending states can feel insecure and vulnerable. Both are likely to perceive the other as a strategic competitor and even as an enemy who can be blamed for a variety of their respective problems. These mirror images, based ironically on a shared logic, abet the dynamic of deadly rivalries. Mistaken beliefs about the other can result in self-fulfilling prophecies such that, for example, by treating a status-quo power as if it were a revisionist power, one's actions can contribute to this state's alienation from the international system. As Joseph Nye cautioned, "the rise of China recalls Thucydides's warning that the belief in the inevitability of conflict can become one of its main causes."[2]

As argued earlier, discourse on international relations, including that on power transitions, includes ideational construction rather than just presenting some objective reality. Commentators, including academics and political entrepreneurs, popularize some interpretations of reality, while other interpretations are overlooked and even dismissed. Thus, for instance, while people are obviously well aware of the demise of the USSR, the peaceful nature of this event has not been generally recognized as a puzzle from the perspective of power transition, whereas much more attention seems to have gone to the analysis of the prospects and consequences of a relative decline in U.S. power. Similarly, whereas the peaceful disposition of a democratic latecomer has been invoked to explain the power transition between the U.S. and the U.K., this logic has not been extended to account for the Spanish–American war. Shuttling logic denies the U.S. the status of a central contender in international relations prior to 1945, but assigns to China such a role even though its current standing falls far short of the U.S. position even prior to 1914.

Second, this book actually agrees with the power-transition theory on several important points. It shares Kenneth Organski's observation that the prevailing international order was established by the leading powers to their advantage, and that these states would be reluctant to make concessions to the latecomers of their own accord. Organski's premise that the distribution of benefits is a source of international disputes offers a fundamental insight. Differential growth rates among the leading states cause constant changes in their relative power, and these power shifts in turn cause discord about the allocation of benefits. Moreover, the perspective offered in this book agrees with the authors of *The War Ledger* that the primary determinants of national growth are located inside a state, especially with regard to its people's productivity. Hence, the quality of a state's human capital, including its people's capacity to master and advance technological innovations, offers a glimpse of its future growth potential. This emphasis on the domestic causes of national growth therefore implies the limited influence external forces can have in shaping a major state's development trajectory. Consequently, preventive war or economic coercion is not likely to alter the target state's long-term growth. My discussion finally also agrees fundamentally with the premise of the power-transition theory that major wars among the leading states represent the subject of the greatest interest to both the academic and policy communities. These conflicts are likely to cause the most devastation in human and financial costs, and present the greatest prospect for changing the nature of the international system. In deciding to adopt some selective aspects of the power-transition theory but not others, my approach is no different from that pursued by some other colleagues.[3]

Third, the power-transition theory invites one to generalize beyond isolated cases, to articulate explicit criteria, and to confront and compare observable data. It offers a remarkably comprehensive formulation of the dynamics of international relations. This theory therefore enables us to address concepts and ideas that are pertinent to any thorough discussion of international relations and, indeed, concepts and ideas that play a central role in many other theories about international relations. As shown in the previous discussion, we are encouraged to inquire about the nature and sources of national power, the policy orientations and role conceptions of the leading states, the nature and distribution of international benefits, the motivations behind choosing between accommodation and confrontation when facing upward or downward mobility, the conditions inclining states to pursue bandwagoning or balancing, and the influence of geography, culture and regime characteristics in the selection of friends and enemies. Whereas researchers may reasonably disagree about the answers to these questions, the identification and summary of these questions in the form of a coherent research program are an important contribution made by scholars working in the tradition of the power-transition theory. This book has accordingly focused on this theory because it affords a systematic agenda, calling attention to questions that are obviously both theoretically important and policy-relevant.

What are this book's major substantive propositions with policy import? One is that the U.S. enjoys a huge preponderance today that is unlikely to be challenged by China or any other state in the next several decades.[4] Michael D. Swaine and Ashley J. Tellis argued:

> China's many weaknesses will not be redressed in any fundamental way before the 2015–2020 timeframe. Assuming that present trends hold, it is only during this timeframe *at the very earliest* that the Chinese economy would *begin* to rival the U.S. economy in size, diversity, and orientation and that the Chinese military will acquire the wherewithal to mount credible denial threats at its strongest regional adversaries such as the United States, Japan, and India, while simultaneously maintaining a modicum of control or exploitative power over smaller competitors such as Taiwan, Vietnam, and the Southeast Asia states [emphases in the original].[5]

This is the most optimistic projection, assuming the best-case scenario for China's growth prospects. Its assumptions about U.S. performance in the interim are unclear.

However, as Dale Copeland has remarked, "the United States is supremely dominant in all three dimensions of power: military, economic, and potential."[6] Therefore, there is little risk of a power transition in the next few decades. This being the case, why is there then a pervasive concern about China's rise and even China's threat? Chinese officials and the Chinese public suspect that exaggerated views of Chinese capabilities and ambitions are part of Washington's concerted effort to mobilize domestic and international support to block China's ascent and contain its influence. Some Chinese scholars believe that an "eastward shift" in U.S. security strategy, aimed at China, is inevitable and that it has just been temporarily postponed by the U.S. campaign against terrorism and its invasion of Iraq.[7]

Given the current and likely continued U.S. preponderance, there is little reason for Washington to contemplate a preventive war against China. Unlike Wilhelmine and Nazi Germany, the U.S. is not being confronted with the prospect of a deep and inevitable decline. The desperation stemming from this expectation of a bleak future is a necessary but insufficient condition for preventive war to be considered a plausible option. Another necessary condition for the preventive motivation is that the leaders of the declining state must be convinced that their country would suffer a severe deficit in benefits should its competitor be allowed to establish a new international order. Still a third necessary condition is that the initiator of the preventive war must obviously believe in its military superiority.[8] Without this belief that gives a reasonable basis for this initiator to expect success on the battlefield, it would not be rational to initiate a preventive war. The purpose of such a war is to secure resources that would add to the initiator's potential power (or to deny such resources to a competitor), so that it may sustain and even expand its current advantages in the future. As already remarked, however, the prospect of nuclear retaliation by the target of a possible preventive war makes this resort to arms an even more dangerous proposition than before the nuclear age.[9] Preventive wars are, by definition, launched by a state that is poised to experience or is already suffering from precipitous and irreversible decline. As already emphasized on several occasions, the U.S. is not a declining power but is in fact enjoying historically unprecedented preponderance in a unipolar world.

A second major proposition of this book is that conflicts and destabilizing policies are unlikely to be initiated by a state that is gaining relative power. Accordingly, I argue that so long as China's economy continues to expand at a respectable pace, there is little reason for Beijing to initiate any destabilizing policy that could threaten to throw its growth trajectory off track. If anything, Beijing would want to maintain a stable internal and external environment in order to sustain its growth. For reasons given earlier, one would not expect Beijing to engage in an arms race or a competitive alliance aimed at the U.S. It would resort instead to policies of evasion, entanglement, and engagement with the intention of restraining rather than confronting Washington. On the one hand, these tactics of soft balancing are intended to distract and wear down a dominant power rather than to out-muscle it. On the other hand, they seek to alleviate other states' concerns, including the dominant power's concerns, about rising Chinese power and to reassure them of the prospects of significant mutual gains to be achieved from cooperation – and the potential costs that can stem from non-cooperation. These characterizations converge with other scholars' analyses, such as the "calculative strategy" attributed by Swaine and Tellis to Beijing and Goldstein's description of China's grand strategy.[10]

In contrast to the existing tendency for scholars to focus on the power shifts among states or their regimes' status-quo orientation, I submit that the discrepancies between states' power shares and their benefit shares represent a fundamental cause of war (a third major proposition advanced by this book). This disequilibrium inclines a state with an under-allocation of benefits relative to its power to consider going to war – that is, to improve its benefit share to an extent that others are unwilling to concede. This attempt can in turn cause those enjoying a surplus of benefits to resist the demand for redistribution.[11] Quite aside from their selfish reason for wanting to hold on to their advantages, the established states' reluctance to accept an increase in the rising state's benefit share can be explained by their awareness of the problems of misrepresentation, private information, and unreliable commitment. They can have serious doubts about whether the state demanding increased benefits really deserves this increase on the basis of its actual power. The state making the demand for increased benefits presumably believes that it deserves this increase due to its increasing capability and that its counterparts should be given less benefits because their capabilities are stagnating or falling. In the absence of their coming to an agreement about the prevailing distribution of power, war becomes necessary for the states involved to demonstrate their actual power on the battlefield. This formulation argues that absent a serious discrepancy between its power share and its benefit share, a state cannot credibly threaten war, regardless of the nature of ongoing or anticipated power shifts. It also suggests that an inability to make timely and proportionate adjustments to the international distribution of benefits constitutes a basic source of international instability, and directs attention to the search for the reasons behind this inadequate adjustment. Although explaining a declining hegemon's inability to reverse its sagging technological lead and competitive productivity, the observation by Rasler and Thompson is equally apposite in this context: "Conceit, complacence, and pride hamper the ability of people to embrace change."[12] In addition to cognitive and emotional resistance to change, the rigidity of domestic social and political institutions further exacerbates this tendency.

A fourth major proposition of this book is that absent serious provocation, states rarely engage in collective action to contain a rising power.[13] Accordingly, instead of trying to balance against China, it is more likely that Beijing's neighbors will try to engage and accommodate it. This does not mean that the security dilemma does not apply to their relations, but that unless Beijing engages in repeated aggression against these countries and accumulates escalating power, one would not expect to see the emergence of an anti-Chinese blocking coalition. Given our earlier discussion, external attempts to contain China are unlikely to succeed in bending its growth curve. This growth is determined primarily by domestic factors. Given China's sheer size, its neighbors are likely to acquire a stake in its continued growth as the Chinese economy assumes a larger role as an engine for regional growth. Interdependence of course also means that China's economic slowdown will have negative repercussions for its trade partners, including Taiwan.

These remarks do not imply the arrival of Camelot in the Asian region. Even though the U.S. is unlikely to seek a preventive war and China is unlikely to wish for a direct confrontation, a crisis between these two countries is still possible due to a clash over Taiwan. The argument advanced earlier is that should a Sino-American armed clash occur because of Taiwan, it would be because Beijing has been unable to prevent U.S. intervention rather than because it has sought such U.S. involvement. Moreover, it would be in Beijing's interest to allow the ongoing processes of cross-Strait exchanges to continue to unfold and expand. Thus, China would want to avoid changing the status quo. The source of destabilization is more likely to come from Taiwan, which, however, is unlikely to precipitate a crisis without U.S. backing. Our analysis of extended deterrence and the logic of selection leads furthermore to the expectation that should there be another Sino-American crisis over Taiwan, it will be more difficult for Washington to turn back a stronger and more determined Beijing. Significantly, although the perceived capability and resolve of a potential defender certainly matter in heading off a possible challenge, the logic of our previous analysis argues that it is even more important to attend to the importance, in terms of both prospective gain and prospective loss, that an issue has for the leaders and people belonging to the challenging state. A weaker state can accept and even initiate a confrontation with a stronger and resolved adversary because it evidently cares about some other policy desiderata even more than avoiding a defeat on the battlefield.

The U.S. has so far adopted a strategy of deliberate ambiguity, refusing to indicate how it would act in case of a military conflict between China and Taiwan. It has so far promoted an arrangement whereby it will try to discourage Taipei from declaring *de jure* independence in exchange for Beijing's willingness to eschew the use of force to resolve the island's current *de facto* independence. Significantly, and as argued previously, with popular support becoming increasingly important for the Chinese leaders' claim to legitimate and representative rule, their bargaining space will become more limited in the coming years. Domestic audience costs would therefore contribute to a less accommodating China on the matter of Taiwan's status. Taiwan's democratization has the same effects on its political processes. The pro- and anti-independence forces on Taiwan are reasonably balanced at this time, although the general trend of events points toward the island's greater economic interdependence and political dialogue with China.[14] Future developments on Taiwan are likely to be pivotal in determining not only cross-Strait relations but also Sino-American relations. Should those political and economic forces favoring eventual reunification prevail in Taiwan's internal deliberations, a leading source of regional instability would be alleviated.

Given Taiwan's past as Japan's colony, Beijing would be especially wary of any involvement by Tokyo.[15] Our earlier discussion suggests that the concern of power-transition theory should be extended beyond the top two countries in the international hierarchy. In other words, one should also be attentive to the possibility of rivalry among the third-, fourth-, fifth- and sixth-ranked powers. This expanded focus calls attention to the evolving Sino-Japanese and Sino-Indian relations beyond a preoccupation with Sino-American relations. Tension on the Korean peninsula and turmoil in Central Asia can potentially engage Tokyo and New Delhi, setting off a contagion effect that engulfs Beijing and Washington. It should also be recognized that just as China's recent rapid rise has meant that Japan's relative position has suffered, in the future China would likely face the same situation as India's and Indonesia's economies start to take off.

Beijing has made it abundantly clear that reunification with Taiwan ranks at the very top of its policy agenda. It has unmistakably staked its reputation on this issue about which it cares more than anything else. This commitment enhances its credibility because any policy reversal will be highly costly to its reputation, externally and especially internally. Beijing's reputation commitment, however, suggests an important concern. St. Petersburg felt that it had compromised in the Balkan crises in 1908–9 and 1912–13, and feared that its reputation as a defender of its ally, Serbia, could suffer even more damage should it seek accommodation again in 1914. The German leaders exploited this Russian concern in order to remove the possibility of a negotiated settlement in their effort to precipitate war. Similarly, Hitler attacked Poland in order to force a showdown with the U.K. and France, presenting these countries with a choice between fighting Germany and succumbing to German domination. He did not want to give London and Paris time in which to prepare themselves to resist Berlin more successfully later. In short, "tying hands" by staking one's reputation heavily and irrevocably to a policy position allows the opposition an opportunity to lock one into a conflict that one would have rather preferred to fight under a different set of circumstances.

The advent of nuclear weapons, as argued above, should make a confrontation between the great powers less likely and, concomitantly, a policy of retrenchment more palatable. A second-strike capability makes a declining power's security concern less acute and, at the same time, the prospect of launching a preventive war much less attractive. This observation in turn implies that should the U.S. establish a successful missile-defense system, it would introduce a destabilizing effect. This development would make another nuclear power – whether rising or declining – less confident about the retaliatory threat provided by its nuclear arsenal. This missile-defense system would have the effect of disarming the other nuclear powers, creating a situation comparable to the time when the U.S. had a nuclear monopoly. During those years immediately after World War II, Washington did in fact consider launching a preventive war against the USSR. It rejected this policy in favor of one of containing rising Soviet power, not for any moral or political consideration but rather because it expected to maintain its power preponderance over Moscow.[16] One may also recall that at the height of the Sino-Soviet dispute, Moscow had secretly approached the Nixon administration to inquire about U.S. reaction to a possible preventive Soviet strike against the Chinese nuclear facilities at Lop Nor.[17] Previously, and ironically, the U.S. had approached the Soviet government under Nikita Khrushchev for assistance in or at least tacit approval of a possible U.S. preventive strike against the Chinese nuclear program.[18] Thus, even among the great powers, an inability to retaliate with nuclear weapons can make one a more tempting target for an attack.

A final remark is in order about the concept of revisionism and its opposite, a state's status-quo orientation. If one assumes, as some realists do, that states' future intentions can never be counted on, then discussions about their current or past revisionist or status-quo orientation are really irrelevant because one can never be sure of the intentions of their future leaders. Indeed, because offensive realists expect all states to be expansionist if given an opportunity, a status-quo power is an oxymoron.[19] If so, all prospective power transitions are alarming and, in the absence of the dominant power's confident expectation that it will continue to retain its lead in the future, preventive wars are likely. According to Copeland, whether the officials of this dominant power feel that their contemporary counterparts are moderate and reasonable people does not matter.[20] Rather, they have to question whether they can count on the future leaders of a rising power to refrain from aggression. This perspective suggests that the personal affinities of the incumbent leaders or the current cultural or regime characteristics of states do not matter because one can never be sure of how these variables may change in the future. Such a view implies a very bleak situation because even in the absence of attributing hostile or aggressive intentions to the other side's current leadership, a state may initiate preventive war or undertake containment policies reminiscent of the Cold War. Leaders would then focus exclusively on the distribution of national power and the changes in this distribution. This phenomenon, if true, would be very unfortunate, because it logically implies that as the world's predominant power, the U.S. will inevitably become the target of a broad blocking coalition.[21] In this scenario, rather than leading other states to contain a rising China, Washington would find itself being opposed by an alliance consisting of all the great powers in Europe and Asia. Significantly, other states have not so far engaged in hard balancing against U.S. preponderance. This situation may yet change in the future. Whether it does, as Stephen Walt wisely counseled,[22] depends not so much on how much power the U.S. has as on how its power is used. This important insight is as applicable to China as it is to the U.S. Other states' reaction to China's rise will reflect not only Beijing's increasing power but, more importantly, what it does with this power. If China avoids behaving in an overbearing or threatening manner, its policies would at least not contribute to exacerbating other states' security concerns.

The power-transition theory resonates with many Americans in part because it combines concerns dear to the hearts of realists and liberals. This formulation calls attention to shifts in national power and also states' shared norms and regime characteristics, topics that occupy a central place in realist and liberal discourse respectively. The U.S. has enjoyed an incomparably more favorable security position than any other country. Objectively, it has been able to achieve a greater degree of national security than any other country. Christopher Layne argued recently that Washington's projection and maintenance of power on a global scale have been motivated and rationalized by domestic impulses to gain commercial access and ideological influence abroad.[23] In his view, the U.S. quest for global primacy and dominance has been driven by a liberal agenda. Significantly, this interpretation accords with the power-transition theory, which stresses a contest for predominance in the *world* and control of international *order*. This characterization implies a U.S. grand strategy aimed at pursuing global hegemony and securing "open door" access abroad to promote economic penetration and regime conversion. Other alternatives, such as the option of offshore balancing, are by default overlooked.[24] Therefore, a theory of international relations can frame and influence actual policy.

While China's recent power gains and ostensible revisionist agenda have naturally been a source of concern and even alarm in American discourse in the context of the power-transition theory, there has been less analysis of how China's actions respond to or interact with U.S. policies and outlook. From China's perspective and that of most other states, a palpable source of international turmoil stems instead from the fact that "[in] the post-September 11 world, [U.S.] exceptionalism, combined with the immensity of American power, hinted at the dangers of a nation so strong that others could not check it, and so self-righteous that it could not check itself."[25]

Notes

Epigraph

1 Thucydides, *The History of the Peloponnesian War*, trans. Rex Warner (New York: Penguin Books, 1954), p. 49.
2 George W. Bush, *National Security Strategy of the United States of America*, September 2, 2002 (Washington, D.C.: Government Printing Office, 2002), p. 15. Rather than pre-emption (a concept that refers to military action taken against an imminent enemy attack), the strategic rationale presented in this document justifies preventive war.
3 Edmund Burke, "Remarks on the Policy of the Allies with Respect to France," in *The Works of Edmund Burke*, Vol. 4 (Boston, MA: Little, Brown, 1901), p. 457.

Preface

1 "China's Century," *Newsweek* (May 9, 2005), pp. 26–45. That China's re-emergence on the center stage of world political economy is on the minds of many Americans is shown by the remarkable coincidence that in addition to *Newsweek*, three other popular U.S. magazines featured cover stories or a lead article on China at about the same time. The June 27, 2005 issue of *Time* presented "China's New Revolution" (pp. 22–53) as its cover story, and the June 20 issue of *U.S. News and World Report* had "China's Turn" (pp. 34–52) as its cover story. Moreover, in the June issue of *The Atlantic Monthly*, "How We Would Fight China" (pp. 49–64), written by Robert D. Kaplan, was the lead article. Coincidentally, the Public Broadcasting Service's Nightly Business Report featured a special series on "China's Century of Change" in the week of June 27, 2005.
2 Aaron L. Friedberg, "The Future of U.S.–China Relations: Is Conflict Inevitable?," *International Security* 30 (2005): 7. See also Jacek Kugler, "The Asian Ascent: Opportunity for Peace or Precondition for War?," *International Studies Perspectives* 7 (2006): 36–42; and Ronald L. Tammen, "The Impact of Asia on World Politics: China and India Options for the United States," *International Studies Review* 8 (2006): 563–580.
3 Stephan Richter, "Repeating History," at http://theglobalist.com/nor/news/2000/07-11-00.html. A more extensive treatment is offered by Avery Goldstein, "Great Expectations: Interpreting China's Arrival," *International Security* 22 (1997/1998): 36–73; and Randall L. Schweller, "Managing the Rise of Great Powers," in *Engaging China: The Management of an Emerging Power*, ed. Alastair Iain Johnston and Robert S. Ross (London: Routledge, 1999), pp. 1–31. In addition to the collection of essays provided by the latter volume, see also Michael E. Brown, Owen R. Cote, Jr., Sean M. Lynn-Jones, and Steven E. Miller, eds, *The Rise of China* (Cambridge, MA: MIT Press, 2000).
4 A.F.K. Organski, *World Politics* (New York: Knopf, 1958); and A.F.K. Organski and Jacek Kugler, *The War Ledger* (Chicago, IL: University of Chicago Press, 1980).

5   As an indication of the mounting level of interest in this theory, a recent conference attended by Chinese and U.S. scholars addressed its central themes. The topic of the Sino-American Security Dialogue Conference, held in Beijing in October 2003, was "'China's Rise' and U.S.–China Relations in the 21st Century: Power Transitions and the Question of 'Revisionism'."
6   Antonio Gramsci, *Selection from the Prison Notebooks of Antonio Gramsci*, ed. and trans. Quintin Hoare and Geoffrey Nowell Smith (New York: International Publishers, 1971).
7   The Bush doctrine seeks to ensure U.S. supremacy and to deter the emergence of a military rival or a regional hegemon outside North America. Under this doctrine, all other states become potential enemies, and a large, rising state such as China poses a special threat to the U.S. goal of maximizing its power and security. To the extent that non-Americans (including the Chinese) believe that the U.S. will actually implement the Bush doctrine, images of reciprocal hostility and the danger of self-fulfilling prophecy will begin to take hold.
8   This concern of course reflects the dominant power's perspective. In the wake of Operation Iraqi Freedom, the rest of the world tends instead to be more concerned about how to manage a hegemon that has increasingly resorted to assertive unilateralism.
9   Although Chamberlain is popularly remembered today for his policy of appeasing Nazi Germany, he was seen by some of his contemporary colleagues as "Britain's best chance for achieving efficiency, coherence, and success in correlating foreign policy, defense, and economic stability" when he became prime minister. The bywords of his regime would be "action, efficiency, and decisiveness" which "would be a unique British reply to vigorous dictatorships abroad." Gaines Post Jr., *Dilemmas of Appeasement: British Deterrence and Defense, 1934–1937* (Ithaca, NY: Cornell University Press, 1993), p. 21.
10 On the use of historical analogies by U.S. officials in making foreign policy, see Yuen Foong Khong, *Analogies at War: Korea, Munich, Dien Bien Phu, and the Vietnam Decisions of 1965* (Princeton, NJ: Princeton University Press, 1992).

1   Introduction: the basic arguments

1   For some prominent examples from the 1970s and 1980s discussing international relations in the wake of a relative decline in U.S. power, see David Calleo, *Beyond American Hegemony: The Future of the Western Alliance* (New York: Basic Books, 1988); Robert O. Keohane, *After Hegemony: Cooperation and Discord in the World Political Economy* (Princeton, NJ: Princeton University Press, 1984); Kenneth Oye, Donald Rothchild, and Robert Lieber, eds, *Eagle Entangled: U.S. Foreign Policy in a Complex World* (New York: Longman, 1979); and Richard Rosecrance, ed., *America as an Ordinary Country* (Ithaca, NY: Cornell University Press, 1976).
2   Jean Jacques Servan-Schreiber, *The American Challenge*, trans. Ronald Steel (New York: Atheneum, 1968); and Ezra Vogel, *Japan As Number 1* (New York: Harper & Row, 1979).
3   Max Weber, *The Protestant Ethic and the Spirit of Capitalism*, trans. Talcott Parsons (New York: Scribner, 1930); and Paul Kennedy, *The Rise and Fall of the Great Powers: Economic Change and Military Conflict from 1500 to 2000* (New York: Random House, 1987). Two classic historical studies on imperial decline are John H. Elliott, *Imperial Spain, 1469–1716* (New York: St. Martin's Press, 1963); and Edward Gibbon, *The Decline and Fall of the Roman Empire* (New York: Dutton, 1910). For a recent analysis of the implications of U.S. hegemony, see Chalmers A. Johnson, *Blowback: The Costs and Consequences of American Empire* (New York: Metropolitan Books, 2000).
4   Charles F. Doran, *Systems in Crisis: New Imperatives of High Politics at Century's End* (Cambridge: Cambridge University Press, 1991); and George Modelski, *Long Cycles in World Politics* (Seattle: University of Washington Press, 1987).

5 Stephan Richter, "Repeating History," at http://theglobalist.com/nor/news/2000/07-11-00.html. See also the following exchange: Lanxin Xiang, "Washington's Misguided China Policy," *Survival* 43 (2001): 7–23; and David Shambaugh, "China or America: Which is the Revisionist Power?," *Survival* 43 (2001): 25–30. For a classic study of Anglo-German relations prior to World War I, see Paul M. Kennedy, *The Rise of the Anglo-German Antagonism, 1860–1914* (London: Allen & Unwin, 1982).

6 The original formulation of this theory may be found in A.F.K. Organski, *World Politics* (New York: Knopf, 1958). It was elaborated and subjected to an initial quantitative test in A.F.K. Organski and Jacek Kugler, *The War Ledger* (Chicago, IL: University of Chicago Press, 1980). An assessment of the research program generated by this theory may be found in Jacek Kugler and Douglas Lemke, eds, *Parity and War: Evaluations and Extensions of The War Ledger* (Ann Arbor: University of Michigan Press, 1996); and Jonathan M. DiCicco and Jack Levy, "Power Shifts and Problem Shifts: The Evolution of the Power Transition Research Program," *Journal of Conflict Resolution* 43 (1999): 675–704.

7 For a major extension of the power-transition theory, see Douglas Lemke, *Regions of War and Peace* (Cambridge: Cambridge University Press, 2002). There is a rather extensive literature seeking empirical verification of hypotheses derived from this theory. The following publications offer but a partial compilation: Brian Efird, Jacek Kugler, and Gaspare M. Genna, "From War to Integration: Generalizing Power Transition Theory," *International Interactions* 29 (2003): 293–313; Daniel S. Geller, "Status Quo Orientation, Capabilities, and Patterns of War Initiation in Dyadic Rivalries," *Conflict Management and Peace Science* 18 (2000): 73–96; Henk Houweling and Jan G. Siccama, "Power Transitions as a Cause of War," *Journal of Conflict Resolution* 32 (1988): 87–102; Woosang Kim, "Power Parity, Alliance, Dissatisfaction, and Wars in East Asia, 1860–1993," *Journal of Conflict Resolution* 46 (2002): 654–672, "Power Transitions and Great Power War from Westphalia to Waterloo," *World Politics* 45 (1992): 153–172, "Alliance Transitions and Great Power War," *American Journal of Political Science* 35 (1991): 833–850, and "Power, Alliance, and Major Wars, 1816–1975," *Journal of Conflict Resolution* 33 (1989): 255–273; Woosang Kim and James D. Morrow, "When Do Power Shifts Lead to War?," *American Journal of Political Science* 36 (1992): 896–922; Douglas Lemke and William Reed, "Power Is Not Satisfaction: A Comment on de Soysa, Oneal, and Park," *Journal of Conflict Resolution* 42 (1998): 511–516, and "Regime Types and Status Quo Evaluations: Power Transition Theory and the Democratic Peace," *International Interactions* 22 (1996): 143–164; Douglas Lemke and Suzanne Werner, "Power Parity, Commitment to Change, and War," *International Studies Quarterly* 40 (1996): 235–260; John R. Oneal, Indra de Soysa, and Yong-Hee Park, "But Power and Wealth *Are* Satisfying: A Reply to Lemke and Reed," *Journal of Conflict Resolution* 42 (1998): 517–520; Frank Whelon Wayman, "Power Shifts and the Onset of War," and Suzanne Werner and Jacek Kugler, "Power Transitions and Military Buildups: Resolving the Relationship between Arms Buildups and War," in *Parity and War: Evaluations and Extensions of The War Ledger*, ed. Jacek Kugler and Douglas Lemke (Ann Arbor: University of Michigan Press, 1996), pp. 145–161 and pp. 187–207.

8 See, for example, Peter H. Gries, "China Eyes the Hegemon," *Orbis* 49 (2005): 401–412; Wang Jisi, "China's Search for Stability with America," *Foreign Affairs* 84 (2005): 39–48; and Zheng Bijian, "China's 'Peaceful Rise' to Great-power Status," *Foreign Affairs* 84 (2005): 18–24. In the latter article (p. 22), Zheng professed that "China will not follow the path of Germany leading up to World War I or those of Germany and Japan leading up to World War II, when these countries violently plundered resources and pursued hegemony." Either implicitly or explicitly, Chinese scholars often invoke the logic of power-transition theory. Sometimes, however, this logic was altered, as when it was suggested that "according to the power transition theory, to maintain its dominance, a hegemon will be tempted to declare war on its challengers while it still

has a power advantage." David Zweig and Bi Jianhai, "China's Global Hunt for Energy," *Foreign Affairs* 84 (2005): 27. The view expressed by the latter writers is the opposite of that proposed by the power-transition theory according to A.F.K. Organski and, later on, Organski and Kugler. This theory's main hypothesis is that "when a dissatisfied great-power challenger achieves parity with the dominant power, the probability of international war rises dramatically." This most recent statement is from Douglas Lemke, "Great Powers in the Post-Cold War World: A Power Transition Perspective," in *Balance of Power: Theory and Practice in the 21st Century*, ed. T.V. Paul, James J. Wirtz, and Michel Fortmann (Stanford, CA: Stanford University Press, 2004), p. 57.

9 The Russo-Japanese war of 1904 to 1905 was initially considered as another case to which the power-transition theory should apply. Organski and Kugler, *op. cit.*, 46.

10 Recent applications of the power-transition theory to China's ascendance are provided by Ronald L. Tammen, Jacek Kugler, Douglas Lemke, Allan C. Stam III, Mark Abdollahian, Carole Alsharabati, Brian Efird, and A.F.K. Organski, *Power Transitions: Strategies for the 21st Century* (New York: Chatham House, 2000); and in a special 2003 issue of the journal *International Interactions* edited by Douglas Lemke and Ronald L. Tammen, with their introductory article "Power Transition Theory and the Rise of China," *International Interactions* 29 (2003): 269–271.

11 For a discussion on the critical importance of technological innovation rather than economic, military or territorial size as a source of national competitiveness, see George Modelski and William R. Thompson, *Leading Sectors and World Powers: The Coevolution of Global Politics and Economics* (Columbia: University of South Carolina Press, 1996); and Rafael Reuveny and William R. Thompson, *Growth, Trade, and Systemic Leadership* (Ann Arbor: University of Michigan Press, 2004).

12 Modelski and Thompson, *Leading Sectors and World Powers*, p. 97; and Harold K. Jacobson, *Networks of Interdependence: International Organizations and the Global Political System* (New York: Knopf, 1984), p. 56.

13 On the importance of cultural and political affinity in contributing to the peaceful transition between the U.K. and the U.S., see Charles A. Kupchan, Emanuel Adler, Jean-Marc Coicaud, and Yuen Foong Khong, eds, *Power in Transition: The Peaceful Change of International Order* (Tokyo: United Nations University Press, 2001); and on the influence of regime character, see Randall L. Schweller, "Domestic Structure and Preventive War: Are Democracies More Pacific?," *World Politics* 44 (1992): 235–269. American images of the Kaiser's Germany have changed over time and more as a result of evolving U.S.–German relations than the latter state's objective attributes. See Ido Oren, "The Subjectivity of the 'Democratic Peace': Changing U.S. Perceptions of Imperial Germany," *International Security* 20 (1995): 147–184.

14 Randolph M. Siverson and Ross A. Miller, "The Power Transition: Problems and Prospects," in *Parity and War: Evaluations and Extensions of The War Ledger*, ed. Jacek Kugler and Douglas Lemke (Ann Arbor: University of Michigan Press, 1996), pp. 57–73; and John A. Vasquez, *The War Puzzle* (Cambridge: Cambridge University Press, 1993), especially ch. 3.

15 The extent to which Spain could be considered to have a democratic regime at the time of the Spanish–American War is important for the theory of democratic peace. David Lake considered Spain in 1898 to be a democracy, and thus treated the Spanish–American war as a violation of this theory. See his "Powerful Pacifists: Democratic States and War," *American Political Science Review* 86 (1992): 24–37.

16 See Steve Chan, "Can't Get No Satisfaction? The Recognition of Revisionist States," *International Relations of the Asia-Pacific* 4 (2004): 207–238.

17 James D. Fearon, "Rationalist Explanations for War," *International Organization* 49 (1995): 379–414; and Daniel Kahneman and Amos Tversky, "Prospect Theory: An Analysis of Decision under Risk," *Econometrica* 47 (1979): 263–291.

18 The major work on preventive war is by Dale C. Copeland, *The Origins of Major War* (Ithaca, NY: Cornell University Press, 2000).

19 The public justification given by the administration of George W. Bush for attacking Iraq in 2003 referred explicitly to the preventive motivation, arguing that the U.S. could not afford to wait for Saddam Hussein to acquire weapons of mass destruction.

20 The Correlates of War Project and the Militarized Interstate Disputes Project offer the most systematic and comprehensive datasets that show the incidence of involvement in these conflicts by different states.

21 The theoretical basis for these observations comes from Robert Powell, *In the Shadow of Power: States and Strategies in International Politics* (Princeton, NJ: Princeton University Press, 1999). On appeasement, see Daniel Treisman, "Rational Appeasement," *International Organization* 58 (2004): 344–373; and Stephen R. Rock, *Appeasement in International Politics* (Lexington: University of Kentucky Press, 2000).

22 David Shambaugh, "Containment or Engagement of China? Calculating Beijing's Responses," *International Security* 21 (1996): 180–209.

23 Paul Schroeder, "History versus Neorealism," *International Security* 20 (1995): 193–195, and "Historical Reality vs. Neo-realist Theory," *International Security* 19 (1994): 108–138.

24 I have already mentioned the Gramscian notion of ideational hegemony. A recent study of ideational construction with general reference to international relations theories and Americans' perceptions of threat from a rising China is David L. Rousseau's *Identifying Threats and Threatening Identities: The Social Construction of Realism and Liberalism* (Stanford, CA: Stanford University Press, 2006). For a discussion of economic statecraft, see David A. Baldwin, *Economic Statecraft* (Princeton, NJ: Princeton University Press, 1985).

25 The general tendency is to assume a more assertive China as this country becomes stronger. Differences of opinion are more likely to be about whether Beijing has already acquired or will likely acquire sufficient capabilities to pursue this assertiveness rather than whether it is inclined to be assertive when it has the wherewithal to do so. See, for example, Richard Bernstein and Ross H. Munro, "The Coming Conflict with America," *Foreign Affairs* 76 (1997): 18–32; Gerald Segal, "East Asia and the 'Constrainment' of China," *International Security* 20 (1996): 107–135; and Denny Roy, "Hegemon on the Horizon? China's Threat to East Asian Security," *International Security* 19 (1994): 149–168. For a different take, see Robert S. Ross, "Beijing as a Conservative Power," *Foreign Affairs* 76 (1997): 33–44; and William H. Overholt, *The Rise of China: How Economic Reform is Creating a New Superpower* (New York: Norton, 1993).

26 Major states have not thus far sought to balance against preponderant U.S. power following the demise of the USSR. See G. John Ikenberry, ed., *America Unrivaled: The Future of the Balance of Power* (Ithaca, NY: Cornell University Press, 2002); and Paul *et al., op. cit.* My description of the Chinese strategy for managing U.S. hegemony contains elements of "soft balancing," though it is not identical to this concept. See Robert A. Pape, "Soft Balancing against the United States," *International Security* 30 (2005): 7–45.

27 On extended deterrence, see Paul K. Huth, *Extended Deterrence and the Prevention of War* (New Haven, CT: Yale University Press, 1988). On "sunk costs" and "tied hands" as deterrence approaches, see James D. Fearon, "Signalling Foreign Policy Interests: Tying Hands versus Sinking Costs," *Journal of Conflict Resolution* 41 (1997): 68–90.

28 Alexander E. Wendt, "The Agent–Structure Problem in International Relations Theory," *International Organization* 41 (1987): 337–370; and Walter Carlsnaes, "The Agency–Structure Problem in Foreign Policy Analysis," *International Studies Quarterly* 36 (1992): 245–279.

29 Jonathan Mercer, *Reputation and International Politics* (Ithaca, NY: Cornell University Press, 1996).

30 For a classic analysis of John Foster Dulles's perception of the USSR, see Ole R. Holsti, "The Belief System and National Images: A Case Study," *Journal of Conflict Resolution* 6 (1962): 244–252.

2 Power scores and the identity of central contenders

1 Power is an elusive and challenging concept to capture and measure. See James March, "Power of Power," in *Varieties of Political Theory*, ed. David Easton (Englewood Cliffs, NJ: Prentice Hall, 1966), pp. 39–70. For a more recent discussion on the evolving and multi-dimensional nature of power, see Ashley J. Tellis, Janise Bially, Christopher Layne, and Melissa McPherson, *Measuring National Power in the Postindustrial Age* (Santa Monica, CA: RAND, 2000).

2 The COW project has spawned a huge literature. For one of the earlier descriptions of this project, see Melvin Small and J. David Singer, *Resort to Arms: International and Civil Wars, 1816–1980* (Beverly Hills, CA: Sage, 1982).

3 The original analysis of national material capabilities may be found in J. David Singer, Stuart Bremer, and John Stuckey, "Capability Distribution, Uncertainty, and Major Power War, 1820–1965," in *Peace, War, and Numbers*, ed. Bruce M. Russett (Beverly Hills, CA: Sage, 1972), pp. 19–48. A subsequent account explaining the expansion of the data coverage to states beyond the original great powers may be found in J. David Singer, "Reconstructing the Correlates of War Dataset on Material Capabilities of States, 1816–1985," *International Interactions* 14 (1987): 115–132.

4 This point accords with the power-transition theory; see A.F.K. Organski and Jacek Kugler, *The War Ledger* (Chicago, IL: University of Chicago Press, 1980), pp. 51, 56, 61. As subsequent discussion will make clear, this statement does not contradict the power-transition theory because it claims that war looms only when a dissatisfied challenger overtakes or is poised to overtake a satisfied dominant power. In practice, however, many previous studies attempting to verify the power-transition theory have overlooked the satisfaction or status-quo orientation of the contesting states. This latter issue will be taken up in Chapter 3.

5 It is difficult to imagine that anyone would seriously propose that under contemporary conditions a state should promote population growth or territorial aggrandizement, or increase its conscription or energy consumption, in order to enhance its national power.

6 Its 2005 *World Factbook* is available at http:www.cia.gov/cia/publications/factbook.

7 Organski and Kugler, *op. cit.*, p. 28. These authors also suggested that the slower the speed of this overtaking and, hence, the more protracted this passage is, the more likely that the problems stemming from power transition can be resolved. At the same time, the longer this transition takes to unfold, the more likely that it may be "punctuated by a number of armed conflicts" (*op. cit.,* pp. 21, 54, 62).

8 As several colleagues have remarked, "It is no exaggeration to assert that any projection of Chinese GDP is fraught with peril. Anyone who has delved into the arcane issues surrounding purchasing power parity (PPP) and exchange rate calculations understands there is no agreed upon standard of measurement. Even among PPP advocates, with expenditure and production approaches, numbers may vary widely" (Ronald L. Tammen, Jacek Kugler, Douglas Lemke, Allan C. Stam III, Mark Abdollahian, Carole Alsharabati, Brian Efird, and A.F.K. Organski, *Power Transitions: Strategies for the 21st Century* (New York: Chatham House, 2000), p. 210).

9 Organski and Kugler, *op. cit.*, pp. 38, 108.

10 Emilio Casetti, "Power Shifts and Economic Development: When Will China Overtake the USA?," *Journal of Peace Research* 40 (2003): 661–675. For other analyses of China's growth prospects, see K.C. Yeh, "China's Economic Growth: Recent Trends and Prospects," and Angang Hu, "The Chinese Economy in Prospect," in *China, the*

United States, and the Global Economy, ed. Shuxun Chen and Charles Wolf, Jr. (Santa Monica: CA: RAND, 2001), pp. 69–97 and pp. 99–146; and Nicholas R. Lardy, *China's Unfinished Economic Revolution* (Washington, D.C.: The Brookings Institution, 1998).

11 See, for example, David Shambaugh, "China Engages Asia: Reshaping the Regional Order," *International Security* 29 (2004/2005): 64–99; Thomas J. Christensen, "Posing Problems without Catching Up: China's Rise and Challenges for U.S. Security Policy," *International Security* 25 (2001): 5–40; Avery Goldstein, "Great Expectations: Interpreting China's Arrival," *International Security* 22 (1997/1998): 36–73; and Robert S. Ross, "Beijing as a Conservative Power," *Foreign Affairs* 76 (1997): 33–44. Note that the statistics for military spending are from U.S. sources that, at least during the Cold War years, had tended to exaggerate the defense expenditures of the communist states. Using data from the U.S. Arms Control and Disarmament Agency, one would have reached the same conclusion of U.S. predominance in military power. In other words, if there is a bias in these data, they tend to understate the extent of U.S. predominance. See Steve Chan, "Is There A Power Transition between the U.S. and China? The Different Faces of Power," *Asian Survey* 45 (2005): 687–701.

12 George Modelski and William R. Thompson, *Leading Sectors and World Powers: The Coevolution of Global Politics and Economics* (Columbia: University of South Carolina Press, 1996).

13 Robert S. Ross, "Bipolarity and Balancing in East Asia," in *Balance of Power: Theory and Practice in the 21st Century*, ed. T.V. Paul, James J. Wirtz, and Michel Fortmann (Stanford, CA: Stanford University Press, 2004), p. 294.

14 Joseph S. Nye, Jr., *Bound to Lead: The Changing Nature of American Power* (New York: Basic Books, 1990), and *The Paradox of American Power* (New York: Oxford University Press, 2002).

15 This is an important point emphasized by Organski and Kugler (*op. cit.*, pp. 21, 33–34).

16 That the gazelles often outperform the elephants is emphasized in the distinction between trading states and strategic states. See Richard Rosecrance, *The Rise of the Trading State: Commerce and Conquest in the Modern World* (New York: Basic Books, 1986). For extensive discussions on historical contests for global leadership, see Karen A. Rasler and William R. Thompson, *War and State Making: The Shaping of the Global Powers* (Boston, MA: Unwin Hyman, 1989), and *The Great Powers and the Global Struggle, 1490–1990* (Lexington: University of Kentucky Press, 1994); see also William R. Thompson, ed., *Great Power Rivalries* (Columbia: University of South Carolina Press, 1999).

17 See, for example, Rafael Reuveny and William R. Thompson, *Growth, Trade, and Systemic Leadership* (Ann Arbor: University of Michigan Press, 2004). For a fascinating historical study on the early modern era, see Carlo M. Cipolla, *Guns, Sails, and Empires: Technological Innovation and the Early Phases of European Expansion, 1470–1700* (New York: Minerva Press, 1965).

18 This point was emphasized by Bruce M. Russett in "The Mysterious Case of Vanishing Hegemony: Or, Is Mark Twain Really Dead?," *International Organization* 39 (1985): 207–232. See also Susan Strange, "The Persistent Myth of Lost Hegemony," *International Organization* 41 (1987): 551–574.

19 The importance of these factors for promoting and sustaining a country's international competitiveness was stressed by David Rapkin and William R. Thompson in "Power Transition, Challenge and the (Re)Emergence of China," *International Interactions* 29 (2003): 315–342. For a populist rendition, see Geoffrey Colvin, "America: The 97-Lb. Weakling," *Fortune* (July 25, 2005): 70–82.

20 However, as already noted, the Japanese had registered a larger number of patent applications than the Americans. The measures used to discern national power have individual weaknesses, but we hope that collectively they may contribute to gaining a more sound understanding of the relative strengths of different countries. Thus, for

instance, exclusive attention to demographic size can exaggerate China's importance whereas, due to its tighter government control of internet hosts, an over-emphasis of this measure can understate China's importance. Which specific measure is most appropriate for China? There is of course no consensus on this question except that perhaps gross national product per capita offers the most succinct summary indicator of national productivity. As should be evident by now, the approach undertaken in this book treats national power as a multi-dimensional phenomenon. Just as a physician would want to check a patient's body temperature, blood pressure, heartbeat, and lung functions in order to gain an initial assessment of his/her health, it would seem odd to insist on just one select measure that is uniquely appropriate for China, as suggested by a reviewer of an earlier draft. Indeed, I deliberately choose a generic approach in this study that avoids treating China as a special case or the only focus of analysis. After all, as instructors, we do not design a test just for one student. Nor do we assign a course grade to this student on the basis of just this one test without additional information about his/her knowledge of the class material – and we certainly do not assign a course grade to other students in the class without requiring them to take the same test, or even any test.

21 Michael D. Swaine and Ashley J. Tellis, *Interpreting China's Grand Strategy: Past, Present, and Future* (Santa Monica, CA: RAND, 2000), pp. 204–205.

22 See, for instance, the discussion in Avery Goldstein, *Rising to the Challenge: China's Grand Strategy and International Security* (Stanford, CA: Stanford University Press, 2005), especially ch. 3.

23 Although this theory was originally concerned about rivalry among the most powerful states, it has recently been extended to study conflict among the minor powers. See Douglas Lemke, *Regions of War and Peace* (Cambridge: Cambridge University Press, 2002).

24 It has been estimated that the U.S. gross domestic product had already grown to be about twice as large as that of the U.K. by the year 1900. Harold K. Jacobson, *Networks of Interdependence: International Organizations and the Global Political System* (New York: Knopf, 1984), p. 56.

25 While recognizing that the U.S. had "passed all countries in potential power by the end of the nineteenth century and . . . maintained her lead from that time to ours," the authors of *The War Ledger* justified its exclusion as a "contender in the central system" on the ground that this country "had not come to view herself as part of the central system" until after World War II (Organski and Kugler, *op. cit.*, p. 45).

26 Ibid., p. 45.

27 In his book *World Politics* (New York: Knopf, 1958), Organski acknowledged that the U.S. had overtaken the U.K. prior to World War I. The political and cultural affinity between these two countries, however, was thought to account for their peaceful power transition.

28 William R. Thompson, "The Evolution of a Great Power Rivalry: The Anglo-American Case," in Thompson, *op. cit.*, p. 201.

29 As acknowledged by a colleague writing in the tradition of power-transition theory, some "might see American omission from contender status during World War I and World War II as odd, specifically since America's contributions to those wars arguably proved decisive to their outcomes" (Lemke, *op. cit.*, pp. 92–93).

30 Douglas Lemke and Suzanne Werner, "Power Parity, Commitment to Change, and War," *International Studies Quarterly* 40 (1996): 235–260.

31 The results of this exercise would be the same, regardless of whether one adds more states to those listed in Table 2.2 in an effort to determine the largest drop-off.

32 If one looks at the size of gross domestic product unadjusted for purchasing-power parity, U.S. predominance would be even more pronounced.

33 Organski and Kugler, *op. cit.*, p. 49.

34 In an essay reviewing recent books on "American imperialism," Campbell Craig stated succinctly: "at present . . . no state besides the United States can be characterized as a

great power, using the standard realist definition of a great power – a nation that can hold its own in a war with any other nation." He also observed: "the system of international relations today is unipolar – there is no balance of power, no other state that is creating a balance by effectively contending with the United States." Campbell Craig, "American Realism Versus American Imperialism," *World Politics* 57 (2004): 168 and 169.

35 The vision of a united Europe, however, has suffered a serious setback in the wake of the French and Dutch voters' rejection of the proposed constitution for the European Union in late May and early June, respectively, of 2005. Prior to these developments, Joseph Nye (*op. cit.*, 2002, p. 168) remarked,

> the one entity with the capacity to challenge the United States in the near future is the European Union if it were to become a tight federation with major military capabilities and if the relations across the Atlantic were allowed to sour. Such an outcome is possible but would require major changes in Europe and considerable ineptitude in American policy to bring it about.

36 Wang Jisi, "China's Search for Stability with America," *Foreign Affairs* 84 (2005): 41.
37 Nye, *op. cit.* (2002), p. 20.
38 Ibid., p. 2.
39 Regional hegemony, or the concentration of regional power, is a significant factor in one variant of the power-transition theory. Karen A. Rasler and William R. Thompson, (*op. cit.*, p. 1990) argued that the decline of a global maritime leader and the concomitant ascent of a regional land power have historically occasioned global wars involving contests for systemic leadership. The designation of Europe as the central (regional) system for international relations prior to 1945, however, in effect precludes considering the rise of the U.S. as a regional hegemon in the Western Hemisphere (if not, as already argued, also as a contender for global leadership and even the *de facto* occupant of that position) in this analytic scheme.

3 Revisionist impulse and the incumbent's strategic selection

1 Condoleezza Rice, "Promoting the National Interest," *Foreign Affairs* 79 (2000): 56.
2 According to Organski and Kugler, "the power-transition model . . . argues that wars occur only when a dissatisfied great power catches up with the dominant nation" (A.F.K. Organski and J. Kugler, *The War Ledger* (Chicago, IL: University of Chicago Press, 1980), p. 39).
3 Ibid., p. 23.
4 As Karen Rasler and William R. Thompson remarked, "declining incumbents select, to some extent, which challengers they will fight and with whom they will ally to meet the intensive challenge." See "Global War and the Political Economy of Structural Change," in *Handbook of War Studies II*, ed. Manus I. Midlarsky (Ann Arbor: University of Michigan Press, 2000), p. 310.
5 John A. Vasquez, "When Are Power Transitions Dangerous? An Appraisal and Reformulation of Power Transition Theory," in *Parity and War: Evaluations and Extensions of The War Ledger*, ed. Jacek Kugler and Douglas Lemke (Ann Arbor: University of Michigan Press, 1996), pp. 41–42. See also William R. Thompson, "Why Rivalries Matter and What Great Powers Rivalries Can Tell Us about World Politics," in *Great Power Rivalries*, ed. William R. Thompson (Columbia: University of South Carolina Press, 1999), p. 12.
6 Kenneth Bourne, *Britain and the Balance of Power in North America: 1815–1908* (Berkeley: University of California Press, 1967), p. 408. For American and British mutual perceptions, see John M. Owens, IV, *Liberal Peace, Liberal War: American Politics and International Security* (Ithaca, NY: Cornell University Press, 1997).

7 William R. Thompson, "The Evolution of a Great Power Rivalry: The Anglo-American Case," in Thompson, *op. cit.*, p. 213.

8 Significantly, if one is to argue that legislative oversight should be the hallmark of a democracy in that era, then Spain could conceivably qualify for this status at the time of the Spanish–American War. See James L. Ray, *Democracy and International Conflict: An Evaluation of the Democratic Peace Proposition* (Columbia: University of South Carolina Press, 1995). In view of the Spanish–American War, this designation for Spain in turn creates a problem for the proposition that democracies do not fight each other.

9 Stephen R. Rock described a series of unilateral British concessions to accommodate the Americans with little expectation that these gestures would be reciprocated. In addition to settling the boundary dispute between Venezuela and British Guyana according to U.S. demands, London also settled the border between Alaska and the Canadian Northwest on terms favorable to Washington and accepted the building of an isthmian canal in Panama (a development that would greatly enhance U.S. naval power). Rock quoted Bradford Perkins, remarking that "in hard diplomatic coin, the Americans took but they did not give." See Stephen R. Rock, *Appeasement in International Politics* (Lexington: University of Kentucky Press, 2000), p. 41.

10 John J. Mearsheimer, *The Tragedy of Great Power Politics* (New York: Norton, 2001), p. 238. Yet by casting the U.S. in the role of an offshore balancer that is *only* interested in preventing another power from gaining the status of a regional hegemon, Mearsheimer offers what Christopher Layne described as a "diet version" of offensive realism. That is, the U.S. was exempted from the central logic of offensive realism that *all* states seek to expand their power. See Christopher Layne, "The 'Poster Child for Offensive Realism': America as a Global Hegemon," *Security Studies* 12 (2002/2003): 120–164; and Steve Chan, "Realism, Revisionism, and the Great Powers," *Issues & Studies* 40 (2004):135–172.

11 Mearsheimer, *op.cit.*, p. 238.

12 Indeed, the designation of some states as status-quo oriented would be an oxymoron from the perspective of offensive realism, which sees all states as motivated by revisionist ambitions. Yet, as already mentioned, offensive realism treats the U.S. as the *only* status-quo power in the world. By treating the U.S. as the only exception to its general logic, offensive realism (or at least John Mearsheimer's formulation of this theory) contradicts its own argument that states will not cease their effort to seek more power until they achieve complete global domination.

13 Dale C. Copeland, "Economic Interdependence and War: A Theory of Trade Expectations," *International Security* 20 (1996): 28–29.

14 That is to say, all states tend to believe that they deserve more good things than they currently possess. Dissatisfaction in this sense then refers to a belief that one is being under-rewarded. I will pursue this topic further in Chapter 6, emphasizing the point that being dissatisfied does not necessarily mean that a country is bent on challenging the international status quo defined as the system's prevailing rules and norms.

15 As one observer remarked, the international relations literature has generally emphasized the threat posed by these and other alleged revisionist states (e.g., Maoist China, Castroite Cuba, or the so-called rogue states of Iraq, Iran, and North Korea) to the international system, while tending to overlook the reciprocal threat that these states have faced from the international system. These states have been the target of economic blockade and/or military intervention by foreign powers seeking their demise. Barry Buzan, *People, States and Fear: An Agenda for International Security Studies in the Post-Cold War Era* (Boulder, CO: Lynne Rienner, 1991), p. 308.

16 Randall L. Schweller, "Managing the Rise of Great Powers," in *Engaging China: The Management of an Emerging Power*, ed. Alastair Iain Johnston and Robert S. Ross (London: Routlege, 1999), pp. 20–21.

17 Japan's delegates failed to even gain recognition for the principle of racial and sovereign equality from the victorious allies at the Versailles Conference, a fact which in turn suggests that this principle was not part of the "international order" at that time.

18 Yuen Foong Khong, "Negotiating 'Order' during Power Transitions," in *Power in Transition: The Peaceful Change of International Order*, ed. Charles A. Kupchan, Emanuel Adler, Jean-Marc Coicaud, and Yuen Foong Khong (Tokyo: United Nations University Press, 2001), p. 40.

19 The U.S chose to stay outside the League of Nations after World War I.

20 Rock, *op. cit.* For an account of Britain's predicament, see Aaron L. Friedberg, *The Weary Titan: Britain and the Experience of Relative Decline, 1895–1905* (Princeton, NJ: Princeton University Press, 1988); and Daniel Treisman, "Rational Appeasement," *International Organization* 58 (2004): 344–373.

21 See Bourne, *op. cit.*

22 William R. Thompson favors the latter interpretation. See his "The Evolution of a Great Power Rivalry," *op. cit.*

23 For an informative account of the different experiences of Japan and China in facing Western imperialist pressure, see Frances V. Moulder, *Japan, China and the Modern World Economy* (New York: Cambridge University Press, 1979).

24 Ido Oren, "The Subjectivity of the 'Democratic Peace': Changing U.S. Perceptions of Imperial Germany," *International Security* 20 (1997): 147–184. Oren's more general point is that perceptions of other states' regimes and cultural characteristics tend to be a product rather than a determinant of one's relations with them. Just as in the case of the current tendency to describe Anglo-American relations in the late 1800s as cordial rather than acrimonious, American views about imperial Germany have altered due to the experience of the Great War. Such perceptions – ideational constructions, if you will – can undergo rather major transformation and sharp reversals in the wake of changed relations, such as in the case of Americans' perceptions of the USSR and Japan after World War II and Iran after the overthrow of the Shah. Americans held a more favorable view of China in 1972 than now, even though the latter's regime was in fact far more oppressive at the time of Richard Nixon's historic visit to Beijing.

25 Thompson, "The Evolution of a Great Power Rivalry," *op. cit.*, p. 213.

26 See David L. Rousseau, *Identifying Threats and Threatening Identities: The Social Construction of Realism and Liberalism* (Stanford, CA: Stanford University Press, 2006).

27 At least according to the perspective of offensive realism, more power is always better. The title of a recent exchange may be construed to suggest that being powerful does not necessarily make a country satisfied. Douglas Lemke and William Reed, "Power Is Not Satisfaction: A Comment on de Soysa, Oneal, and Park," *Journal of Conflict Resolution* 42 (1998): 511–516.

28 It would of course not be correct to suggest that the U.S. administration under George W. Bush rejects the idea of national sovereignty. Indeed, leading American neo-conservatives, such as the U.S. Ambassador to the United Nations (John Bolton), want to withdraw from "meddling" international institutions and remove constraints on sovereignty that limit Washington's policy discretion. There is therefore an inconsistency in the American insistence that, on the one hand, other states' claims of sovereignty should not stop U.S. efforts to promote democracy and capitalism in their countries and that, on the other hand, rejects constraints on its own sovereignty in matters such as the prosecution of war criminals, the use of land-mines or nuclear weapons, and the emission of gases that damage the earth's ozone. This predicament is not limited to officials. I attended an academic conference several years ago. At this conference, several prominent scholars advocated that the U.S. should intervene abroad in order to promote democracy in China and the African countries. One of the participants advocated that one should "fetishize elections" in this effort to spread democracy. This advocacy is ironic because the leading scholars present were members of professional associations (such as the American Political Science Association and the International Studies Association) and had held official positions (such as association president, department chair, and center director) without the benefit of contested

elections or even any election. While arguing that democracy and human rights are universal values for an international community, many of these colleagues and the nongovernmental organizations expressing similar views are likely to recoil, as Joseph Nye (*op. cit.*, 2002, p. 19) acknowledged forthrightly, from the "nightmare" of a prospective world without sovereignty, where "a billion Chinese and a billion Indians," joined by the citizens of other poorer countries, are in a position to continually outvote the citizens of the wealthy countries. The Chinese are also not beyond reproach for inconsistencies. Considerations of sovereignty and non-interference in others' domestic affairs did not stop them supporting sanctions against South African apartheid.

29   A.R.F. Crganski and Jaceh Kugler, *The War Ledger* (Chicago, IL: University of Chicago Press, 1980), p. 23.

30   Naturally, the opportunity for states to participate in intergovernmental organizations varies according to their affluence, the time since their political independence, and the number of their immediate neighbors. The point being pursued here of course refers to the states' willingness to join IGOs after these differences in their opportunity to do so have been controlled for. For a more extended discussion on the rationale behind using participation in IGOs as an index of states' revisionist or status-quo orientation, see Steve Chan, "Can't Get No Satisfaction? The Recognition of Revisionist States," *International Relations of the Asia-Pacific* 4 (2004): 207–238. For a discussion of the logic of opportunity and willingness, see Benjamin A. Most and Harvey Starr, *Inquiry, Logic and International Politics* (Columbia: University of South Carolina Press, 1989).

31   Robert O. Keohane and Lisa L. Martin, "The Promise of Institutionalist Theory," *International Security* 20 (1995): 39–51; and Harold K. Jacobson, *Networks of Interdependence: International Organizations and the Global Political System* (New York: Knopf, 1984).

32   China is not included in this table because it did not belong to many IGOs during the years in question and because it was clearly not a principal actor involved in the initiation of World Wars I and II. As already reported, as late as 1970, Beijing belonged to only two IGOs. Parenthetically, if participation in IGOs may be used to indicate the degree to which a country is isolationist or isolated, then this characterization applies more to China even for the relatively recent past than to the U.S. from the late 1800s to the mid-1900s. This point is relevant to the debate about why the U.S. should or should not be designated as a central contender in the international system. Whether it should be disqualified from this designation on the ground of its ostensible isolationism is pertinent to the question of whether China should be similarly disqualified for, say, the first three decades of the People's Republic.

33   This remark corresponds with the observation that there was a "decline in the growth of participation in IGOs on the part of the governments initiating the two world wars" (William K. Domke, *War and the Changing Global System* (New Haven, CT: Yale University Press, 1988), p. 150).

34   Bruce M. Russett and John R. Oneal, *Triangulating Peace: Democracy, Interdependence, and International Organizations* (New York: Norton, 2001), p. 304.

35   Nico Krish, "Weak as Constraint, Strong as Tool: The Place of International Law in U.S. Foreign Policy," in *Unilateralism and U.S. Foreign Policy: International Perspectives*, ed. David M. Malone and Yuen Foong Khong (Boulder, CO: Lynne Rienner, 2003), p. 47.

36   David M. Malone and Yuen Foong Khong, "Unilateralism and U.S. Foreign Policy: International Perspectives," in Malone and Yuen, *op. cit.*, p. 5.

37   For a discussion of Washington's exceptionalist logic applied in defense of its resort to preventive war against Iraq, see Benjamin R. Barber, *Fear's Empire: War, Terror, and Democracy* (New York: Norton, 2003).

38   Alastair Iain Johnston, "Is China a Status Quo Power?," *International Security* 7 (2003): 49.

39   David C. Kang, "Getting Asia Wrong: The Need for New Analytical Frameworks," *International Security* 27 (2003): 68.

40 David Shambaugh, "China Engages Asia: Reshaping the Regional Order," *International Security* 29 (2004/2005): 64. See also Lanxin Xiang, "Washington's Misguided China Policy," *Survival* 43 (2001): 7–23; and David Shambaugh, "China or America: Which is the Revisionist Power?," *Survival* 43 (2001): 25–30.

41 M. Taylor Fravel, "Regime Insecurity and International Cooperation: Explaining China's Compromises in Territorial Disputes," *International Security* 30 (2005): 46–83.

42 Other scholars have noticed similar patterns. See, for example, Stephen M. Walt, "Taming American Power," *Foreign Affairs* 84 (2005): 107.

43 Vasquez, p. 51.

44 Felix Oppenheim offered the injunction that "avoidance of unnecessary departures from common usage" is an important analytic virtue. Quoted in Randall L. Schweller, "Bandwagoning for Profit: Bringing the Revisionist State Back In," *International Security* 19 (1994): 81.

45 David M. Edelstein, "Managing Uncertainty: Beliefs about Intentions and the Rise of Great Powers," *Security Studies* 12 (2002): 10. See also Andrew Kydd, "Trust, Reassurance, and Cooperation," *International Organization* 54 (2000): 325–357.

46 Although continuing with a vigorous program of colonial expansion, France had by the end of the nineteenth century turned to a posture of strategic defense in Europe, seeking to promote an alliance network for the containment of rising German power. During much of the period of contemporary history of international relations (typically dating from the Congress of Vienna in 1815), China had been trying to fend off foreign encroachment.

47 See, for example, Jeffrey W. Taliaferro, "Security Seeking under Anarchy: Defensive Realism Revisited," *International Security* 25 (2000/2001): 128–161. For a penetrating analysis on the conflicting presentations of realism, see Jeffrey W. Legro and Andrew Moravcsik, "Is Anybody Still a Realist?," *International Security* 24 (1999): 5–55.

48 Andrew Kydd, "Sheep in Sheep's Clothing: Why Security Seekers Do Not Fight Each Other," *Security Studies* 7 (1997): 114–155.

49 The basic thrust of the Bush doctrine is that "the United States must remain the only great power on the planet: it should develop a military force so vast that it deters any rival from contending with it and it should use all means at its disposal – most notoriously, preventive war – to deal with nations or groups not deterred by this military preponderance." See Campbell Craig, "American Realism Versus American Imperialism," *World Politics* 57 (October 2004): 161. For a discussion of "The National Security Strategy of the United States of America" of September 2002 (available at http://www.whitehouse.gov/nsc/html), see Andrew J. Bacevich, *American Empire: The Realities and Consequences of U.S. Diplomacy* (Cambridge, MA: Harvard University Press, 2002); and Robert Jervis, *American Foreign Policy in a New Era* (New York: Routledge, 2005). Authors such as Craig, Bacevich, and Jervis have called attention to a fundamental shift in the U.S. strategic vision under George W. Bush. The policy of deterrence and containment, as practiced during the Cold War years, tacitly accepted the existence of competing powers such as the USSR and China. In contrast, the Bush doctrine enunciated in the 2002 document stated that "our forces will be strong enough to dissuade adversaries from a military build-up in hopes of surpassing, or equaling, the United States." Its declared goal is to perpetuate U.S. dominance indefinitely by, in Craig's words (p. 162), "[instilling] fear in any potential rivals, declaring that [Washington] will not allow them to contend with the United States and that it will deal with them if they make any serious attempt to do so." The logic of preventive war follows from this new U.S. doctrine, which has the effect of "[turning] world politics into a permanent game of the U.S. against the world."

50 David L. Cingranelli and David L. Richards, "Measuring the Level, Pattern, and Sequence of Government Respect for Physical Integrity Rights," *International Studies Quarterly* 43 (1999): 407–417, and "Respect for Human Rights After the End of the Cold War," *Journal of Peace Research* 36 (1999): 511–534.

51 The physical-quality-of-life index is a composite indicator based on a people's average infant mortality rate, literacy rate, and life expectancy. See Morris D. Morris, *Measuring the Condition of the World's Poor: The Physical Quality of Life Index* (New York: Pergamon Press, 1979).

52 A survey by the Pew Research Center published in June 2005 confirms the general conclusion that people in other countries (even in countries such as the U.K., France, and Germany that are traditional U.S. allies) hold a poor image of the U.S. In most of the sixteen countries that participated in this poll, more respondents reported a favorable image of China than those expressing the same view about the U.S. See http://pewglobal.org. Several leading American scholars have remarked recently that in view of Washington's announced policy agenda under the administration of George W. Bush, "the U.S. is not a status-quo power" and that it is a "revisionist state." See Robert Jervis, "Explaining the Bush Doctrine," *Political Science Quarterly* 118 (2003): 365–388; and G. John Ikenberry, "America's Imperial Ambition," *Foreign Affairs* 81 (2002): 44–60. The commentary by historian Paul W. Schroeder is also highly relevant. See his "The Mirage of Empire Versus the Promise of Hegemony," in *Systems, Stability, and Statecraft: Essays on the International History of Modern Europe*, ed. Paul W. Schroeder (New York: Palgrave, 2004), pp. 297–305.

53 Ivo H. Daalder and James M. Lindsay, *America Unbound: The Bush Revolution in Foreign Policy* (New York: Wiley, 2005); Stephen M. Walt, *Taming American Power: The Global Response to U.S. Primacy* (New York: Norton, 2005); and Jervis, *op. cit.* (2005).

54 Walt, *op. cit.*, p. 23.

55 Daalder and Lindsay, *op. cit.*

56 See, for example, Peter H. Gries, *China's New Nationalism: Pride, Politics, and Diplomacy* (Berkeley: University of California Press, 2004).

4   Imperial overstretch and loss aversion as sources of war

1 According to Organski and Kugler, "the aggressor will come from a small group of dissatisfied strong countries; and it is the weaker, rather than the stronger, power that is most likely to be the aggressor"; and "the powerful and satisfied do not start wars." They also hypothesized that "wars occur only when a dissatisfied great power catches up with the dominant nation. Satisfied powers do not fight" (A.F.K. Organski and Jacek Kugler, *The War Ledger* (Chicago, IL: University of Chicago Press, 1980), pp. 19, 23, 39).

2 The power-transition theory is about those "conflicts whose outcomes will affect the very structure and operation of the international system" (ibid., p. 45).

3 It is possible for a war to have this effect in transforming the international system without the belligerents being motivated by a desire to change the rules and principles of this system. That is, two status-quo states can fight a war without any intention to change the system's rules and principles, and yet the outcome of this war can cause a major transformation of the system's structure. Bruce Bueno de Mesquita argued that this was what happened in the case of the Seven Weeks' War between Austria and Prussia in 1866. Bruce Bueno de Mesquita, "Pride of Place: The Origins of German Hegemony," *World Politics* 43 (1990): 1–27.

4 James D. Fearon, "Rationalist Explanations for War," *International Organization* 49 (1995): 379–414; Erik Gartzke, "War Is in the Error Term," *International Organization* 53 (1999): 567–587; and R. Harrison Wagner, "Bargaining and War," *American Journal of Political Science* 44 (2000): 469–484.

5 In addition to private information, other factors such as misrepresentation and the commitment problem can hamper efforts to reach a settlement so that war may be avoided. The relevant points were developed and discussed by Fearon, *op. cit.* In a

series of other publications, he elaborated and expanded on the rationalist perspective with respect to phenomena such as extended deterrence and civil war. See James D. Fearon, "Selection Effects and Deterrence," *International Interactions* 28 (2000): 5–29; "Commitment Problems and the Spread of Ethnic Conflict," in *The International Spread of Ethnic Conflict: Fear, Diffusion, and Escalation,* ed. David A. Lake and Donald Rothchild (Princeton, NJ: Princeton University Press, 1998), pp. 107–126; "Signalling Foreign Policy Interests: Tying Hands Versus Sinking Costs," *Journal of Conflict Resolution* 41 (1997): 68–90; "Domestic Political Audiences and the Escalation of International Disputes," *American Political Science Review* 88 (1994): 577–592; and "Signaling versus the Balance of Power and Interests: An Empirical Test of a Crisis Bargaining Model," *Journal of Conflict Resolution* 38 (1994): 236–269.

6　Note that this generalization refers to the parties' capabilities, not their resolve. Surely, consideration about the latter factor can still play a huge role in asymmetric contests. Thus, for instance, in the war between the U.S. and North Vietnam, private information about each contestant's resolve to accept heavy costs, run the risk of escalation, and persevere throughout a protracted struggle was critical in influencing both sides' expectations about the likely outcome of their conflict. When, however, the contestants' power asymmetry becomes hugely lopsided, the weaker party's higher resolve would at some point be insufficient to offset its capability disadvantage and therefore influence the war's ending.

7　That the German leaders might have miscalculated does not imply that the British leaders had got it right. After all, both sides to a conflict could be mistaken in their anticipation of how a possible war would turn out.

8　Paul Kennedy, "The First World War and the International Power System," *International Security* 9 (1984): 29.

9　The same logic would lead one to expect that in contrast to an ordinary power, a superpower is better positioned to signal that it has a stake in a distant conflict and that it is more resolved to defend its interest there.

10　A state may change its mind even when it had not intended to bluff initially. This change can simply stem from a motivation to deny an adversary making potential gains. Thus, for instance, even though the Truman administration had implicitly acknowledged that Korea was located outside the U.S. defense perimeter in the Pacific, North Korea's attack on South Korea led to Washington's intervention in the Korean War. Moreover, even though the Truman administration had declared a neutral position in the Chinese Civil War, the outbreak of the Korean War led to its decision to interpose the Seventh Fleet in the Taiwan Strait. This decision in turn saved Chiang Kai-shek from being defeated by the communist forces that were poised to invade Taiwan, causing the separation of this island from China to this day.

11　This remark does not deny that duplicity such as the Nazi–Soviet pact can also apply to the stronger side. After all, Hitler's Germany was set on invading the USSR and used this pact only as a ruse.

12　Thus, the U.K. is "stuck" with the Falklands even though its control of these islands is expensive and unlikely to constitute a long-term solution.

13　States' concern for their reputation, however, tends to be exaggerated. Their concessions are more likely to be interpreted by their opponents as a lack of capability than as a lack of will. See Jonathan Mercer, *Reputation and International Politics* (Ithaca, NY: Cornell University Press, 1996).

14　Fearon (*op. cit.*, 1997) discussed the two strategies of "sunk costs" and "tied hands." These strategies are ideal types and actual conduct can obviously consist of elements from both approaches. Moreover, these are not mutually exclusive approaches. Thus, for example, troop mobilization and military deployment can serve to both signal resolve and contribute to battlefield victory should war break out. See Branislav Slantchev, "Military Coercion in International Crises," *American Political Science Review* 99 (2005): 533–547.

15 In the case of the Falklands conflict between the U.K. and Argentina, the officials of the latter country doubted their counterparts' commitment to defending the islands because London had failed to accept "sunk costs," for example stationing a large number of troops and building transportation infrastructures in the contested territory. The recall of the British ice-breaker, *The Endurance*, due to budgetary constraints further persuaded Buenos Aires that London would not resist Argentina's takeover of the islands.

16 With respect to its possible intention to defend Taiwan and the offshore islands, Washington has over the years moved away from an emphasis on "sinking costs" but has not at the same time resorted to "tying its hands." Its current policy is deliberate "strategic ambiguity." As Fearon noted (*op. cit.*, 1997: 82), however, there is no bluffing in the equilibrium. China is not unaware of how a fully committed defender would have acted. A fully committed defender would surely want to convey the message that "we will fight" a deterrence challenge rather than "we may fight" as implied by a posture of "strategic ambiguity." Significantly, however, a policy of "tying hands" turns over the initiative to the other side. Once one party (regardless of its status as a defender or challenger) is fully committed, it enables the other party to decide whether and, if so, when and how to initiate a confrontation. Repeated declarations made by Beijing about the importance of national reunification have in effect tied China's hands in response to a possible move by Taipei, with or without Washington's support, to declare *de jure* independence.

17 Still another reason hypothesized to cause war is that the goods being fought over tend to be lumpy or indivisible. Consequently, these resources cannot be easily allocated to satisfy competing demands. An example may be the competing claims of sovereignty advanced by China and Taiwan although, even in this case, creative arrangements may be designed to skirt this challenge.

18 This generalization does not deny that states sometimes decide to abandon their commitments even after incurring heavy "sunk costs." The U.S. withdrawal from South Vietnam offers an exemplary illustration.

19 That the U.K. and France had failed to resist German challenges on previous occasions increased Hitler's doubts about their intention to defend Poland.

20 As already discussed in the last chapter, the U.K. did adopt a policy of retrenchment even though one may question whether it came too little and too late. Imperial overstretch appears to be a common problem for declining hegemons. See Paul Kennedy, *The Rise and Fall of the Great Powers* (New York: Random House, 1987). For additional studies on the causes and consequences of imperial decline, see Carlo M. Cipolla, ed., *The Economic Decline of Empires* (London: Methuen, 1970); and Robert Gilpin, *War and Change in World Politics* (New York: Cambridge University Press, 1981). Karen A. Rasler and William R. Thompson provide an informative analysis seeking to determine whether an increasingly acute trade-off between consumption and investment has been an antecedent of imperial decline, or vice versa. They conclude that imperial decline tends to exacerbate the consumption-versus-investment trade-off, which constitutes a secondary rather than a primary factor in bringing about the decline in the first place. Declining technological advantage, rising foreign competition, and domestic rigidities are likely to be the primary causes. See Karen A. Rasler and William R. Thompson, *The Great Powers and Global Struggle, 1490–1990* (Lexington: University of Kentucky Press, 1994), chs 5 and 6.

21 For major works on prospect theory, see Daniel Kahneman, Paul Slovic, and Amos Tversky, eds, *Judgment under Uncertainty: Heuristics and Biases* (Cambridge: Cambridge University Press, 1982); and Daniel Kahneman and Amos Tversky, eds, *Choices, Values, and Frames* (Cambridge: Cambridge University Press, 2000), and "Prospect Theory: An Analysis of Decision under Risk," *Econometrica* 47 (1979): 263–291. For applications of prospect theory to international relations, see Jack S. Levy, "Prospect Theory, Rational Choice, and International Relations," *International*

Studies Quarterly 41 (1997): 87–112, and "Loss Aversion, Framing, and Bargaining: The Implications of Prospect Theory for International Conflict," *International Political Science Review* 17 (1996): 179–195; Mark L. Haas, "Prospect Theory and the Cuban Missile Crisis," *International Studies Quarterly* 45 (2001): 241–270; Rose McDermott, *Risk-Taking in International Politics: Prospect Theory in American Foreign Policy* (Ann Arbor: University of Michigan Press, 1998); Barbara Farnham, ed., *Avoiding Losses/Taking Risks: Prospect Theory and International Conflict* (Ann Arbor: University of Michigan Press, 1994); William A. Boettcher, III, *Presidential Risk Behavior in Foreign Policy: Prudence or Peril?* (New York: Macmillan, 2005); and Jeffrey W. Taliaferro, *Balancing Risks: Great Power Intervention in the Periphery* (Ithaca, NY: Cornell University Press, 2004), and "Realism, Power Shifts, and Major War," *Security Studies* 10 (2001): 145–178.

22 I am indebted to an anonymous reviewer for pointing out this tendency and the other two points made in this paragraph. Studies mentioned in Note 21, such as historical analyses of Germany's policies before World War I and Japan's policies before World War II, offer substantive evidence in support of these propositions derived from prospect theory.

23 Kennedy, *op. cit.*

5 Preventive war and alternative responses to decline

1 According to the power-transition theory, "the coalition which the hitherto dominant nation has put together cannot be overtaken because the challenger has fewer and weaker friends than the dominant nation, and cannot muster a coalition capable of overcoming the combination of powers ranged against it" (A.F.K. Organski and Jacek Kugler, *The War Ledger* (Chicago, IL: University of Chicago Press, 1980), p. 60).

2 Ibid., p. 62.

3 There is of course a huge literature on the two World Wars. Some leading accounts include V.R. Berghahn, *Germany and the Approach of War in 1914* (London: St. Martin's Press, 1973); Fritz Fischer, *The War of Illusions* (New York: Norton, 1975); Andreas Hillgruber, *Germany and the Two World Wars* (Cambridge, MA: Harvard University Press, 1981); A.J.P. Taylor, *The Origins of the Second World War* (New York: Atheneum, 1961); and Barbara W. Tuchman, *The Guns of August* (New York: Dell, 1962). I have developed some of the ideas in this and previous chapters in Steve Chan, "Exploring Some Puzzles in Power-Transition Theory: Some Implications for Sino-American Relations," *Security Studies* 13 (2004): 103–141.

4 Randall L. Schweller, *Deadly Imbalances: Tripolarity and Hitler's Strategy of World Conquest* (New York: Columbia University Press, 1998), p. 114.

5 He was reportedly furious that British and French appeasement at Munich had forced him to postpone a confrontation with them.

6 On May 10, 1941, Rudolf Hess flew to Scotland, ostensibly on a mission to secure peace with the U.K. and to coordinate a joint Anglo-German attack on the USSR. Whether Hess was delusional or had Hitler's private blessing for his mission has been a matter of historical controversy.

7 Dale C. Copeland, *The Origins of Major War* (Ithaca, NY: Cornell University Press, 2000), and also "Neorealism and the Myth of Bipolar Stability: Toward a New Dynamic Realist Theory of Major War," *Security Studies* 5 (1996): 29–89. For a quantitative investigation, see Douglas Lemke, "Investigating the Preventive Motive for War," *International Interactions* 29 (2003): 273–292. A preventive war is not the same as a pre-emptive war. The latter concept refers to a state taking military action in the face of an imminent assault from an enemy. It is not a very common phenomenon. See Dan Reiter, "Exploding the Powder Keg Myth," *International Security* 20 (1995): 5–34.

8 Ibid. (2000), p. 8.

9 This is the major insight of the power-cycle theory, originally appearing in Charles F. Doran and Wes Parsons, "War and the Cycle of Relative Power," *American Political Science Review* 74 (1980): 947–965. More recent publications pertaining to this theory may be found in Charles F. Doran, *Systems in Crisis: New Imperatives of High Politics at Century's End* (Cambridge: Cambridge University Press, 1991); "System Disequilibrium, Foreign Policy Role, and the Power Cycle: Challenges for Research Design," *Journal of Conflict Resolution* 33 (1989): 371–401; and a special edition of the journal *International Political Science Review* published in January 2003.

10 On the public rationale given by the U.S. administration for waging a preventive war against Iraq, see John J. Mearsheimer and Stephen M. Walt, "An Unnecessary War," *Foreign Policy* (January/February 2003): 50–59.

11 See, for instance, the statements by Theobald von Bethmann-Hollweg, Helmut von Moltke, and Gottlieb von Jagow, quoted in Copeland, *op. cit.*, (2000), pp. 63, 71, and 90.

12 Ibid., p. 80.

13 Robertson quoted in ibid. Esmonde M. Robertson, *Hitler's Pre-war Policy and Military Plans, 1933–1939* (London: Longmans, 1963), p. 54.

14 Copeland, *op. cit.*, (2000), p. 135.

15 Ibid.; and Schweller, *op. cit.*, pp. 137–139.

16 People in general and government leaders in particular are strategic in the sense that they try to anticipate the future and formulate their current policy so that they can promote wanted developments and avoid unwanted ones.

17 Karen A. Rasler and William R. Thompson, *The Great Powers and the Global Struggle, 1490–1990* (Lexington: University of Kentucky Press, 1994), p. 84.

18 The U.S., as noted previously, had already become the leading global power.

19 Thomas J. Christensen and Jack Snyder, "Chain Gangs and Passed Bucks: Predicting Alliance Patterns in Multipolarity," *International Organization* 44 (1990): 137–168.

20 See Barton Whaley, *Codeword Barbarossa* (Cambridge, MA: MIT Press, 1973).

21 Michael A. Barnhart, *Japan Prepares for Total War: The Search for Economic Security, 1919–1945* (Ithaca, NY: Cornell University Press, 1987), p. 267.

22 John J. Mearsheimer, *The Tragedy of Great Power Politics* (New York: Norton, 2001).

23 Of course, the situation would have been even more worrisome for Washington should the two Axis powers join their forces in an anti-U.S. coalition.

24 The Lusitania incident and the Zimmerman telegram contributed to bringing the U.S. into World War I, a conflict that Germany could not hope to win in the long run. Berlin committed the same mistake again by declaring war on the U.S. after Japan attacked Pearl Harbor. In their moments of private candor, the Japanese leaders acknowledged the hopelessness of their cause in the event that the Pacific War dragged on for more than a few years. They were aware that the U.S. was eight or nine times stronger than Japan when they planned to mount the surprise attack on Pearl Harbor. Roberta Wohlstetter, *Pearl Harbor: Warning and Decision* (Stanford, CA: Stanford University Press, 1962).

25 Paul Schroeder, "Historical Reality vs. Neo-realist Theory," *International Security* 19 (1994): 108–138.

26 As already noted, the USSR qualified as a candidate for this role.

27 If anything, other states should bandwagon with a rising challenger against a declining hegemon. For a discussion on the motivation behind this behavior, see Randall L. Schweller, "Bandwagoning for Profit: Bringing the Revisionist State Back In," *International Security* 19 (1994): 72–97.

28 Germany invaded the USSR in 1941 despite the existence of a non-aggression pact between the two countries. It invaded France in 1914, setting off World War I when the initial dispute had involved Austria-Hungary and Serbia. As for Japan, it attacked the U.S. in 1941 because Washington had opposed its bid for regional hegemony in the Asia Pacific. Like Germany, Japan made the error of fighting multiple adversaries that included China and the European colonial powers in Southeast Asia. In the 1920s and

1930s, Japan also initiated several military clashes with the USSR. Moscow, however, did not declare war against Japan until the very last days of World War II.

29 On wars waged by the weak against the strong, see Andrew Mack, "Why Big Nations Lose Small Wars: The Politics of Asymmetric Conflict," *World Politics* 27 (1975): 175–200; and T.V. Paul, *Asymmetric Conflicts: War Initiations by Weaker Powers* (New York: Cambridge University Press, 1994).

30 Copeland offered an important caveat, suggesting that a dominant state would not launch a preventive war if it has available more acceptable ways to preserve its status. Among other things, the officials in question must believe that their country's fundamental resources are suffering sharp and irreversible decline. The fundamental resources pertain to this state's tangible economic and military power, its intangible soft power, and the potential to realize and sustain both these forms of power in the future.

31 Conversely, when a state possesses a temporary advantage but faces a seemingly inevitable long-term economic decline, it would be more tempted to undertake such a venture.

32 These colleagues described this phenomenon as the Phoenix factor. See Organski and Kugler, *op. cit.*, pp. 104–106.

33 The scorched-earth policy undertaken by Rome against Carthage in the Punic War offers an example of making sure that the enemy will never be able to recover from its defeat. The division of Germany following World War II illustrates another attempt to ensure that a former adversary will not re-emerge as a great power. With the reunification of Germany, however, this country has re-emerged as the dominant European power.

34 This part of the discussion draws from Steve Chan and Brock Tessman, "Relative Decline: Why Does It Induce War or Sustain Peace?," manuscript (Boulder: University of Colorado, 2005).

35 See Aaron L. Friedberg, *The Weary Titan: Britain and the Experience of Relative Decline, 1895–1905* (Princeton, NJ: Princeton University Press, 1988); and Stephen R. Rock, *Appeasement in International Politics* (Lexington: University of Kentucky Press, 2000).

36 The term "lateral pressure" has been used to describe this push to look for foreign resources in order to meet rising domestic consumption and demographic growth. See Nazli Choucri and Robert C. North, *Domestic Growth and International Violence* (San Francisco, CA: Freeman, 1975).

37 For discussions of the predicament faced by Gorbachev's USSR, see Stephen G. Brooks and William C. Wohlforth, "Power, Globalization, and the End of the Cold War: Reevaluating a Landmark Case for Ideas," *International Security* 25 (2000/2001): 5–53; Randall L. Schweller and William C. Wohlforth, "Power Test: Evaluating Realism in Response to the End of the Cold War," *Security Studies* 9 (2000): 60–107; William C. Wohlforth, "Realism and the End of the Cold War," *International Security* 19 (1994/1995): 91–129; and Stephen G. Brooks and Willliam C. Wohlforth, "Economic Constraints and the End of the Cold War," in *Cold War Endgame: Oral History, Analysis, Debates*, ed. William C. Wohlforth (University Park: Pennsylvania State University Press, 2003), pp. 273–309.

38 Copeland (*op.cit.*, 2000) showed that the weaker party has sometimes resorted to crisis diplomacy in order to extract concessions from the stronger party. He introduced the concept of power oscillation, referring to short-term shifts in the military balance brought about by armament development or alliance politics. These are occasions when the weaker side may precipitate crises in the hope of stopping a further deterioration of its position.

39 By the way, this coalition also included China. Brooks and Wohlforth (*op. cit.*, 2000/2001, pp. 22–23) reported that Soviet military expenditures were consuming about 40 percent of the budget and 15 to 20 percent of the gross domestic product.

40 Brooks and Wohlforth (*op. cit.*, 2000/2001, p. 29) quoted Mikhail Gorbachev as saying:

> "our goal is to prevent the next round of the arms race. If we do not accomplish it, the threat to us will only grow. We will be pulled into another round of the arms race that is beyond our capabilities, and we will lose it, because we are already at the limit of our capabilities. Moreover, we can expect that Japan and the FRG [West Germany] could very soon join the American potential. . . . If the new round begins, the pressure on our economy will be unbelievable."

41 For a discussion on this alliance dynamic, see Christensen and Snyder, *op. cit.*
42 In contrast to a bipolar situation, a multi-polar situation affords weak or declining states more opportunities to hide or pass bucks.
43 Italy bandwagoned with Germany in World War II, and Germany chained itself to Austria-Hungary in World War I.
44 Kenneth Waltz, *Theory of International Politics* (New York: Random House, 1979); and John Mearsheimer, "Why We Will Soon Miss the Cold War," *The Atlantic* (August 1990): 35–50, and "Back to the Future: Instability in Europe after the Cold War," *International Security* 15 (1990): 5–56.
45 See, for instance, Charles W. Kegley and Gregory A. Raymond, *A Multipolar Peace? Great-power Politics in the Twenty-First Century* (New York: St. Martin's Press, 1994). It seems warranted to consider not only the frequency of wars in bipolar and multi-polar systems, but also the scope, severity, and duration of wars under these two structural conditions. For three earlier studies on this topic, see J. David Singer and Melvin Small, "Alliance Aggregation and the Onset of War, 1815–1945," in *Quantitative International Politics: Insights and Evidence*, ed. J. David Singer (New York: Free Press, 1968), pp. 247–286; Michael Haas, "International Subsystems: Stability and Polarity," *American Political Science Review* 64 (1970): 98–123; and Manus I. Midlarsky, *On War: Political Violence in the International System* (New York: Free Press, 1975).
46 Copeland *op. cit.*, (1996).
47 The public logic given by the U.S. administration for attacking Iraq in 2003 was to prevent Saddam Hussein from acquiring weapons of mass destruction. Had the Iraqis already possessed these weapons, a U.S. invasion would have been much less likely. When asked about what conclusion he would draw from the air campaign waged by the U.S. against the Serbs in 1999, an Indian general reportedly quipped: "Don't fight the U.S. unless you have nuclear weapons."
48 William Burr and Jeffrey T. Richelson, "Whether to 'Strangle the Baby in the Cradle': The United States and the Chinese Nuclear Program, 1960–64," *International Security* 25 (2000/2001): 54–99; Gordon Chang, "JFK, China, and the Bomb," *Journal of American History* 74 (1988): 1289–1310; and Edward Luttwak, *The Grand Strategy of the Soviet Union* (New York: St. Martin's Press, 1983), p. 40.
49 Although not presented explicitly in terms of the preventive motivation, Paul Schroeder gave a cogent presentation of the predicament faced by Germany and especially Austria-Hungary with respect to both the competitive dynamic on the European continent and the race to expand globally. These macro-trends were operating to the disadvantage of these countries prior to 1914, presenting the prospect of their almost inevitable clash with the U.K., France, and Russia. See Paul W. Schroeder, "Embedded Counterfactuals and World War I as an Unavoidable War," in *Systems, Stability, and Statecraft: Essays on the International History of Modern Europe*, ed. Paul W. Schroeder (New York: Palgrave, 2004), pp. 157–191.
50 This argument suggests that an effective missile-defense system would have the reverse effect, because it nullifies a potential adversary's second-strike capability.
51 G. John Ikenberry, ed., *America Unrivaled: The Future of the Balance of Power* (Ithaca, NY: Cornell University Press, 2002).

52 We are of course speaking about transitions between not just the two most powerful states. Should we limit ourselves to the two most powerful states, there had been only one transition involving the U.K. and the U.S. since the Congress of Vienna in 1815.

53 Randall Schweller offers the best-known analysis, arguing that regime characteristics should affect whether a power transition would produce war. See Randall L. Schweller, "Domestic Structure and Preventive War: Are Democracies More Pacific?," *World Politics* 44 (1992): 235–269.

54 Of course, one could argue that U.S. power was the crucial reason for the USSR to eschew preventive war against Germany, Japan, and China. However, U.S. power was obviously insufficient for deterring Germany from resorting to preventive war in 1914 and again in 1939. Nor was it sufficient to deter Japan from attacking China, the European colonies in Southeast Asia, and even the U.S. itself in World War II.

55 As just implied in the discussion, the U.S. was never in any danger of being overtaken by Iraq.

6 Appeasement and the distribution of benefits

1 Douglas Lemke and William Reed, "Power Is Not Satisfaction: A Comment on de Soysa, Oneal, and Park," *Journal of Conflict Resolution* 42 (1998): 511–516.

2 In his original discussion of the power-transition theory, Kenneth Organski pointed out that the dominant nation "always benefits disproportionately" from the existing international order at the expense of the weaker states, and that "the dominant nation and its supporters are not usually willing to grant the newcomers more than a small part of the advantages they receive" (A.F.K. Organski, *World Politics* (New York: Knopf, 1958), pp. 327–328). More recently, Randall Schweller expressed the same view, indicating that "after all, states that find the status quo most agreeable are usually the ones that created the existing order; as the principal beneficiaries of the status quo, they more than anyone else have a vested interest in preserving it" (Randall L. Schweller, *Deadly Imbalances: Tripolarity and Hitler's Strategy of World Conquest* (New York: Columbia University Press, 1998), p. 84). This chapter takes up many points presented originally for Steve Chan, "Exploring Some Puzzles in Power-Transition Theory: Some Implications for Sino-American Relations," *Security Studies* 13 (2004): 103–141.

3 For examples of the status-discrepancy theory, see Maurice A. East, "Status Discrepancy and Violence in the International System: An Empirical Analysis," in *The Analysis of International Politics*, ed. James N. Rosenau, Vincent Davis, and Maurice A. East (New York: Free Press, 1972), pp. 299–319; Johan Galtung, "A Structural Theory of Aggression," *Journal of Peace Research* 1 (1964): 95–119; and Michael D. Wallace, *War and Rank Among Nations* (Lexington, KY: Heath, 1973).

4 Robert Gilpin, *War and Change in World Politics* (New York: Cambridge University Press, 1981), p. 31.

5 Ibid., pp. 13–15.

6 Naturally, I am not taking for granted that these assumptions are met in the real world. In fact, by positing these conditions under which war may be averted, one is calling attention to the fact that they are often implausible in the real world and thereby pointing to the reasons why wars can happen even though they are an inefficient way to settle international disputes. A recent study argued that hegemons do not distribute private goods to their allies as one would expect from the power-transition theory. See Margit Bussman and John R. Oneal, "Do Hegemons Distribute Private Goods? A Test of Power-Transition Theory," *Journal of Conflict Resolution* 51 (2007): 88–111.

7 This argument accords with Organski's original discussion of the power-transition theory. Organski saw the prevailing international order as a source of privileges for the powerful, and had warned that a peace enforced by the powerful should not be confused with "a peace with justice" (*op. cit.*, pp. 328, 332). Gilpin agreed with this view, stating

that "in international society the distribution of power among coalitions [of states] determines who governs the international system and whose interests are principally promoted by the functioning of the system," and that the "dominant states have sought to exert control over the system in order to advance their self-interests" (*op. cit.*, p. 29).

8 Note that this statement does not contradict the proposition that an already dominant state may seek to further advance its interests. The key here is whether the dominant state's power share would entitle it to an even larger share of the benefits. That, as the dominant power, this state is already receiving more benefits from the international system than the other less powerful states does not deny the possibility that its power advantage can encourage and enable it to claim even more benefits. Therefore, the emphasis of my formulation is on the extent of surplus or deficit that characterizes the discrepancy between a state's relative power and its relative benefits.

9 Robert Powell, *In the Shadow of Power: States and Strategies in International Politics* (Princeton, NJ: Princeton University Press, 1999), p. 199.

10 A.F.K. Organski and Jacek Kugler, *The War Ledger* (Chicago, IL: University of Chicago Press, 1980), p. 23.

11 This line of reasoning conforms to the earlier discussion on prospect theory, which suggests that people tend to be risk averse when they are in the domain of gains.

12 Powell, *op. cit.* See also Robert Powell, "Uncertainty, Shifting Power, and Appeasement," *American Political Science Review* 90 (1996): 749–764.

13 When a latecomer's growth slows or even reverses, it finds itself in a domain of losses. This discovery in turn brings about its greater willingness to accept risks as suggested by prospect theory. Concomitantly, the power-cycle theory postulates that the turning points at which a country's power decelerates or peaks are likely to induce stressful situations (brought about by anxiety, panic, and disappointment) that can trigger war. Accordingly, the propositions advanced here converge with observations made by researchers employing both rationalist and non-rationalist approaches.

14 Organski and Kugler, *op. cit.*, pp. 21, 54, 62.

15 For an informative historical account contrasting the approaches adopted by two imperial powers in decline, namely Spain and Britain, see Daniel Treisman, "Rational Appeasement," *International Organization* 58 (2004): 344–373. On different interpretations of the end of the Cold War (including the role played by Soviet concessions), see William C. Wohlforth, ed., *Cold War Endgame: Oral History, Analysis, Debates* (University Park: Pennsylvania State University Press, 2003); and Richard Ned Lebow and Thomas Risse-Kappen, eds, *International Relations Theory and the End of the Cold War* (New York: Columbia University Press, 1995). Finally, for a comparative analysis of appeasement policies (including British accommodation of a rising U.S.), see Stephen R. Rock, *Appeasement in International Politics* (Lexington: University of Kentucky Press, 2000).

16 During 1934 to 1937, the British government under Neville Chamberlain faced a resurgent Germany and an expansionist Italy in the domestic context of fiscal stringency and policy disarray. It sought coordination and accommodation abroad in order to buy time for Britain to ramp up its defense. See Gaines Post, Jr., *Dilemmas of Appeasement: British Deterrence and Defense, 1934–1937* (Ithaca, NY: Cornell University Press, 1993).

17 Mercer's book, however, shows that concessions to an adversary seldom cause the conceding state to be perceived as irresolute. Instead of being seen to have a weak resolve, these concessions tend to be taken as a sign that this state has a weak capability. See Jonathan Mercer, *Reputation and International Politics* (Ithaca, NY: Cornell University Press, 1996).

18 "Britain's global adversaries did not infer lack of resolve from its acquiescence to U.S. demands" (Treisman, *op. cit.*, p. 364).

19 Roberta Wohlstetter, *Pearl Harbor: Warning and Decision* (Stanford, CA: Stanford University Press, 1962). See also Bruce M. Russett, "Refining Deterrence Theory: The Japanese Attack on Pearl Harbor," in *Theory and Research on the Causes of War*,

ed. Dean G. Pruitt and Richard C. Snyder (Englewood Cliffs, NJ: Prentice-Hall, 1969), pp. 127–135; Iriye Akira, *Power and Culture: The Japanese–American War, 1941–1945* (Cambridge, MA: Harvard University Press, 1981); and Michael A. Barnhart, *Japan Prepares for Total War: The Search for Economic Security, 1919–1941* (Ithaca, NY: Cornell University Press, 1987).

20 Treisman, *op. cit.*

21 Bruce Bueno de Mesquita offered an example of grappling with this problem. In his study of the Austro-Prussian War in 1866, he used currency exchange rates as an indicator of relative national benefits being accorded by the international system. His rationale was that countries with discounted currencies would be less able to afford imported goods, and vice versa. As Jacek Kugler and Douglas Lemke pointed out, however, this reasoning presumes that a state is more interested in purchasing imports than promoting exports. See Bruce Bueno de Mesquita, "Pride of Place: The Origins of German Hegemony," *World Politics* 43 (1990): 1–27; and Jacek Kugler and Douglas Lemke, "The Power Transition Research Program," in *Handbook of War Studies II*, ed. Manus I. Midlarsky (Ann Arbor: University of Michigan Press, 2000), pp. 129–163.

22 In its May 9, 2005 issue (p. 36), *Newsweek* reported that 24,000 American students between grades 7 and 12 took Chinese as a foreign language, compared to one million who were learning French.

23 Bruce M. Russett, "The Mysterious Case of Vanishing Hegemony: Or, Is Mark Twain Really Dead?," *International Organization* 39 (1985): 207–232.

24 This privilege refers to the medieval monarchs' resort to debasing coins, a private benefit, which they derived from the performance of a public good (the issuance of coins to facilitate commerce). The U.S. has been accused of using its financial power to export its domestic inflation. Campbell Craig made the point that American dominance in the global capitalist system enabled the U.S. to practice exuberant consumption without the kind of fiscal restraint that would apply to other "ordinary" countries. This observation underscores again the connection between national power and national benefits. See Campbell Craig, "American Realism Versus American Imperialism," *World Politics* 57 (2004): 166–167.

25 Americans' heavy, even seemingly unbridled, consumption of foreign oil was emphasized by Campbell Craig, in an essay otherwise addressing other larger points, as an evident example of "the material exploitation of U.S. global preponderance by American society" (ibid., p. 165). For a more extensive discussion of the strategic importance of oil for national wealth and security, see Daniel Yergin, *The Prize: The Epic Quest for Oil, Money, and Power* (New York: Touchstone, 1991). That the level of a state's energy consumption may be considered as an indicator of its international benefit has recently gained additional credibility in view of increasing American concerns about how rising Chinese energy demand can have costly consequences for the U.S. economy. James R. Barber offered a parallel analysis on the world's uneven and unfair pattern of energy consumption based on what he called "Justice-of-Energy Distribution Index." See his *Jihad vs. McWorld: How Globalism and Tribalism Are Reshaping the World* (New York: Random House, 1995).

26 Significantly, direct sales made by foreign-owned companies in the host country's domestic market are not reflected in standard trade accounts. Similarly, the location of production rather than the nationality of a company's owners tends to be the focus of attention. There is therefore a tendency to overlook the investments made by national companies to manufacture goods abroad for the purpose of re-exporting them back to the home market. Thus, as Joseph Nye (*op. cit.*, 2002, pp. 55–56) remarked

imports and exports provide a very incomplete picture of global economic linkages. For example, overseas production by American transnational corporations was more than twice the value of American exports; sales by foreign-owned companies inside the United States were nearly twice the value of imports.

27 Brian M. Pollins, "Does Trade Follow the Flag? A Model of International Diplomacy and Commerce," *American Political Science Review* 83 (1989): 465–480.

28 The U.S. Congress voted 398 to 15 to oppose a bid by CNOOC (China National Offshore Oil Corporation) to buy UNOCAL, the ninth largest U.S. energy company, for $18.5 billion in June 2005. In face of the strong opposition it encountered in U.S. domestic politics, CNOOC eventually decided to withdraw its bid. This anecdote highlights the strategic motivation for securing energy supply and the commercial incentives for making foreign direct investment. Nelson D. Schwartz, "Why China Scares Big Oil?," *Fortune* (July 25, 2005): 89–94; and David Zweig and Bi Jianhai, "China's Global Hunt for Energy," *Foreign Affairs* 84 (2005): 25–38.

29 Which of the different calculations presents the most accurate view of reality? The figures used are of course estimates and the computations seek to bracket the range of uncertainty. As already mentioned with respect to the multiple indicators used in chapters 2 and 3, each individual measure has shortcomings. I seek, however, convergent validation by examining an ensemble of measures so that one can be reasonably confident about one's empirical observations.

30 It has been estimated that China was consuming 6.9 million barrels of oil per day compared to 20.9 million barrels for the U.S. in August 2005. These figures put the U.S. level at about three times higher than the Chinese level. "Rising Oil Prices Will Impact Taiwan Economy: Economist," August 31, 2005 at http://english.ww.gov.tw/.

31 That is, it can both invest in foreign countries and receive foreign investment from other countries. It can also disinvest its operations abroad.

32 Naturally, this generic characterization is subject to modification. For instance, foreign investments in extractive resources and cash crops have less industrial spin-off benefits for the host country than foreign investments in manufacturing operations. Countries with a large domestic market, such as China, command more bargaining power in negotiating with multinational corporations than others without the benefit of a large population. The proficiency of the host government's civil service is another factor. Bureaucratic incompetence allows the multinational corporations to keep and repatriate more profits. For a thoughtful discussion on these considerations, see Theodore H. Moran, "Multinational Corporations and Dependency: A Dialogue for Dependentistas and Non-Dependentista," *International Organization* 32 (1978): 79–100.

33 Gary C. Hufbauer and Yee Wong, "China Bashing 2004," *International Economics Policy Briefs*, No. PB04-5 (September 2004): 2–3; available at http://www.iie.com/publications/pb/pb04-5.pdf.

34 Significantly, two developed countries, Germany and Italy, also turned out to be major net importers of investment capital.

35 An example of such reform would be the introduction of changes to the provision of permanent membership of the U.N. Security Council.

36 Organski and Kugler argued that gross national product offers the most appropriate indicator of national power (*op. cit.*, pp. 38, 108).

37 This observation does not deny that during the 1980s, Japan was the focus of American commercial antagonism and was widely seen as an economic challenger to the U.S.

38 Charles A. Kupchan, "Benign States and Peaceful Transition," in *Power in Transition: The Peaceful Change of International Order*, ed. Charles A. Kupchan, Emanuel Adler, Jean-Marc Coicaud, and Yuen Foong Khong (Tokyo: United Nations University Press, 2001), pp. 18–33.

39 Just because some of the victims of these programs of aggrandizement were not powerful enough to mount effective resistance does not of course mean that the sponsors and operators of these programs were not aggressive. Plainly, Germany's aggrandizement

met more effective resistance than the U.S. pursuit of its "manifest destiny" in their respective neighborhoods.

40 The Monroe Doctrine was a unilateral declaration used by Washington to justify its right to intervene in *any* controversy in the Western Hemisphere involving a non-resident power. In this context, it is perhaps instructive to quote from a recent comment by Benjamin Schwarz which offers a possible perspective from Beijing: American

> [h]ardliners and moderates, Republicans and Democrats, agree that America is strategically dominant in East Asia and the eastern Pacific – China's backyard. They further agree that America should retain its dominance there. Thus U.S. military planners define as a threat Beijing's efforts to remedy its own weak position in the face of overwhelming superiority that they acknowledge the United States holds right up to the edge of the Asian mainland. This probably reveals more about our ambitions than it does about China's. Imagine if the situation is reversed, and China's air and naval power were a dominant and potentially menacing presence on the coastal shelf of North America. Wouldn't we want to offset that preponderance?
> (Benjamin Schwarz, "Comment: Managing China's Rise," *Atlantic Monthly* (June 2005): 27)

7 Conundra of containment and engagement

1 See David Shambaugh, "Containment or Engagement of China? Calculating Beijing's Responses," *International Security* 21 (1996): 180–209. Shambaugh questions the applicability of standard liberal or realist paradigms to contemporary Asian reality, especially the theory of offensive realism advocating pre-emptive containment of China in "China Engages Asia: Reshaping the Regional Order," *International Security* 29 (2004/2005): 64–99. On offensive realism, see John J. Mearsheimer, *The Tragedy of Great Power Politics* (New York: Norton, 2001). For a recent discussion on a mixed strategy of engagement and containment, see Thomas J. Christensen, "Fostering Stability or Creating a Monster?," *International Security* 31 (2006): 81–126.

2 This view is shared by those who subscribe to John Mearsheimer's theory of offensive realism, which treats all states as expansionist (except for a regional hegemon such as the U.S.). However, the proposition that states are accordingly always motivated to balance against their counterparts' power is not shared by other realists. For instance, Stephen Walt argued that states tend to balance against the source of the greatest threat to them rather than necessarily the holder of the greatest amount of power. Similarly, David Edelstein showed that historically, officials have not always assumed the worst about a rising power, especially when they expect that this state's intentions are malleable and when there are domestic and international pressures to cooperate with this state. He concluded, however, that it is generally difficult to alter other countries' intentions, and therefore officials who had not assumed the worst about their counterparts would have been better off if they did. David M. Edelstein, "Managing Uncertainty: Beliefs about Intentions and the Rise of Great Powers," *Security Studies* 12 (2002): 1–40; and Stephen M. Walt, *The Origins of Alliances* (Ithaca, NY: Cornell University Press, 1987).

3 According to Organski and Kugler, "losers begin and maintain a steadily accelerating recovery rate after the war, and overtake the winners in the eighteenth year of the postwar period. At the conclusion of that period, differences in power distribution among all groups have been eradicated: their levels of power return to points one would have anticipated had no war occurred." They also remarked: "in the long run (from fifteen to twenty years), the effects of war are dissipated, because losers accelerate their recovery and resume antebellum rates. They may even overtake winners. Soon, the power distribution in the system returns to levels anticipated had

wars not occurred" (A.F.K. Organski and Jacek Kugler, *The War Ledger* (Chicago, IL: University of Chicago Press, 1980), pp. 133, 145).

4 The insurgency movement challenging the U.S. occupation of Iraq is illustrative. Whether or not one can succeed in attempts at converting a defeated country into a democracy is another matter. It is not likely, however, that one can replicate in Iraq the post-1945 experience of occupied Germany and Japan.

5 Karen A. Rasler and Williams R. Thompson, *War and State Making: The Shaping of Global Powers* (Boston, MA: Unwin Hyman, 1989), p. 173.

6 Organski and Kugler argued that national power trajectories cannot be influenced in the long run by war or other kinds of external intervention, stating that their "model insists that attempts to arrest the gains of the faster-growing nation will fail. Whatever the fortunes of war, the challenger will probably 'win' sooner or later" (Organski and Kugler, *op. cit.*, p. 28).

7 Ibid., p. 24. In the same vein, they remarked: "the origins of the independent variables in evidence in international relations are *not* found in international relations but in the growth of the units that constitute the system" (Ibid., p. 146).

8 Ibid.

9 George Modelski and William R. Thompson, *Leading Sectors and World Powers: The Coevolution of Global Politics and Economics* (Columbia: University of South Carolina Press, 1996).

10 Dale Copeland "Economic Interdependence and War: A Theory of Trade Expectations," *International Security* 20 (1996): 4–41.

11 Michael A. Barnhart, *Japan Prepares for Total War: The Search for Economic Security, 1919–1941* (Ithaca, NY: Cornell University Press, 1987), p. 265.

12 Edward D. Mansfield and Jack Snyder, *Electing to Fight: Why Emerging Democracies Go to War* (Cambridge, MA: MIT Press, 2005), p. 268.

13 Gary C. Hufbauer, Jeffrey Schott, and Kimberly A. Elliott, *Economic Sanctions Reconsidered: History and Current Policy* (2nd edn) (Washington, D.C.: Institute of International Economics, 1990), p. 106.

14 Robert A. Pape, "Why Economic Sanctions Do Not Work," *International Security* 22 (1997): 90–136. For exchanges on the effectiveness of sanctions, see also Kimberly A. Elliott, "The Sanctions Glass: Half Full or Completely Empty?," *International Security* 23 (1998): 50–65; Robert A. Pape, "Why Economic Sanctions Still Do Not Work," *International Security* 23 (1998): 66–77; and the correspondence between David A. Baldwin and Robert A. Pape on "Evaluating Economic Sanctions," *International Security* 23 (1998): 189–198.

15 Pape, *op. cit.* (1997), p. 109.

16 The large trade deficit (reaching almost $202 billion in 2005) which the U.S. has incurred with China may incline Americans to see a source of bargaining leverage. The size of this deficit, however, tends to be inflated because it refers to the gross amount of China's trade surplus with the U.S. rather than the net amount calculated on the basis of China's portion of the value-added of these exports to the U.S. Ostensibly Chinese goods sold to the U.S. are often "Chinese" only to the extent that China was the final assembler of materials that it had imported from third countries. Foreign multinational companies located inside China supply about half of its global exports. Oded Shenkar, *The Chinese Century: The Rising Chinese Economy and Its Impact on the Global Economy, the Balance of Power and Your Job* (Philadelphia, PA: Wharton School Publishing, 2005), p. 12. Punitive action taken against China's exports would therefore largely have the effect of relocating the points of final assembly from China to other countries offering low-cost assembly. This point was underscored in Gary C. Hufbauer and Yee Wong, "China Bashing 2004," *International Economics Policy Briefs*, No. PB04-5 (September 2004): 3; available at http://www.iie.com/publica-tions/pb/pb04-5.pdf. These same authors also pointed out that the actual size of China's trade surplus with the U.S. is subject to debate, because the U.S. Department of Commerce includes Hong Kong's entrepôt trade and makes its calculations based

on free-alongside-ship (FAS) figures. If adjustments are made for re-exports and freight-on-board (FOB) figures are used, China's trade surplus with the U.S. in 2003 would be 26 percent lower than the U.S. estimate (ibid.).

17 See Lisa L. Martin, *Coercive Cooperation: Explaining Multilateral Economic Sanctions* (Princeton, NJ: Princeton University Press, 1992), and "Credibility, Costs, and Institutions: Cooperation on Economic Sanctions," *World Politic* 45 (1993): 406–432. Naturally, an attempt to coordinate a multilateral effort to sanction a target state also signals that the leading sender state is serious about this project rather than undertaking it for purposes of domestic partisan gain or public relations. The willingness of this leading sender state to incur the transaction costs in organizing this coalition and to engage its reputation in this joint enterprise also serves the important purpose of signaling its commitment to the declared course of action to the target state and to the other sanctioning states. For further discussion on this topic, see Daniel W. Drezner, "Bargaining, Enforcement, and Multilateral Sanctions: When Is Cooperation Counterproductive?," *International Organization* 54 (2000): 73–102.

18 Mancur Olson, *The Logic of Collective Action: Public Goods and the Theory of Groups* (Cambridge, MA: Harvard University Press, 1965).

19 The attempt by the Arab members of the Organization of Petroleum-Exporting Countries to influence U.S. and Dutch foreign policy toward Israel is well publicized. Less known has been the U.S. effort to use grain as a weapon to influence Soviet policy. For a classic statement on economic coercion, see David A. Baldwin, *Economic Statecraft* (Princeton, NJ: Princeton University Press, 1985). A collection of more recent studies on economic sanctions may be found in Steve Chan and A. Cooper Drury, eds, *Sanctions as Economic Statecraft: Theory and Practice* (London: Macmillan, 2000).

20 Michael Mastanduno, *Economic Containment: CoCom and the Politics of East–West Trade* (Ithaca, NY: Cornell University Press, 1992).

21 Import-competing industries, for example, would support trade restrictions, whereas export-oriented industries would be opposed to these restrictions. Similarly, American capital – which stands to profit more from foreign commerce and investment – is likely to be more disposed to oppose sanctioning China than American labor. See Steve Chan, "The Politics of Economic Exchange: Carrots and Sticks in Taiwan–China–U.S. Relations," *Issues & Studies* 42 (2006): 1–22.

22 The U.S. had threatened to curb its export of weapons technology to Europe and even to raise questions about its more general military cooperation with the latter if the European Union lifted its arms embargo against China. Similarly, Israel had also come under intense U.S. pressure on several occasions to cancel its arms contracts with China. Parenthetically, should the E.U. lift its arms embargo against China in the future, this decision will signal an important shift toward its soft balancing against U.S. power, a topic to be addressed in the next chapter.

23 Robert Putnam, "Diplomacy and Domestic Politics: The Logic of Two-Level Games," *International Organization* 42 (1988): 427–460.

24 Large U.S. retailers, for instance, have a vested interest in the import of labor-intensive Chinese imports. Similarly, U.S. companies seeking to expand their presence in the Chinese market – such as those selling heavy construction equipment, agricultural products, civilian aircraft, and financial services – would be averse to a proposed trade or investment boycott. Whether a Republican administration would be more attentive to these interests than, say, to the pleas of textile and steel workers whose jobs are threatened by low-cost Chinese imports offers an example highlighted by the perspective of two-level games alluded to above.

25 Jack. S. Levy has called attention to the scope conditions of traditional balance-of-power formulations that were derived from the European context and focused on the great powers in that region with large land forces. His discussion therefore suggests that there is a mismatch between these scope conditions inherited from European history and current Asian circumstances. For an argument that Chinese continental power and U.S. maritime power can co-exist, see Robert S. Ross,

"The Geography of the Peace: East Asia in the Twenty-first Century," *International Security* 23 (1999): 81–118; and "Bipolarity and Balancing in East Asia," in *Balance of Power: Theory and Practice in the 21st Century*, ed. T.V. Paul, James J. Wirtz, and Michel Fortmann (Stanford, CA: Stanford University Press, 2004), pp. 267–304. Levy's chapter, "What Do Great Powers Balance Against and When?," can also be found in the latter volume, pp. 29–51.

26 Randall L. Schweller, "Bandwagoning for Profit: Bringing the Revisionist State Back In," *International Security* 19 (1994): 72–97.

27 Paul W. Schroeder, "Historical Reality versus Neo-realist Theory," *International Security* 19 (1994): 108–138. See also Paul W. Schroeder, *The Transformation of European Politics, 1763–1848* (Oxford: Clarendon Press, 1994); and also Randall L. Schweller, *Deadly Imbalances: Tripolarity and Hitler's Strategy of World Conquest* (New York: Columbia University Press, 1998).

28 One of the more puzzling questions for traditional realists is the apparent absence of second-tier states to balance against U.S. preponderance after the end of the Cold War. See G. John Ikenberry, ed., *America Unrivaled: The Future of the Balance of Power* (Ithaca, NY: Cornell University Press, 2002).

29 See the excellent discussion of British diplomacy on the eve of World War I in Timothy W. Crawford, *Pivotal Deterrence: Third-Party Statecraft and the Pursuit of Peace* (Ithaca, NY: Cornell University Press, 2003), especially pp. 78 and 93.

30 David C. Kang, "Getting Asia Wrong: The Need for New Analytical Frameworks," *International Security* 27 (2003): 57–85; and "Why China's Rise Will be Peaceful: Hierarchy and Stability in the East Asian Region," *Perspectives on Politics* 3 (2005): 551–554. See also Zhiqun Zhu, "Power Transition and U.S.–China Relations: Is War Inevitable?," *Journal of International and Area Studies* 12 (2005): 1–24. Zhu argued that a peaceful power transition between the U.S. and China is possible.

31 Kang, *op. cit.* (2005): p. 552.

32 Robert Powell introduced a second variable that would incline a rising power's neighbors to rally against it. The repeated aggressions by this rising power must raise the specter that these campaigns would bring about correspondingly large political, military, and psychological gains. Such gains can exacerbate the security concerns of the other states and thus cause them to engage in containment policies. See Robert Powell, *In the Shadow of Power: States and Strategies in International Politics* (Princeton, NJ: Princeton University Press, 1999).

33 Moscow's absorption of Lithuania, Latvia, and Estonia, and the installation of communist regimes in East and Central European states under Red Army occupation, had this effect on the formation of the North Atlantic Treaty Organization. Moreover, prior to being attacked by Nazi Germany, the USSR had itself invaded Poland and Finland. These episodes had a bearing on the decisions by the West Europeans to join the U.S. in an effort to contain Moscow. They were also pertinent to the acute concerns about Moscow's large returns to scale following the defeat of the Nazis, the other factor encouraging balancing behavior in Powell's view. Finally, problems pertaining to the organization of collective action are more likely to be overcome when the largest contributor is willing and able to assume a disproportionate burden of the relevant costs, as was the case with the U.S.'s role in the formation of the North Atlantic Treaty Organization. For a classic analysis on the uneven distribution of alliance burden, see Mancur Olson and Richard Zeckhauser, "An Economic Theory of Alliances," *Review of Economics and Statistics* 48 (1966): 266–279.

34 Kang, *op. cit.* (2003), pp. 82–83. In a similar vein, Australian Foreign Minister Alexander Downer reportedly said: "Washington should not automatically assume that Australia would help it defend Taiwan against a Chinese military attack" (David Zweig and Bi Jianhai, "China's Global Hunt for Energy," *Foreign Affairs* 84 (2005): 30).

35 David Shambaugh, "China Engages Asia: Reshaping the Regional Order," *International Security* 29 (2004/2005): 99. In a subsequent editorial correspondence,

Shambaugh emphasized accommodation rather than bandwagoning on the part of China's neighbors. See the exchange between Nicholas Khoo and Michael L.R. Smith, "China Engages Asia? Caveat Lector," and David Shambaugh, "The Author Replies," *International Security* 30 (2005): 196–205; and 205–213.

36 On the need to consider alternative explanations for behavior that is often taken to be "soft balancing," see Stephen G. Brooks and William C. Wohlforth, "Hard Times for Soft Balancing," *International Security* 30 (2005): 72–108. On the absence of balancing against the U.S., see Keir A. Lieber and Gerard Alexander, "Waiting for Balancing: Why the World Is Not Pushing Back," *International Security* 30 (2005): 109–139.

37 Interestingly, M. Taylor Fravel argued that potential domestic challenges from ethnic minorities have disposed Beijing to make substantial concessions in settling its territorial disputes with neighbors. Whether the same tendency may apply to China's neighbors in Southeast Asia, or may have the reverse effect, is an empirical question that deserves analysis. See M. Taylor Fravel, "Regime Insecurity and International Cooperation: Explaining China's Compromises in Territorial Disputes," *International Security* 30 (2005): 46–83.

38 There was of course a time when Western missionaries flocked to China to proselytize its people. What are the appropriate norms for a state to follow is a question that turns us back to the discussion on revisionist conduct and orientation. As discussed in Chapter 3, it is not clear that objective indicators of foreign policy conduct and orientation would necessarily place China more outside the international community than the U.S.

39 Antonio Gramsci, *Selection from the Prison Notebooks of Antonio Gramsci*, ed. and trans. Quintin Hoare and Geoffrey Nowell Smith (London: International Publishers, 1971); and Stephen Gill, ed., *Gramsci, Historical Materialism, and International Relations* (Cambridge: Cambridge University Press, 1993).

40 One can agree with these values and still recognize and acknowledge forthrightly that the global spread of these values is what a policy of engagement has as one of its primary goals. "McWorld" refers to Macintosh, MTV, and McDonald's. See James R. Barber, *Jihad vs. McWorld: How Globalism and Tribalism Are Reshaping the World* (New York: Random House: 1995).

41 On soft power, see Joseph S. Nye, *Bound to Lead: The Changing Nature of American Power* (New York: Basic Books, 1990). Described sometimes as "coca-colonization," the adoption of imported ideas and loss of indigenous tradition are not taken up as a serious topic for debate among those who propose engagement as a path to conversion. A particularly graphic example from consumer behavior is the introduction of formula milk to replace breast-feeding among the poor in the developing countries, a development that tends to cause more harm than good for mothers and their babies. Benjamin R. Barber referred to the so-called McWorld with its intense promotion of what he described as American monocultural hegemonism with an emphasis on a lifestyle of consumerism. Barber's discussion made clear that the U.S. has a huge dominance in the "infortainment telesector," and he expected the forces of McWorld to eventually prevail over nationalistic and nativist "Jihad." Elsewhere, Barber warned against "confusing democratization with economic liberalization," which is tantamount to confounding the spread of liberty with the contagion of McWorld. He admonished that "today America is not in the business of exporting free market democracy, it is in the business of freeing up markets and globalizing corporate capital and calling it democracy." See his *Fear's Empire: War, Terrorism, and Democracy* (New York: Norton, 2003), pp. 156, 158.

42 Quoted in Barber, *op. cit.* (1995), p. 82.

43 Karl W. Deutsch, Sidney A. Burrell, Robert A. Kann, Maurice Lee, Jr., Martin Lichtenman, Raymond E. Lindgren, Francis L. Loewenheim, and Richard W. Van Wagenen, *Political Community and the North Atlantic Area: International Organization in the Light of Historical Experience* (New York: Greenwood Press, 1957).

44 Following the work on security community by Karl Deutsch and his colleagues, these ideas received further amplification in Robert O. Keohane and Joseph S. Nye, *Power and Interdependence: World Politics in Transition* (Boston, MA: Little, Brown, 1977); and Bruce M. Russett and John R. Oneal, *Triangulating Peace: Democracy, Interdependence, and International Organizations* (New York: Norton, 2001).

45 Beijing launched missiles in Taiwan's vicinity in 1996 in an effort to influence the latter's presidential election. The last war it fought was against Vietnam in 1979. A list of incidents involving the use of armed force by the other permanent members of the U.N. Security Council over the past quarter century or so would include Afghanistan, Bosnia, the Falklands, Grenada, Haiti, Iran, Iraq, Kosovo, Kuwait, Lebanon, Libya, Nicaragua, Panama, and Somalia.

46 Steve Chan, "Discerning the Causal Relationships between Great Powers' IGO Membership and Their Initiation of Militarized Disputes," *Conflict Management and Peace Science* 22 (2005): 239–256.

47 Parenthetically, if these international standards include mass acceptance of secular liberal values, American attitudes tend to be the exception rather than the norm among the advanced industrialized democracies, and popular support for and confidence in democratic institutions have suffered a sharper decline in the United States in recent decades than in its cohorts. Moreover, the response patterns given by the World Values Survey show that the Chinese are no less supportive of or receptive to democratic values than the Americans. See, for example, Russell J. Dalton, "Political Support in Advanced Industrial Democracies," in *Critical Citizens: Global Support for Democratic Government*, ed. Pippa Norris (Oxford: Oxford University Press, 1999), pp. 57–77; Ronald Inglehart, Miguel Basanez, Jaime Diez-Medrano, Loek Halman, and Ruud Luijkx, eds, *Human Beliefs and Values: A Cross-cultural Sourcebook based on the 1999–2002 Values Surveys* (Mexico City: Siglo Veintiuno Editories, 2004); Ronald Inglehart and Wayne E. Baker, "Modernization, Cultural Change, and the Persistence of Traditional Values," *American Sociological Review* 65 (2000): 19–51; and Seymour Martin Lipset, *American Exceptionalism: A Double-Edged Sword* (New York: Norton, 1996).

48 See William J. Long, *Economic Incentives and Bilateral Cooperation* (Ann Arbor: University of Michigan Press, 1996).

49 Russett and Oneal, *op. cit.* But see also Katherine Barbieri, *The Liberal Illusion: Does Trade Promote Peace?* (Ann Arbor: University of Michigan Press, 2002).

50 This is so that they would not thereby create a dependency relationship with or confer a commercial advantage on a potential adversary. This motivation therefore causes a selection effect, with friendly states being more inclined to trade with each other and potential adversaries eschewing commercial relations lest these ties are exploited as a "hostage" in possible attempts at economic coercion.

51 Parenthetically, although the U.S. looms large for China's exports, the latter has diversified its commercial relations so that the rest of the world, especially China's Asian neighbors, has recently become more important in its external trade and vice versa. That is, the Asian countries are trading more with each other. They have thus become less dependent on the U.S. market.

52 R. Harrison Wagner offers a very informative discussion on this and other points. See his "Economic Interdependence, Bargaining Power, and Political Influence," *International Organization* 42 (1988): 461–463.

53 Albert O. Hirschman, *National Power and the Structure of Foreign Trade* (Berkeley: University of California Press, 1945).

54 This observation suggests in turn that sanctions are a two-way street. What would be the implications for the U.S. capital market if the Chinese were to boycott the purchase of U.S. debt instruments? In mid-2005, China was estimated to hold about $244 billion in U.S. Treasury securities. As shown in the episodes of the grain and oil embargoes, the international financial market is sufficiently efficient to overcome the threatened

disruptions and disturbances. In line with the earlier remarks about replacement cost and alternative sources of supply and demand, a pertinent question to ask about any implied Chinese threat to withdraw from the U.S. debt market is: What does Beijing plan to do with its cash? Investment in domestic consumption or in alternative foreign securities inevitably changes the cost and supply of money, thereby encouraging and enabling other capital owners to buy and hold U.S. debt instruments. Moreover, even the prospect that Beijing is considering a withdrawal from the U.S. debt market would cause a sharp financial loss for its existing holdings, thus reminding one that (just as in the case of U.S. threats to bar the import of Chinese goods) sanctions and boycotts can be painful to the sender state as well as the target state.

55 As in other kinds of international communication, states may bluff about their intention to impose sanctions or make such declarations for the sake of domestic (often partisan) consumption. One clue about the seriousness of a state's threat to impose trade sanctions is whether it is willing to deny its own exports to the target state (as opposed to barring its imports of goods from the target state). The former course of action, such as when applied to Rhodesia and South Africa, would be more effective against the target state but also more costly to the sender state. The sender state's willingness to bear the heavy costs of self-denial communicates the seriousness of its intent. That the U.S. administration under Ronald Reagan wanted its European allies to boycott the sale of equipment for an oil pipeline to the USSR while lifting the embargo against the sale of American wheat to Moscow diminished the credibility of its sanction threat. If the White House was unwilling to withstand political pressure from American farmers, how likely was it to jeopardize the much more important alliance relationship with Europe?

56 Erik Gartzke, Quan Li, and Charles Boehmer, "Investing in the Peace: Economic Interdependence and International Conflict," *International Organization* 55 (2001): 391–438.

57 Immanuel Kant, *Perpetual Peace*, trans. Lewis White Beck (New York: Bobbs-Merrill, 1957).

58 On the topic of self-enforcing agreements, see Beth V. Yarbrough and Robert M. Yarbrough, *Cooperation and Governance in International Trade* (Princeton, NJ: Princeton University Press, 1992), and these authors' article, "Reciprocity, Bilateralism, and Economic 'Hostage': Self-Enforcing Agreements in International Trade," *International Studies Quarterly* 30 (1986): 7–21. For a classic analysis on how cooperation can develop despite mutual fears of defection and opportunism, see Robert Axelrod, *The Evolution of Cooperation* (New York: Basic Books, 1984).

59 Examples include Washington's effort to create a "coalition of the willing" outside the United Nations framework for the invasion of Iraq, and its earlier boycott of the International Labor Organization and the U.N. Education, Scientific and Cultural Organization. William H. Overholt warned that heavy-handed U.S. pressure on China, even for laudable goals such as promoting human rights, would not be supported by other Asian countries and would meet resistance from Beijing for which sovereignty is a primary policy concern. He invited his readers to imagine a scenario in which the roles were reversed.

If Beijing were demanding independence for Alaska, sending emissaries to impose immediate changes in the governance of New York, and giving advanced weapons to independence fighters in Puerto Rico, while voting in favor of economic war [an allusion to the earlier congressional debates on whether to extend the most-favored-nation trading status to China] and having its foreign minister declare the transformation of the United States into a communist state a primary objective of Chinese foreign policy, Washington would be concerned.
(*The Rise of China: How Economic Reform is Creating a Superpower* (New York: Norton, 1993), p. 414)

8   Managing the hegemon: in lieu of frontal confrontation

1 Michael D. Swayne and Ashley J. Tellis, *Interpreting China's Grand Strategy: Past, Present, and Future* (Santa Monica, CA: RAND, 2000), p. 112.

2 Avery Goldstein, *Rising to the Challenge: China's Grand Strategy and International Security* (Stanford, CA: Stanford University Press, 2005), p. 12.

3 See, for example, Timothy W. Crawford's discussion of Germany's policy on the so-called Eastern Question, involving rivalry between Austria-Hungary and Russia in the 1870s. After taking Alsace and Lorraine, Bismarck believed that Germany "no longer had any objective that could profitably be attained by war" and sought to be an "honest-broker who gets the business done." Quoted in Timothy W. Crawford, *Pivotal Deterrence: Third-Party Statecraft and the Pursuit of Peace* (Ithaca, NY: Cornell University Press, 2003), pp. 52 and 70. Avery Goldstein was explicit in invoking Bismarckian Germany as an appropriate analogue for the policy circumstances and motivations characterizing contemporary China. See ibid., ch. 9.

4 Thus, as Stephen Walt remarked, even though the U.S. had intervened in European affairs with some reluctance during the earlier years of its history, preferring to play the role of an offshore balancer, "this behavior . . . stands in sharp contrast to U.S. conduct in North America and the Western Hemisphere, where it proceeded to conquer a continent, subjugate the indigenous inhabitants, evict the other Great Powers, and openly proclaim its own hegemony over the region" (*Taming American Power: The Global Response to U.S. Primacy* (New York: Norton, 2005), p. 125).

5 Allen S. Whiting, "China's Use of Force, 1950–96, and Taiwan," *International Security* 26 (2001): 103–131; and Steve Chan, "Chinese Conflict Calculus and Behavior: Assessment from a Perspective of Conflict Management," *World Politics* 30 (1978): 391–410.

6 Japan was reluctant to give up the fruits of its conquest in China. Given the U.S. embargo, however, it had only about eighteen months of strategic oil reserves. Once this time ran out, its military forces would not be able to wage an effective war. In that event, the U.S. would have prevailed without having to fire a shot. This strategic predicament explains the Japanese leaders' risky decision to attack Pearl Harbor. As already noted, these officials were quite aware of the tremendous potential power of the U.S., and yet they still went ahead with their plan to attack. Japan in 1941 was not a confident rising power but one whose relative position had already peaked. With the passage of time, it would become weaker *vis-à-vis* the U.S.

7 Allen S. Whiting, *China Crosses the Yalu: The Decision to Enter the Korean War* (New York: Macmillan, 1960).

8 This interpretation suggests that China's intervention stemmed from a defensive motive; it accords with the conclusion of most Sinologists. See, for example, Thomas J. Christensen, *Useful Adversaries: Grand Strategy, Domestic Mobilization and Sino-American Conflict, 1947–1958* (Princeton, NJ: Princeton University Press, 1996), p. 158.

9 The following is just a partial list of studies on Chinese crisis decision-making. Jian Chen, "China's Involvement in the Vietnam War, 1964–69," *China Quarterly* 142 (1995): 356–387, and *China's Road to the Korean War: The Making of the Sino-American Confrontation* (New York: Columbia University Press, 1994); Christensen, *op. cit.*; Melvin Gurtov, "The Taiwan Strait Crisis Revisited: Politics and Foreign Policy in Chinese Motives," *Modern China* 2 (1976): 49–103; Chi-kin Lo, *China's Policy Towards Territorial Disputes: The Case of the South China Sea Islands* (London: Routledge, 1989); Thomas W. Robinson, "The Sino-Soviet Border Dispute: Background, Development, and the March 1969 Clashes," *American Political Science Review* 66 (1972): 1175–1202; Robert S. Ross, *The Indochina Triangle: China's Vietnam Policy 1975–1979* (New York: Columbia University Press, 1988), and "The 1995–1996 Taiwan Strait Confrontation: Coercion, Credibility, and Use of Force," *International Security*

25 (2000): 87–123; Marwyn S. Samuels, *Contest for the South China Sea* (New York: Methuen, 1982); Thomas E. Stolper, *China, Taiwan, and the Offshore Islands: Together with an Implication for Outer Mongolia and Sino-Soviet Relations* (Armonk, NY: Sharpe, 1985); Allen S. Whiting, "New Light on Mao; Quemoy 1958: Mao's Miscalculation," *China Quarterly* 62 (1975): 263–270, and *The Chinese Calculus of Deterrence: India and Indochina* (Ann Arbor: University of Michigan Press, 1975); and Richard Wich, *Sino-Soviet Crisis Politics: A Study of Political Change and Communication* (Cambridge, MA: Harvard University Press, 1980).

10 The diversionary theory of war suggests that elites start foreign crises in order to distract public attention from their domestic problems.

11 As Andrew Nathan and Robert Ross noted,

> China has been a reactive power, striving not to alter but to maintain regional patterns of power. Its diplomacy has been in support of the status quo, aiming not to undermine but to join international regimes. China's policies toward Russia, the new Central Asian republics, India, the two Koreas, Japan, and the countries of Indochina have sought to consolidate bilateral relationships and to stabilize subregional power balances. Its military threats against Taiwan were aimed at deterring Taiwan from changing the status quo rather than at compelling it to accelerate the pace of reunification. In the South China Sea, China has acted to maintain historical claims when others challenged them, rather than to extend new claims.
>
> (Andrew J. Nathan and Robert S. Ross, *The Great Wall and the Empty Fortress: China's Search for Security* (New York: Norton, 1997), p. 230)

12 Peter H. Gries, *China's New Nationalism: Pride, Politics, and Diplomacy* (Berkeley: University of California Press, 2004).

13 Edward D. Mansfield and Jack Snyder, "Democratization and the Danger of War," *International Security* 20 (1995): 5–38. Other analysts hold the view that democratization makes states more peaceful. For a thoughtful discussion of various optimistic and pessimistic prognoses of future Sino-American relations, see Aaron L. Friedberg, "The Future of U.S.–China Relations," *International Security* 30 (2005): 7–45.

14 See, for example, Samuel P. Huntington, *Political Order in Changing Societies* (New Haven, CT: Yale University Press, 1968); Roland Paris, *At War's End: Building Peace after Civil Conflict* (New York: Cambridge University Press, 2004); and Edward D. Mansfield and Jack Snyder, *Electing to Fight: Why Emerging Democracies Go to War* (Cambridge, MA: MIT Press, 2005).

15 Mansfield and Snyder, ibid., p. 35. Thus, proper sequence is important as shown in "nineteenth-century Britain's example in establishing institutions before unleashing mass political participation" (p. 260).

16 *Nightly Business Report*, July 28, 2006.

17 Indeed, recent moves by Chen Shui-Bian's administration include attempts to revise the Republic of China constitution which, drafted originally by the Kuomintang on the Mainland, claims to represent China, with Taiwan being a Chinese province. In his discussion of whether the U.S. should abandon strategic ambiguity in favor of strategic clarity, Timothy W. Crawford pointed out the critical assumption that "China's intentions to [possibly] attack Taiwan are less motivated by greed than by 'Beijing's fears of eventual Taiwanese independence with U.S. backing'" (Crawford, *op. cit.*, p. 201, with the latter phrase quoted from a letter from Thomas Christensen). Of course, although Taiwan has thus far not declared *de jure* independence, its *de facto* independence from China (with U.S. backing) has been a real, not hypothetical, situation for Beijing for over 55 years. Why should Beijing such great fears need to be allayed in order to avoid a conflict over the Taiwan Strait when the supposed issue at stake for China is just Taiwan's *de jure* but not its *de facto* status? One possible answer advanced here is that the stakes have increased for Beijing because of the

Chinese leaders' new-found sensitivity to public opinion – or, if you will, because of the onset of the democratization process. Another possible answer is that the ongoing processes of closer economic, cultural, and political accommodation and even cooperation between the two sides of the Taiwan Strait may be jeopardized by Taipei's or Washington's policies from Beijing's point of view, so that it perceives the prospect of eventual peaceful reunification as more distant and perhaps even out of reach. Significantly, and ironically, this interpretation suggests that just as the U.S. has declared its opposition to unilateral actions by Taipei or Beijing to change the status quo in the Taiwan Strait, China's fears are that the ongoing processes favoring its goals of reunification may be interrupted by unilateral actions by its counterparts. The basic argument advanced in this book is that as a rising power, China can benefit from the unfolding processes and take advantage of the ongoing momentum. It can afford to let time work to its advantage absent efforts by others to abort or intercept current trends.

18 Thomas J. Christensen, "Posing Problems without Catching Up: China's Rise and Challenges for U.S. Security Policy," *International Security* 25 (2001): 5–40.

19 Ibid.

20 Kishore Mahbubani, "Understanding China," *Foreign Affairs* 84 (2005): 55.

21 For pertinent discussions, see G. John Ikenberry, ed., *America Unrivaled: The Future of the Balance of Power* (Ithaca, NY: Cornell University Press, 2002); and T.V. Paul, James J. Wirtz, and Michel Fortmann, eds, *Balance of Power: Theory and Practice in the 21st Century* (Stanford, CA: Stanford University Press, 2004).

22 See, for example, Steve Chan and Alex Mintz, eds, *Defense, Welfare, and Growth: Perspectives and Evidence* (London: Routledge, Chapman and Hall, 1992).

23 Wang Jisi, "China's Search for Stability with America," *Foreign Affairs* 84 (2005): 43.

24 Robert A. Pape, "Soft Balancing against the United States," *International Security* 30 (2005): 10. See also Stephen M. Walt, *Taming American Power: The Global Response to U.S. Primacy* (New York: Norton, 2005), ch. 3.

25 Other pertinent discussions on soft balancing, including skeptical views, are available in T.V. Paul, "Introduction: The Enduring Axioms of Balance of Power Theory and Their Contemporary Relevance," in *Balance of Power: Theory and Practice in the 21st Century*, ed. T.V. Paul, James J. Wirtz, and Michel Fortmann (Stanford, CA: Stanford University Press, 2004), pp. 1–25, and "Soft Balancing in the Age of U.S. Primacy," *International Security* 30 (2005): 46–71; Stephen G. Brooks and William C. Wohlforth, "Hard Times for Soft Balancing," *International Security* 30 (2005): 72–108; and Keir A. Lieber and Gerard Alexander, "Waiting for Balancing: Why the World is not Pushing Back," *International Security* 30 (2005): 109–139.

26 Ralph D. Sawyer, *Sun Tzu: Art of War* (Boulder, CO: Westview Press, 1994).

27 Ibid.

28 For these and other views attributed to Chinese strategic thinking, see Davis B. Bobrow, Steve Chan, and John A. Kringen, *Understanding Foreign Policy Decisions: The Chinese Case* (New York: Free Press, 1979).

29 Davis B. Bobrow, "Challenges to U.S. Preferences: Strategies of Resistance and Modification," manuscript (University of Pittsburgh, 2004). A discussion on how others may try to manage the U.S. as a hegemon can also be found in Stephen M. Walt, "Taming American Power," *Foreign Affairs* 84 (2005): 105–120.

30 This and other points are taken from Steve Chan, "Soft Deterrence, Passive Resistance: American Lenses, Chinese Lessons," presented at the annual meeting of the International Studies Association, Honolulu, March 1–5, 2005.

31 See Bobrow, *op. cit.*

32 Sawyer, *op. cit.*

33 In this respect, Stephen M. Walt warned that Washington's aggressive unilateralism would alienate other states. Even when they choose not to actively balance against or challenge the U.S., these states can still be motivated to circumvent or decline to

cooperate with American policies. Thus, he advised U.S. self-restraint in order to avoid making others fearful and resentful. See his "Keeping the World 'Off Balance': Self Restraint and U.S. Foreign Policy," in *America Unrivaled: The Future of the Balance of Power*, ed. G. John Ikenberry (Ithaca, NY: Cornell University Press, 2002), pp. 121–154.

34 This abbreviation refers to the Association of Southeast Asian Nations, Plus China, Japan, and South Korea. Peter H. Gries, "China Eyes the Hegemon," *Orbis* 49 (2005): 407.

35 The Shanghai Cooperation Organization consists of China, Kazakhstan, Kyrgyzstan, Tajikistan, Uzbekistan, and Russia. Iran attended the 2006 meeting as an observer. On the increasing Chinese engagement with and involvement in multilateral regional groups, see David Shambaugh, "China Engages Asia: Reshaping the Regional Order," *International Security* 29 (2004/2005): 64–99.

36 This injunction incorporates the ideas of reversing roles, turning tables on the opposition, and administering to the other its own medicine, but its subtlety extends beyond these meanings. The story from which this injunction is supposed to have originated also refers to the exposure of contradictions in another person's arguments or rationale. Indeed, the Chinese concept for contradiction derives from the combination of characters for spear and shield.

37 Paul W. Schroeder, *The Transformation of European Politics, 1763–1848* (New York: Oxford University Press, 1994), and "Historical Reality vs. Neo-realist Theory," *International Security* 19 (1994): 108–148.

38 A.J.P. Taylor, *The Origins of the Second World War* (New York: Atheneum, 1961), p. 278.

39 Paul Kennedy, *The Rise and Fall of the Great Powers: Economic Change and Military Conflict from 1500 to 2000* (New York: Random House, 1987). Karen A. Rasler and William R. Thompson argue that a failure to sustain technological innovation has been the most important reason for hegemonic decline, with imperial overstretch playing a secondary role. See *The Great Powers and Global Struggle, 1490–1990* (Lexington: University of Kentucky Press, 1994).

40 William C. Wohlforth, ed., *Cold War Endgame: Oral History, Analysis, Debates* (University Park: Pennsylvania State University Press, 2003).

41 See Rasler and Thompson (*op. cit.*) for evidence on the nature and strength of trade-off in the U.S. and British cases.

42 These injunctions and their application during the Warring States period of Chinese history received extensive treatment in classic Chinese military texts (the *Seven Military Classics*, including Sun Tzu's *Art of War*). The following passages offer two exemplary references to the pertinent strategic ideas at work: "By acting submissively, feigning loyalty, and playing upon King Fu-ch'ai's desires for victory and power over the northern Chou states through Po P'i's persuasions, [the kingdom of] Yueh insidiously deflected attention away from itself and ensured that [the kingdom of] Wu would dissipate its military strength and energy"; and "Whenever possible [King Kou-chien] increased [King] Fu-ch'ai's arrogance, played upon his desires, and encouraged him in his deluded campaigns against Ch'i in the north" (Sawyer, *op. cit.*, pp. 108, 121). For all their supposed comparative advantage in appreciating and capturing the nuances of traditional cultural perspectives, there is a general dearth of sensitive and sophisticated scholarship on Chinese strategic thought and conduct among Sinologists writing about contemporary military and diplomatic affairs. Much of their research fails to go beyond ritualistic references to the so-called Middle-Kingdom syndrome and the supposed importance of "face" to the Chinese. Indeed, the prevalent mode of analysis by U.S. academics writing on Chinese foreign policy tends to follow the Western Clausewitzean tradition emphasizing armament procurement and alliance behavior. For an exceptional study of Chinese cultural legacies in strategic matters, see Alastair Iain Johnston, *Cultural Realism: Strategic Culture and Grand Strategy in Chinese History* (Princeton, NJ: Princeton University Press, 1995).

43 Thus, much of the standard work on "China threat," focusing narrowly on military instrumentation, can be seriously flawed. See, for example, Robert D. Kaplan, "How We Would Fight China," *Atlantic Monthly* (June 2005): 49–64. This type of work provides a clear contrast to the strategic style and rationale that I attribute to the Chinese. For a response to Kaplan's article, see Benjamin Schwarz, "Comment: Managing China's Rise," pp. 27–28 in the same issue of *Atlantic Monthly*.

44 Joseph S. Nye, Jr., *The Paradox of American Power* (New York: Oxford University Press, 2002), p. 22.

45 Dale C. Copeland, *The Origins of Major War* (Ithaca, NY: Cornell University Press, 2000), p. 243.

46 "Deng Puts Forward New 12-Character Guiding Principle for Internal and External Policies," *Ching Pao* (November 5, 1991): 84–86, quoted in Max Sung-chi Yu, Alexander C. Tan, Tim Chen, and Karl Ho, "Is China an Upcoming Threat or a Peaceful Ascendance? The Determining Factor of Taiwan in Hegemonic Power Transition," presented at the annual meeting of the American Political Science Association, Washington, D.C., September 1–4, 2005.

47 Jonathan D. Pollack, "The Transformation of the Asian Security Order: Assessing China's Impact," in *Power Shift: China and Asia's New Dynamics*, ed. David Shambaugh (Berkeley: University of California Press, 2005), pp. 329–346. See also Yunling Zhang and Shiping Tang, "China's Regional Strategy," in ibid., pp. 48–68; and Robert G. Sutter, *China's Rise in Asia: Promises and Perils* (Lanham, MD: Rowman & Littlefield, 2005).

9   Extended deterrence and the logic of selection

1 James D. Morrow, "The Logic of Overtaking," in *Parity and War: Evaluations and Extensions of The War Ledger*, ed. Jacek Kugler and Douglas Lemke (Ann Arbor: University of Michigan Press, 1996), p. 328.

2 Paul Huth has written informatively about extended deterrence. See Paul K. Huth, *Extended Deterrence and the Prevention of War* (New Haven, CT: Yale University Press, 1988), and "Extended Deterrence and the Outbreak of War," *American Political Science Review* 82 (1988): 423–443; Paul K. Huth and Bruce M. Russett, "General Deterrence between Enduring Rivals: Testing Three Competing Models," *American Political Science Review* 87 (1993): 61–73, "Deterrence Failure and Crisis Escalation," *International Studies Quarterly* 32 (1988): 29–45, and "What Makes Deterrence Work? Cases from 1900 to 1980," *World Politics* 36 (1984): 496–526; and Paul K. Huth, Christopher Gelpi, and D. Scott Bennett, "The Escalation of Great Power Disputes: Testing Rational Deterrence Theory and Structural Realism," *American Political Science Review* 87 (1993): 609–623. See also the exchange between Paul K. Huth and Bruce M. Russett, "Testing Deterrence Theory: Rigor Makes a Difference," *World Politics* 52 (1990): 466–501; and Richard Ned Lebow and Janice Gross Stein, "Deterrence: The Elusive Dependent Variable," *World Politics* 52 (1990): 336–369.

3 I adopt the labels "defender" and "challenger" in conformity with the conventional terminology in the study of deterrence. Naturally, the dominant power and the late-comer may assume either role. For instance, in its effort to reunify Korea under an anti-communist government, the U.S. in 1950 was in the role of a challenger to the status quo whereas China took on the role of a defender. Conversely, in the following discussion on Taiwan, China is assumed to be the challenger because it seeks to bring this island under Beijing's control whereas the U.S. is taken to be the defender. Nevertheless, actors can have different reference points with respect to the status quo. Therefore, if Taipei declares *de jure* independence, it would be perceived by Beijing as challenging the status quo. Concomitantly, Beijing becomes in that event a defender of the principle that there is only one China and that Taiwan is part of China

(a principle which has been accepted by Beijing, Washington, and, until relatively recently, Taipei as well). From Beijing's perspective, the U.S. intervention in 1950 (by interposing the Seventh Fleet in the Taiwan Strait to prevent an impending communist invasion of Chiang Kai-shek's last bastion) was tantamount to a revision of the status quo because this action separated Taiwan from China. The reference point adopted by an actor is important because it determines whether this actor perceives itself to be situated in a domain of gain or a domain of loss. Therefore, attributions – indeed, self-attributions – of the role of a defender and challenger may be subjective.

4 A war between the defender and the challenger is not inevitable because the latter still has a chance to back down at that stage, as when Beijing de-escalated its bombardment of the offshore islands of Quemoy and Matsu in 1958.

5 German leaders, however, were not really interested in deterring a Russian attack on their ally Austria-Hungary. As argued previously, they were more motivated to use the escalating crisis to initiate a preventive war against St. Petersburg.

6 In the case of Japan's attack against Pearl Harbor, the European colonies in Southeast Asia were the protégés that the U.S. was trying to defend.

7 In the case of World War I, Germany's invasion of neutral Belgium settled the issue of whether the U.K. would intervene. This German invasion of course represented another case of failure in extended deterrence by the U.K. and France, which had guaranteed Belgium's neutrality in perpetuity.

8 See, however, the explanation given earlier that the roles of defender and challenger may change depending on the reference point used to describe the status quo. Given their different reference points, the two contesting parties could perceive each other as attempting to undermine the status quo. Thus, for instance, if Beijing uses the state of affairs in the late 1940s as its reference point, Taiwan was part of China, and its current effort to reincorporate Taiwan would be a restoration of the status quo ante.

9 Thomas C. Schelling, *Arms and Influence* (New Haven, CT: Yale University Press, 1966), p. 36.

10 A pertinent example from Sino-American relations is when Washington did not take seriously Beijing's warnings that it would intervene on behalf of Pyongyang in the Korean War. See Allen S. Whiting, *China Crosses the Yalu: The Decision to Enter the Korean War* (New York: Macmillan, 1960).

11 Alan N. Sabrosky, "Interstate Alliances: Their Reliability and the Expansion of War," in *Correlates of War II*, ed. J. David Singer (New York: Free Press, 1980), pp. 161–198.

12 Huth, *Extended Deterrence and the Prevention of War*, *op. cit.*, p. 5.

13 Robert Jervis, "What Do We Want to Deter and How Do We Deter It?," in *Turning Point: The Gulf War and the U.S. Military Strategy*, ed. L. Benjamin Edington and Michael J. Mazarr (Boulder, CO: Westview Press, 1994), pp. 122–124, and *System Effects: Complexity in Political Social Life* (Princeton, NJ: Princeton University Press, 1997); and Timothy W. Crawford, *Pivotal Deterrence: Third-Party Statecraft and the Pursuit of Peace* (Ithaca, NY: Cornell University Press, 2003).

14 In his book, Crawford presented detailed case studies on Germany's diplomacy in the Austro-Russian rivalry in the Balkans in the 1870s, Britain's diplomacy immediately prior to the outbreak of World War I in 1914, and U.S. diplomacy in the conflict between Greece and Turkey over Cyprus, and that between India and Pakistan over Kashmir in the 1960s.

15 How a possible cross-Strait conflict is popularly framed in the American public's mind has important consequences. Compared to cases of foreign aggression and humanitarian relief, public opinion tends to be generally much less supportive of U.S. military intervention in others' civil wars. See Bruce W. Jentleson, "The Pretty Prudent Public: Post-Vietnam American Opinion on the Use of Military Force," *International Studies Quarterly* 36 (1992): 47–74; Bruce W. Jentleson and Rebecca L. Britton, "Still Pretty Prudent: Post-Cold War American Public Opinion on the Use of Military Force," *Journal of Conflict Resolution* 42 (1998): 395–417; and Richard C. Eichenberg,

"Victory Has Many Friends: U.S. Public Opinion and the Use of Military Force, 1981–2005," *International Security* 30 (2005): 140–177.

16   Kishore Mahbubani, "Understanding China," *Foreign Affairs* 84 (2005): 56. On the occasion of a U.S. Senate hearing on the Vietnam War, Senator Frank Church called attention to a parallel from America's own Civil War, remarking,

> had England, which favored the South, adhered to the same principle that now seems to govern American policy, and had sent troops in the name of self-determination into the Confederacy, I think the English government would have been hard put to convince Abraham Lincoln that there should be an election to determine the ultimate outcome of the war.
> (Quoted in Yuen Foong Khong, *Analogies at War: Korea, Munich, Dien Bien Phu, and the Vietnam Decisions of 1965* (Princeton, NJ: Princeton University Press, 1992), p. 236)

17   Crawford, *op. cit.*, p. 217.
18   Ibid., p. 212.
19   States sometimes try to contrive an appearance of neutrality in projecting an ostensible policy of pivotal deterrence, when in fact they were partisans in a dispute. One example of such contrivance comes from the Suez Canal crisis of 1956. The U.K. and France reached a secret accord with Israel at Sevres, France. It was agreed that Israel would attack Egypt on October 29. By pre-arrangement the U.K. and France issued an ultimatum on October 30 to both Israel and Egypt to cease fire. When Egypt, as expected, rejected their ostensible attempt at deterring a further escalation of the conflict, the British and French attacked Egypt's airfields on the following day. By November 2, Israeli forces were able to complete their occupation of the Sinai and Gaza. Ostensibly acting to protect the Suez Canal and to secure regional stability, the British and French dropped paratroopers at Port Said and Port Fuad on November 5. Their amphibious forces landed at Port Said the following day.
20   Ibid.
21   The wording "may" suggests that Taipei, like Beijing and Washington, does not represent a unitary actor. There are elements of Taiwan that do not encourage or support independence, and seek instead to promote closer economic integration and political accommodation with China.
22   Anne E. Sartori, "The Might of the Pen: A Reputational Theory of Communication in International Disputes," *International Organization* 56 (2002): 129. Although I agree with Sartori's general argument, her specific illustration about China's failure to deter the U.S. from invading North Korea seems problematic. She attributes this Chinese failure to Beijing's not following through its earlier threats to invade Taiwan. In her view, that Beijing did not invade Taiwan caused it to be seen by Washington as bluffing again when it threatened to intervene in Korea. This interpretation seems to be problematic because the Truman administration ordered the Seventh Fleet to intervene in the Taiwan Strait shortly after the outbreak of the Korean War. Thus, China would have to risk a military confrontation with the U.S. should Beijing follow through on its plan to invade Taiwan in 1950 (Beijing had already amassed troops and made other preparations for such an invasion). Given that Chinese leaders thought that a military confrontation with the U.S. was likely, it became important to consider whether it would be to China's advantage to fight in the Taiwan Strait or on the Korean peninsula. It would not require a great deal of imagination to infer that geographic, military, and political considerations would incline Beijing to select the Korean peninsula rather than the Taiwan Strait as a more advantageous battleground if war were to be waged against the U.S. Therefore, a failure to invade Taiwan in 1950 could not be interpreted as a sign of Chinese bluffing, as Beijing's invasion plan had to be revised in view of the U.S. naval intervention in the opening days of the Korean War and then postponed and abandoned after the escalation of the Korean War.

23 Sartori, ibid:131.

24 In Chapter 8, I argued that Khrushchev's decision to introduce missiles to Cuba suggests a gamble by the USSR to catch up with the U.S. lead in nuclear weapons. That argument implies an attempt of desperation by a state that was falling further behind the dominant power, whereas the alternative interpretation offered here suggests a deterrence motive. In both cases, however, the illustration points to risky behavior stemming from a desire to avoid losses. Attribution of a deterrence motivation to the USSR would suggest that Khrushchev's gambit paid off because in exchange for the withdrawal of Soviet missiles, the U.S. made a secret pledge not to invade Cuba again.

25 Evidently, Douglas MacArthur did not believe Beijing's warnings that it would intervene in the Korean War. His "home by Christmas" offensive turned into a long retreat after the Chinese attacked.

26 At that time, China was ostensibly testing its missiles in waters near the island in an obvious effort to influence Taiwan's presidential election. For a discussion of this episode, see Robert S. Ross, "The 1995–1996 Taiwan Strait Confrontation: Coercion, Credibility, and Use of Force," *International Security* 25 (2000): 87–123. For more general discussions on deterrence in the Taiwan Strait, see Thomas J. Christensen, "The Contemporary Security Dilemma: Deterring a Taiwan Conflict," *Washington Quarterly* 25 (2002): 7–21; and Steve Chan, "Prognosticating about Extended Deterrence in the Taiwan Strait: Implications from Strategic Selection," *World Affairs* 168 (2005): 13–25, and "Extended Deterrence in the Taiwan Strait: Learning from Rationalist Explanations in International Relations," *World Affairs* 166 (2003): 109–125.

27 This acknowledgment was stated as early as February 27, 1972 in the Shanghai communiqué issued by the U.S. and China during Richard Nixon's historic trip to China. Other U.S. presidents have reaffirmed this principle publicly on subsequent occasions.

28 Henry Kissinger captured well the U.S. predicament when he said: "for us to go to war with a recognized country . . . over a part of what we would recognize as their country would be preposterous." Quoted in Crawford, *op. cit.*, p. 190. For extended treatments of Sino-American relations, see Robert S. Ross, *Navigating Cooperation: US–China Relations, 1969–1989* (Stanford, CA: Stanford University Press, 1995); and Roderick MacFarquhar, *Sino-American Relations, 1949–71* (New York: Praeger, 1972).

29 Harry Truman ordered the Seventh Fleet to interpose itself in the Taiwan Strait after the Korean War broke out, preventing a communist invasion of the Kuomintang's final refuge.

30 Crawford, *op. cit.*, p. 203.

31 Nancy Bernkopf Tucker, "Strategic Ambiguity or Strategic Clarity," in *Dangerous Strait: The U.S.-Taiwan-China Crisis*, ed. Nancy Bernkopf Tucker (New York: Columbia University Press, 2005), pp. 186–211; and Frank C. Zagare and D. Marc Kilgour, "The Deterrence-versus-Restraint Dilemma in Extended Deterrence: Explaining British Policy in 1914," *International Studies Review* 8 (2006): 623–641.

32 James D. Fearon, "Signalling Foreign Policy Interests: Tying Hands versus Sinking Costs," *Journal of Conflict Resolution* 41 (1997): 70–71.

33 Thus, these officials had omitted South Korea as a U.S. protégé. In giving this impression, Washington might have misled the communist North into believing that the U.S. would not intervene against its invasion of the South. See Whiting, *op. cit.*, p. 39.

34 Quoted in John J. Mearsheimer and Stephen M. Walt, "An Unnecessary War," *Foreign Policy* (January/February 2003): 54.

35 http://torquecentral. Com/archive/index.php/t-26144.

36 According to this interpretation, Egypt would assume the status of a U.S. protégé.

37 It is perhaps striking that the term "mutual partisan adjustment" is derived from a book on democratic politics. See Charles E. Lindblom, *The Intelligence of Democracy: Decision Making Through Mutual Adjustment* (New York: Free Press, 1965).

38 Although there were periods of rigidity and confrontation in Sino-American relations, recent research based on declassified archives shows that officials in Beijing and Washington were aware of their counterparts' concerns and constraints, and were remarkably cautious and adept in adjusting their policies to limit the danger of conflict spiral. See, for example, Robert S. Ross and Jiang Changbin, eds, *Re-examining the Cold War: U.S.–China Diplomacy, 1954–1973* (Cambridge, MA: Harvard University Press, 2001).

39 Prospect theory argues that a state in the domain of gain will seek to consolidate its gains rather than taking risks that might jeopardize these gains. Kishore Mahbubani attributed to the Chinese leaders a calculation that "in due course circumstances will favor [Beijing's] goals and undermine any hope of an independent Taiwan" (*op. cit.*, p. 56).

40 See T.J. Cheng, "China–Taiwan Economic Linkage: Between Insularity and Superconductivity," in Tucker, *op. cit.*, pp. 93–130; and Tse-Kang Leng, *The Taiwan–China Connection: Democracy and Development across the Taiwan Straits* (Boulder, CO: Westview Press, 1996).

41 Most polls show that the majority of Taiwan's voters favor the status quo of continuing with Taiwan's current ambiguous status so that it neither submits to Beijing nor provokes it. That is, they prefer to play for time. Those in favor of the polar positions of immediate reunification and immediate independence are in the minority.

42 Laws governing referendum are controversial because their introduction implies a possible preparation for secession to be voted on in a special election. Under the former Kuomintang regime, there were a national government and a provincial government on the island. The existence of a provincial government was supposed to lend credence to the claim that the government in Taipei was a national government representing all of China. Thus, ironically, the old Kuomintang regime had agreed with Beijing that there was only one China and that Taiwan was a Chinese province, except that it saw itself as the legitimate government for all Chinese. After the death of Chiang Ching-kuo, Taipei moved gradually to demote and even abolish provincial institutions, thus removing the island's implied status as a Chinese province. Under Chen Shui-Bian, there was a campaign to change the name of leading government and quasi-public institutions so that the word "China" in their title would be replaced by the word "Taiwan." Many of Taiwan's largest corporations also have the word "China" in their title (for example, China Airlines and China Petroleum), thus again implying an association with China. The sensitivity of this issue is demonstrated by Taiwan's formal title as "the Republic of China." Chen Shui-Bian has pledged not to change this name during his second presidential term. Such a change would be likely to be interpreted by Beijing as tantamount to a formal declaration of Taiwan independence. Significantly, and as noted previously, public statements may not indicate true intentions because of the problem of misrepresentation and due to possible changes in circumstances exacerbating the commitment problem. On February 28, 2006, Chen abolished the National Unification Council and the Guidelines for National Unification. This move highlights another important symbolic break with past policies and repeated pledges made previously to refrain from this action – such as given in Chen's inaugural speech in 2000 and again in 2004. See Richard C. Bush, *Untying the Knot: Making Peace in the Taiwan Strait* (Washington, D.C.: Brookings Institution Press, 2005), pp. 63, 317, 319.

43 This characterization conjures up the image of a Chinese saying, which has been adopted as the title of a book on Sino-American relations written by David M. Lampton, *Same Bed, Different Dreams: Managing U.S.–China Relations, 1989–2000* (Berkeley: University of California Press, 2001).

44 For some examples of analysis on selection effect, see Vesna Danilovic, "Conceptual and Selection Biases in Deterrence," *Journal of Conflict Resolution* 45 (2001): 97–125; James D. Fearon, "Selection Effects and Deterrence," *International Interactions* 28 (2000): 5–29; Scott Sigmund Gartner and Randolph M. Siverson, "War Expansion

and War Outcome," *Journal of Conflict Resolution* 40 (1996): 4–15; and Alastair Smith, "To Intervene or Not to Intervene: A Biased Decision," *Journal of Conflict Resolution* 40 (1996): 16–40.

45 See, for example, Dean Lacy and Emerson M.S. Niou, "A Theory of Economic Sanctions and Issue Linkage: The Roles of Preferences, Information, and Threats," *Journal of Politics* 66 (2004): 25–42.

46 Scott Bennett and Allan C. Stam, III, "The Declining Advantages of Democracy: A Combined Model of War Outcomes and Duration," *Journal of Conflict Resolution* 42 (1998): 344–366; and "The Duration of Interstate Wars: 1816–1985," *American Political Science Review* 90 (1996): 239–257.

47 Bruce Bueno de Mesquita and Randolph M. Siverson, "War and the Survival of Political Leaders: A Comparative Study of Regime Types and Political Accountability," *American Political Science Review* 89 (1995): 841–853; and Bruce Bueno de Mesquita, Randolph M. Siverson, and Gary Woller, "War and the Fate of Regimes: A Comparative Analysis," *American Political Science Review* 86 (1992): 638–646.

48 Note that here I am contrasting the American and Chinese officials' sensitivity to domestic political fallout as a result of war. Earlier I advanced a different hypothesis, suggesting that as China's political process becomes more open and pluralistic, leaders in Beijing will become more constrained by domestic public opinion, especially in the form of popular nationalism, than previously in an era when the government and the Communist Party exercised greater control over Chinese society.

49 The distinction being made here points to the monadic and dyadic versions of the democratic peace theory. The monadic version refers to a generally peaceful posture adopted by democracies towards all other countries regardless of their regime characteristic. The dyadic version restricts the phenomenon of democratic peace to the relations between democracies (that is, when a democracy is paired with another democracy).

50 Authoritarian leaders know that their own kind will not suffer serious domestic repercussions as a result of foreign policy setback and therefore may be expected to accept a lower threshold of confidence for starting international disputes. This realization in turn implies that authoritarian leaders are more likely to bluff and to have their bluffs called by their counterparts, whether these counterparts are democratic or other authoritarian leaders. Moreover, other leaders expect their authoritarian counterparts to be less resolute because the authoritarian officials can afford to back down from international disputes due to the perception that they are less likely to face severe domestic repercussions as a result.

51 See Kenneth A. Schultz, "Do Democratic Institutions Constrain or Inform? Contrasting Two Institutional Perspectives on Democracy and War," *International Organization* 53 (1999): 133–162, "Looking for Audience Costs," *Journal of Conflict Resolution* 45 (2001): 32–60, and "Domestic Opposition and Signaling in International Crises," *American Political Science Review* 92 (1998): 829–844.

52 Fearon, *op. cit.*

53 James D. Fearon, "Domestic Political Audiences and the Escalation of International Disputes," *American Political Science Review* 88 (1994): 577–592.

54 Fearon, *op. cit.* (1997), p. 82.

55 Erik Gartzke and Kristian S. Gleditsch, "Why Democracies May Actually Be Less Reliable Allies," *American Journal of Political Science* 48 (2004): 775–795.

56 One reason for this tendency is that special interest groups with intense preferences are likely to dominate the ratification of a defense treaty. When the time comes to honor this treaty, however, a wider array of actors will become engaged. These latter actors are unlikely to be motivated by the same selective incentives that mobilized those who were initially responsible for the treaty's passage. See Gartzke and Gleditsch (ibid.) for further discussion on the logic of collective action behind this inference.

57 John W. Garver, *Face Off: China, the United States, and Taiwan's Democratization* (Seattle: University of Washington Press, 1997); and Ross, (2000) *op. cit.*

58 The inherent contradictions between executive declarations acknowledging the principle of one China and congressional sentiments expressed in the Taiwan Relations Act offer but one prominent example. This phenomenon also suggests that when dealing with the U.S., China faces competing demands from the administration and from Congress. A multiplication of demands lends credence to the impression that one is on a treadmill (compliance with demands from one source does not necessarily settle a matter, but may instead have the effect of encouraging the other source to increase its demands).

59 There is a debate in the literature about whether international treaties *just* "screen" or whether they also "constrain" state behavior. According to the "screening" hypothesis, states sign treaties not due to an interest to demonstrate credible commitment (by deliberately engaging their reputation to upholding their contractual obligations) but rather because they want to use treaties as a device to separate (i.e., distinguish) themselves from others which have not already paid the high *ex-ante* price of preparing themselves to comply with the treaty terms. This view suggests that international legal obligations have little effect on states' behavior independent of those considerations that led them to sign the treaties in the first place. The "constraining" hypothesis contends that treaties commit states to certain courses of action by tying their hands, implying that in the absence of this binding commitment states may act differently. See the exchange between Jana Von Stein, "Do Treaties Constrain or Screen? Selection Bias and Treaty Compliance," *American Political Science Review* 99 (2005): 611–622; and Beth A. Simmons and Daniel J. Hopkins, "The Constraining Power of International Treaties: Theory and Methods," *American Political Science Review* 99 (2005): 623–631. Note that according to both hypotheses, states that are parties to a treaty may be expected to behave differently from others that have chosen to refrain from assuming such international commitment.

60 The paradox of the situation is no different from the difficulty a potential borrower faces in dealing with a bank. When this person is in the greatest need of a loan, the bank is more reluctant to extend it (or else it will charge a very high interest rate for this loan). Conversely, the bank is most eager to lend to a person who is financially sufficient and secure.

61 Fearon, *op. cit.* (1997), p. 77.

62 This asymmetry in benefits implies of course that a suspension of the ongoing economic exchanges will be more costly to the challenger than to the defender, everything else being equal.

63 Joanne Gowa made these arguments based on the security externalities of trade. See *Allies, Adversaries, and International Trade* (Princeton, NJ: Princeton University Press, 1994).

64 Vasna Danilovic, *op. cit.*, and "The Sources of Threat Credibility in Extended Deterrence," *Journal of Conflict Resolution* 45 (2001): 341–369.

65 Kenneth E. Boulding, *Conflict and Defense* (New York: Harper & Row, 1962).

66 Thomas J. Christensen, "Posing Problems without Catching Up: China's Rise and Challenges for U.S. Security Policy," *International Security* 25 (2001): 5–40; and Robert S. Ross, "Navigating the Taiwan Strait: Deterrence, Escalation Dominance, and US–China Relations," *International Security* 27 (2002): 48–85.

67 Andrew Mack, "Why Big Nations Lose Small Wars: The Politics of Asymmetric Conflict," *World Politics* 27 (1975): 175–200; and T.V. Paul, *Asymmetric Conflicts: War Initiations by Weaker Powers* (New York: Cambridge University Press, 1994).

68 Robert Ross concluded: "Chinese leaders respect not only U.S. military capabilities but also U.S. resolve, and thus believe that American retaliatory threats are credible" (Ross, *op. cit.*, p. 50). There is little reason to suspect that Chinese leaders would take Washington's military capabilities casually or its declared resolve lightly. At the same

time, however, even if they are convinced that the U.S. has superior military capabilities and is politically resolved, my argument is that these conditions are in themselves not sufficient for concluding that Beijing will not challenge the U.S. effort at extended deterrence.

69 When Egypt and Syria launched the Yom Kippur War against Israel, they did not expect to win on the battlefield and in fact expected at best a military draw in view of Israel's superior forces. The Arab motivation behind starting this war (especially in the case of Anwar Sadat) had more to do with political calculations, both in terms of gaining international support and preventing domestic discontent. In this conflict, however, one is dealing with direct deterrence rather than extended deterrence because this contest was not about the protection of a protégé that Israel had wanted to defend. In addition to Japan's decision to attack Pearl Harbor, Egypt's and Syria's initiation of the Yom Kippur War showed that neither doubt about an opponent's will to resist nor skepticism about its military strength was the cause behind deterrence failure. See Zeev Maoz, *Paradoxes of War: On the Art of National Self-Entrapment* (Boston, MA: Unwin Hyman, 1990).

70 In the cases of Panama, Serbia, and Iraq, however, the U.S. was applying not so much deterrence as compulsion.

71 See Fearon (*op. cit.*, 1997), and "Signaling versus the Balance of Power and Interests: An Empirical Test of a Crisis Bargaining Model," *Journal of Conflict Resolution* 38 (1994): 236–269.

72 This observation implies that journalists and scholars cannot claim any unique source of wisdom. What these colleagues write about is likely to be already known to the relevant officials, whose decisions would have already incorporated this public information. Thus, for instance, one would assume that leaders in Beijing already know about the strength and capability of U.S. forces (including such mundane information as that the U.S. has carrier battle groups and a formidable nuclear arsenal). If they decide to challenge the U.S. in face of this knowledge about American power and even resolve, their decision must have been based on some private information that allows them to offset Washington's known strength and declared intentions.

73 "Feigning a challenge" is meant to acknowledge the suggestion advanced by some researchers that Beijing had actually wanted to strengthen, not weaken, Taipei's and Washington's commitment to the defense of Quemoy and Matsu in order to avert a process leading to the *de facto* realization of "two Chinas." This is so because had Taipei and Washington abandoned these two offshore islands located within very close proximity to the Mainland, this development would have severed one of the remaining social, political, and geographic associations that links Taiwan to China. These associations help to sustain the claim that Taiwan is part of China and forestalls any attempt to create "two Chinas" as a *de facto* and perhaps even *de jure* situation. This interpretation suggests that, rather than seeking to force their withdrawal, China's intent was to ensure that the Kuomintang forces remained in Quemoy and Matsu. For a recent account of the crises involving the offshore islands, see Thomas J. Christensen, *Useful Adversaries: Grand Strategy, Domestic Mobilization and Sino-American Conflict, 1947–1958* (Princeton, NJ: Princeton University Press, 1996), pp. 198 and 232.

74 For example, Nikita Khrushchev was dismissed from power shortly after the Cuban Missile Crisis. Although we do not know the specific extent to which his role in the Soviet experience in that episode led to his political demise, there is little doubt that it was a factor, as has been acknowledged by internal government circular within the USSR.

75 This important idea comes from Robert Axelrod, *The Evolution of Cooperation* (New York: Basic Books, 1984).

76 Taking out the emotional issues of nationalism, domestic legitimacy, and contested sovereignty, one can still appreciate the salience of Taiwan in the eyes of Chinese leaders. Why should they be any less interested in the status of this island than American leaders

are in Cuba? After all, the U.S. has tried to isolate Fidel Castro's government politically and economically, sought his demise through assassination attempts and the Bay of Pigs invasion, and confronted the USSR in the world's closest encounter with a nuclear war thus far.

77 Ross, *op. cit.* (2000), p. 49. Christensen (*op. cit.*, 2001) was more skeptical about whether superior U.S. capability and even its demonstrable resolve to oppose China would deter Beijing from using force against Taiwan. My earlier reference to Japan's attack on Pearl Harbor emphasized the point that a weaker country can challenge a stronger one even if it is convinced that the latter will retaliate.

10 Conclusion: theoretical and policy implications

1 Kishore Mhabubani observed: "a conviction is growing among Chinese policymakers that the United States is bent on curtailing China's rise" (Kishore Mahbubani, "Understanding China," *Foreign Affairs* 84 (2005): 50).

2 Joseph S. Nye, Jr., *The Paradox of American Power* (New York: Oxford University Press, 2002), p. 19. On officials' perceptual tendencies, see the classic study by Robert Jervis, *Perception and Misperception in International Relations* (Princeton, NJ: Princeton University Press, 1976).

3 Two examples come to mind: Douglas Lemke, *Regions of War and Peace* (Cambridge: Cambridge University Press, 2002); and Karen A. Rasler and William R. Thompson, *The Great Powers and the Global Struggle, 1490–1990* (Lexington: University of Kentucky Press, 1994).

4 The absence of any hard balancing by Washington's potential competitors is underscored by the contributors to G. John Ikenberry, ed., *America Unrivalled: The Future of the Balance of Power* (Ithaca, NY: Cornell University Press, 2002). The very preponderance of U.S. power has been cited as one reason for the absence of such balancing behavior. See Keir A. Lieber and Gerard Alexander, "Waiting for Balancing: Why the World Is Not Pushing Back," *International Security* 30 (2005): 109–139.

5 Michael D. Swaine and Ashley J. Tellis, *Interpreting China's Grand Strategy: Past, Present, and Future* (Santa Monica, CA: RAND, 2000), p. 179.

6 Dale C. Copeland, *The Origins of Major War* (Ithaca, NY: Cornell University Press, 2000), p. 241.

7 Zhang Yebai quoted in Peter Gries, "Forecasting US–China Relations, 2015," manuscript (Boulder, CO: University of Colorado, 2005), pp. 29–30. Parenthetically, David L. Rousseau reported that in the years prior to the terrorist attack on September 11, 2001, a rising number of lead articles in the *New York Times* described China as an enemy. Through October 2002, however, this number fell to zero from thirty-two in the previous year.

8 Importantly and as already noted, a state enjoying a short-term military advantage but at the onset of long-term economic decline may be tempted to start a preventive war. However, a state that possesses a strong economic foundation for future growth will not attempt this gamble even when undergoing a short-term military weakness, because the latter disadvantage can be hopefully erased in the future.

9 The U.S. plan to develop and deploy a missile-defense system can introduce a severe concern for China because, if successful, such a system will nullify the retaliatory threat posed by China's meager and vulnerable nuclear arsenal.

10 Swaine and Tellis, *op. cit.*; and Avery Goldstein, *Rising to the Challenge: China's Grand Strategy and International Security* (Stanford, CA: Stanford University Press, 2005).

11 This formulation implies that the allocation of benefits involves a zero-sum game. To the extent that the benefits being contested are inherently indivisible (e.g., status recognition), it becomes more difficult for the contestants to negotiate a settlement to

avoid war. As emphasized earlier, a currently dominant state may still be dissatisfied with its benefits and seek to maximize these benefits using the power advantage available to it. Therefore, war may also happen for this reason. The U.S. invasion of Iraq is a case in point, and was at least partly motivated by a desire to secure control of Iraqi oil.

12 Rasler and Thompson, *op. cit.*, p. 10.

13 The concerted actions covered by this proposition speak to collective measures for defense. In contrast, the logic of preventive war points to offensive actions, even if they are primarily motivated by a desire to avoid losses.

14 The leaders of the two main opposition parties on Taiwan, the Kuomintang and the People First Party, traveled to China in April and May 2005. They agreed with Beijing's officials on working toward eventual reunification based on the principle of "one China." This principle was the crux of the so-called 1992 consensus reached by the two sides' semi-official delegates in talks held in Singapore. Taiwan's current administration, under the ruling Democratic Progressive Party, denies the existence of such a consensus.

15 See, for instance, Wang Jisi's concerns that "the historical conflicts between China and Japan and the mutual antagonism of their peoples can become political problems," especially in the context of a conflict over Taiwan's status, in "China's Search for Stability with America," *Foreign Affairs* 84 (2005): 44.

16 Copeland, *op. cit.*, ch. 6. See also Marc Trachtenberg, "A Wasting Asset: American Strategy and the Shifting Nuclear Balance, 1949–1954," in *History and Strategy*, ed. Marc Trachtenberg (Princeton, NJ: Princeton University Press, 1991), pp. 100–152, and *A Constructed Peace: The Making of the European Settlement, 1945–1963* (Princeton, NJ: Princeton University Press, 1999), pp. 160–166 and 292–294; and Stephen Van Evera, *Causes of War: Power and the Roots of Conflict* (Ithaca, NY: Cornell University Press, 1999), ch. 4.

17 Edward Luttwak, *The Grand Strategy of the Soviet Union* (New York: St. Martin's Press, 1983), p. 40.

18 William Burr and Jeffrey T. Richelson, "Whether to 'Strangle the Baby in the Cradle': The United States and the Chinese Nuclear Program, 1960–64," *International Security* 25 (2000/2001): 54–99; and Gordon Chang, "JFK, China, and the Bomb," *Journal of American History* 74 (1988): 1289–1310.

19 John J. Mearsheimer, *The Tragedy of Great Power Politics* (New York: Norton, 2001). Curiously, however, Mearsheimer also claimed that having secured its own position as a regional power in the Western Hemisphere, the U.S. seeks *only* to play the role of an offshore balancer. That is, the U.S. is the world's only status-quo power, and it has no ambition to conquer Europe or Asia. Consequently, offensive realism exempts the U.S. from its own axiom that "states do not become status quo powers until they completely dominate the system" (ibid., p. 35). As Christopher Layne remarked, this formulation by Mearsheimer offers a "diet" version of offensive realism because it eschews the central logic that a great power such as the U.S. will not cease to expand until it has achieved global hegemony. Christopher Layne, "The 'Poster Child for Offensive Realism': America as a Global Hegemon," *Security Studies* 12 (2002/2003): 120–164.

20 Copeland argued that U.S. leaders, including Harry Truman, liked Josef Stalin and did not feel that he was bent on aggression. They nevertheless undertook actions that initiated the Cold War because they did not feel that they could trust future Soviet leaders. See Copeland, *op. cit.*, ch. 6. This worry about the future goes beyond the question of whether states can communicate their benign intentions effectively, so that the so-called status-quo states can distinguish themselves from the so-called revisionist states. On the latter question, see Andrew Kydd, "Trust, Reassurance, and Cooperation," *International Organization* 54 (2000): 325–357, and "Sheep in Sheep's Clothing: Why Security Seekers Do Not Fight Each Other," *Security Studies* 7 (1997): 114–155.

21 The view that all states are potentially expansionist and should therefore be assumed to be dangerous is not shared by all realists. For example, some believe that states do not necessarily balance against the strongest power but focus instead on the most menacing one. This view in turn implies that officials differentiate between those states that are more threatening and others that do not pose a serious danger. They do not make the worst-case assumption about the intentions of all other states. See Stephen M. Walt, *The Origins of Alliances* (Ithaca, NY: Cornell University Press, 1987); and also David M. Edelstein, "Managing Uncertainty: Beliefs about Intentions and the Rise of Great Powers," *Security Studies* 12 (2002): 1–40.

22 Stephen M. Walt, "Keeping the World 'Off Balance': Self Restraint and U.S. Foreign Policy," in Ikenberry, *op. cit.*, pp. 121–154. In a similar vein, Christopher Layne repeated Edmund Burke's memorable warning:

> Among precautions against ambition, it may not be amiss to take one precaution against our own. I must fairly say, I dread our own power and our own ambition: I dread our being too much dreaded. . . . It is ridiculous to say we are not men, and that, as men we shall never wish to aggrandize ourselves in some way or other . . . we say that we shall not abuse this astonishing and hitherto unheard of power. But every other nation will think we shall abuse it. It is impossible but that, sooner or later, this state of affairs must produce a combination against us which may end in our ruin.
>
> (Edmund Burke, "Remarks on the Policy of the Allies with Respect to France," *The Works of Edmund Burke*, vol. 4 (Boston, MA: Little, Brown, 1901), p. 457. Quoted in Christopher Layne, *The Peace of Illusions: American Grand Strategy from 1940 to the Present* (Ithaca, NY: Cornell University Press, 2006), p. 204)

23 Lagne, *op. cit.*, (2006).

24 Christopher Layne makes a forceful case for the U.S. to abandon its current grand strategy of global hegemony in favor of a policy of offshore balancing. See ibid., as well as others such as Robert Pape and Stephen Walt (*op. cit.*), who have warned that assertive and expansive applications of U.S. power can cause blowback and induce other states to engage in balancing behavior.

25 Walter LaFeber, "The Bush Doctrine," *Diplomatic History* 26 (2002): 558. Quoted in Layne, *op. cit.* (2006), p. 204.

Bibliography

Axelrod, Robert, *The Evolution of Cooperation*, New York: Basic Books, 1984.

Bacevich, Andrew J., *American Empire: The Realities and Consequences of U.S. Diplomacy*, Cambridge, MA: Harvard University Press, 2002.

Bailey, Sydney D. and Sam Daws, *The Procedure of the UN Security Council* (3rd edn), Oxford: Clarendon Press, 1998.

Baldwin, David A., *Economic Statecraft*, Princeton, NJ: Princeton University Press, 1985.

—— "Evaluating Economic Sanctions," *International Security* 23 (1998): 189–198.

Barber, Benjamin R., *Fear's Empire: War, Terror, and Democracy*, New York: Norton, 2003.

Barber, James R., *Jihad vs. McWorld: How Globalism and Tribalism Are Reshaping the World*, New York: Random House, 1995.

Barbieri, Katherine, *The Liberal Illusion: Does Trade Promote Peace?*, Ann Arbor: University of Michigan Press, 2002.

Barnhart, Michael A., *Japan Prepares for Total War: The Search for Economic Security, 1919–1945*, Ithaca, NY: Cornell University Press, 1987.

Bennett, Scott and Allan C. Stam, III, "The Duration of Interstate Wars: 1816–1985," *American Political Science Review* 90 (1996): 239–257.

—— "The Declining Advantages of Democracy: A Combined Model of War Outcomes and Duration," *Journal of Conflict Resolution* 42 (1998): 344–366.

Berghahn, V.R., *Germany and the Approach of War in 1914*, London: St. Martin's Press, 1973.

Bernstein, Richard and Ross H. Munro, "The Coming Conflict with America," *Foreign Affairs* 76 (1997): 18–32.

Bobrow, Davis B., "Challenges to U.S. Preferences: Strategies of Resistance and Modification." Manuscript (University of Pittsburgh, 2004).

Bobrow, Davis B., Steve Chan, and John A. Kringen, *Understanding Foreign Policy Decisions: The Chinese Case*, New York: Free Press, 1979.

Boettcher, William A., III, *Presidential Risk Behavior in Foreign Policy: Prudence or Peril?*, New York: Macmillan, 2005.

Boulding, Kenneth E., *Conflict and Defense*, New York: Harper & Row, 1962.

Bourne, Kenneth, *Britain and the Balance of Power in North America: 1815–1908*, Berkeley: University of California Press, 1967.

Brooks, Stephen G. and William C. Wohlforth, "Power, Globalization, and the End of the Cold War: Reevaluating a Landmark Case for Ideas," *International Security* 25 (2000/2001): 5–53.

—— "Economic Constraints and the End of the Cold War," in *Cold War Endgame: Oral History, Analysis, Debates*, ed. William C. Wohlforth, University Park: Pennsylvania State University Press, 2003, pp. 273–309.

—— "Hard Times for Soft Balancing," *International Security* 30 (2005): 72–108.

Brown, Michael E., Owen R. Cote, Jr., Sean M. Lynn-Jones, and Steven E. Miller, eds, *The Rise of China*, Cambridge, MA: MIT Press, 2000.

Bueno de Mesquita, Bruce, "Pride of Place: The Origins of German Hegemony," *World Politics* 43 (1990): 1–27.

—— and Randolph M. Siverson, "War and the Survival of Political Leaders: A Comparative Study of Regime Types and Political Accountability," *American Political Science Review* 89 (1995): 841–853.

Bueno de Mesquita, Bruce, Randolph M. Siverson, and Gary Woller, "War and the Fate of Regimes: A Comparative Analysis," *American Political Science Review* 86 (1992): 638–646.

Burke, Edmund, "Remarks on the Policy of the Allies with Respect to France," *The Works of Edmund Burke*, vol. 4, Boston, MA: Little, Brown, 1901.

Burr, William and Jeffrey T. Richelson, "Whether to 'Strangle the Baby in the Cradle': The United States and the Chinese Nuclear Program, 1960–64," *International Security* 25 (2000/2001): 54–99.

Bush, George W., *National Security Strategy of the United States of America*, Washington, D.C.: Government Printing Office, 2002.

Bush, Richard C., *Untying the Knot: Making Peace in the Taiwan Strait*, Washington, D.C.: Brookings Institution Press, 2005.

Bussman, Margit and John R. Oneal, "Do Hegemons Distribute Private Goods? A Test of Power-Transition Theory," *Journal of Conflict Resolution* 51 (2007): 88–111.

Buzan, Barry, *People, States and Fear: An Agenda for International Security Studies in the Post-Cold War Era*, Boulder, CO: Lynne Rienner, 1991.

Calleo, David, *Beyond American Hegemony: The Future of the Western Alliance*, New York: Basic Books, 1988.

Carlsnaes, Walter, "The Agency-Structure Problem in Foreign Policy Analysis," *International Studies Quarterly* 36 (1992): 245–279.

Casetti, Emilio, "Power Shifts and Economic Development: When Will China Overtake the USA?," *Journal of Peace Research* 40 (2003): 661–675.

Central Intelligence Agency, *2005 World Factbook* available at http:www.cia.gov/cia/publications/factbook.

Chan, Steve, "Chinese Conflict Calculus and Behavior: Assessment from a Perspective of Conflict Management," *World Politics* 30 (1978): 391–410.

—— "Extended Deterrence in the Taiwan Strait: Learning from Rationalist Explanations in International Relations," *World Affairs* 166 (2003): 109–125.

—— "Power, Satisfaction, and Popularity: A Poisson Analysis of U.N. Security Council Vetoes," *Cooperation and Conflict* 38 (2003): 339–359.

—— "Can't Get No Satisfaction? The Recognition of Revisionist States," *International Relations of the Asia-Pacific* 4 (2004): 207–238.

—— "Exploring Some Puzzles in Power-Transition Theory: Some Implications for Sino-American Relations," *Security Studies* 13 (2004): 103–141.

—— "Realism, Revisionism, and the Great Powers," *Issues & Studies* 40 (2004): 135–172.

—— "Discerning the Causal Relationships between Great Powers' IGO Membership and Their Initiation of Militarized Disputes," *Conflict Management and Peace Science* 22 (2005): 239–256.

—— "Is There a Power Transition between the U.S. and China? The Different Faces of Power," *Asian Survey* 45 (2005): 687–701.

—— "Prognosticating about Extended Deterrence in the Taiwan Strait: Implications from Strategic Selection," *World Affairs* 168 (2005): 13–25.

—— "Soft Deterrence, Passive Resistance: American Lenses, Chinese Lessons," presented at the annual meeting of the International Studies Association, Honolulu, March 1–5, 2005.

—— "The Politics of Economic Exchange: Carrots and Sticks in Taiwan–China–U.S. Relations," *Issues & Studies* 42 (2006): 1–22.

—— and A. Cooper Drury, eds, *Sanctions as Economic Statecraft: Theory and Practice*, London: Macmillan, 2000.

—— and Alex Mintz, eds., *Defense, Welfare, and Growth: Perspectives and Evidence*, London: Routledge, Chapman and Hall, 1992.

—— and Brock Tessman, "Relative Decline: Why Does It Induce War or Sustain Peace?" Manuscript (Boulder, CO: University of Colorado, 2005).

Chang, Gordon, "JFK, China, and the Bomb," *Journal of American History* 74 (1988): 1289–1310.

Chen, Jian, *China's Road to the Korean War: The Making of the Sino-American Confrontation*, New York: Columbia University Press, 1994.

—— "China's Involvement in the Vietnam War, 1964–69," *China Quarterly* 142 (1995): 356–387.

Cheng, T.J., "China–Taiwan Economic Linkage: Between Insularity and Super-conductivity," in *Dangerous Strait: The U.S.–Taiwan–China Crisis*, ed. Nancy Bernkopf Tucker, New York: Columbia University Press, 2005, pp. 93–130.

"China's Century," *Newsweek* (May 9, 2005): 26–45.

"China's New Revolution," *Time* (June 27, 2005): 22–53.

"China's Turn," *U.S. News and World Report* (June 20, 2005): 34–52.

Choucri, Nazli and Robert C. North, *Domestic Growth and International Violence*, San Francisco, CA: Freeman, 1975.

Christensen, Thomas J., *Useful Adversaries: Grand Strategy, Domestic Mobilization and Sino-American Conflict, 1947–1958*, Princeton, NJ: Princeton University Press, 1996.

—— "Posing Problems without Catching Up: China's Rise and Challenges for U.S. Security Policy," *International Security* 25 (2001): 5–40.

—— "The Contemporary Security Dilemma: Deterring a Taiwan Conflict," *The Washington Quarterly* 25 (2002): 7–21.

—— "Fostering Stability or Creating a Monster?," *International Security* 31 (2006): 81–126.

—— and Jack Snyder, "Chain Gangs and Passed Bucks: Predicting Alliance Patterns in Multipolarity," *International Organization* 44 (1990): 137–168.

Cingranelli, David L. and David L. Richards, "Measuring the Level, Pattern, and Sequence of Government Respect for Physical Integrity Rights," *International Studies Quarterly* 43 (1999): 407–417.

—— "Respect for Human Rights After the End of the Cold War," *Journal of Peace Research* 36 (1999): 511–534.

Cipolla, Carlo M., *Guns, Sails, and Empires: Technological Innovation and the Early Phases of European Expansion, 1470–1700*, New York: Minerva Press, 1965.

—— ed., *The Economic Decline of Empires*, London: Methuen, 1970.

Colvin, Geoffrey, "America: The 97-lb. Weakling," *Fortune* (July 25, 2005): 70–82.

Copeland, Dale C., "Economic Interdependence and War: A Theory of Trade Expectations," *International Security* 20 (1996): 4–41.

—— "Neorealism and the Myth of Bipolar Stability: Toward a New Dynamic Realist Theory of Major War," *Security Studies* 5 (1996): 29–89.

—— *The Origins of Major War*, Ithaca, NY: Cornell University Press, 2000.

Craig, Campbell, "American Realism Versus American Imperialism," *World Politics* 57 (2004): 143–171.

Crawford, Timothy W., *Pivotal Deterrence: Third-Party Statecraft and the Pursuit of Peace*, Ithaca, NY: Cornell University Press, 2003.

Daalder, Ivo H. and James M. Lindsay, *America Unbound: The Bush Revolution in Foreign Policy*, New York: Wiley, 2005.

Dalton, Russell J., "Political Support in Advanced Industrial Democracies," in *Critical Citizens: Global Support for Democratic Government*, ed. Pippa Norris, Oxford: Oxford University Press, 1999, pp. 57–77.

Danilovic, Vesna, "Conceptual and Selection Biases in Deterrence," *Journal of Conflict Resolution* 45 (2001): 97–125.

—— "The Sources of Threat Credibility in Extended Deterrence," *Journal of Conflict Resolution* 45 (2001): 341–369.

Deutsch, Karl W., Sidney A. Burrell, Robert A. Kann, Maurice Lee, Jr., Martin Lichtenman, Raymond E. Lindgren, Francis L. Loewenheim, and Richard W. Van Wagenen, *Political Community and the North Atlantic Area: International Organization in the Light of Historical Experience*, New York: Greenwood Press, 1957.

DiCicco, Jonathan M. and Jack Levy, "Power Shifts and Problem Shifts: The Evolution of the Power Transition Research Program," *Journal of Conflict Resolution* 43 (1999): 675–704.

Domke, William K., *War and the Changing Global System*, New Haven, CT: Yale University Press, 1988.

Doran, Charles F., "System Disequilibrium, Foreign Policy Role, and the Power Cycle: Challenges for Research Design," *Journal of Conflict Resolution* 33 (1989): 371–401.

—— *Systems in Crisis: New Imperatives of High Politics at Century's End*, Cambridge: Cambridge University Press, 1991.

—— and Wes Parsons, "War and the Cycle of Relative Power," *American Political Science Review* 74 (1980): 947–965.

Drezner, Daniel W., "Bargaining, Enforcement, and Multilateral Sanctions: When Is Cooperation Counterproductive?," *International Organization* 54 (2000): 73–102.

East, Maurice A., "Status Discrepancy and Violence in the International System: An Empirical Analysis," in *The Analysis of International Politics*, ed. James N. Rosenau, Vincent Davis, and Maurice A. East, New York: Free Press, 1972, pp. 299–319.

Edelstein, David M., "Managing Uncertainty: Beliefs about Intentions and the Rise of Great Powers," *Security Studies* 12 (2002): 1–40.

Efird, Brian, Jacek Kugler, and Gaspare M. Genna, "From War to Integration: Generalizing Power Transition Theory," *International Interactions* 29 (2003): 293–313.

Eichenberg, Richard C., "Victory Has Many Friends: U.S. Public Opinion and the Use of Military Force, 1981–2005," *International Security* 30 (2005): 140–177.

Elliott, John H., *Imperial Spain, 1469–1716*, New York: St. Martin's Press, 1963.

Elliott, Kimberly A., "The Sanctions Glass: Half Full or Completely Empty?," *International Security* 23 (1998): 50–65.

European Union, Directorate General Press and Communication, "Iraq and Peace in the World," November 2003.

Farnham, Barbara, ed., *Avoiding Losses/Taking Risks: Prospect Theory and International Conflict*, Ann Arbor: University of Michigan Press, 1994.

Fearon, James D., "Domestic Political Audiences and the Escalation of International Disputes," *American Political Science Review* 88 (1994): 577–592.

—— "Signaling versus the Balance of Power and Interests: An Empirical Test of a Crisis Bargaining Model," *Journal of Conflict Resolution* 38 (1994): 236–269.

—— "Rationalist Explanations for War," *International Organization* 49 (1995): 379–414.

—— "Signalling Foreign Policy Interests: Tying Hands versus Sinking Costs," *Journal of Conflict Resolution* 41 (1997): 68–90.

—— "Commitment Problems and the Spread of Ethnic Conflict," in *The International Spread of Ethnic Conflict: Fear, Diffusion, and Escalation*, ed. David A. Lake and Donald Rothchild, Princeton, NJ: Princeton University Press, 1998, pp. 107–126.

—— "Selection Effects and Deterrence," *International Interactions* 28 (2000): 5–29.

Fischer, Fritz, *The War of Illusions*, New York: Norton, 1975.

Formal alliance data are available at http://cow2.la.psu.edu.

Fravel, M. Taylor, "Regime Insecurity and International Cooperation: Explaining China's Compromises in Territorial Disputes," *International Security* 30 (2005): 46–83.

Friedberg, Aaron L., *The Weary Titan: Britain and the Experience of Relative Decline, 1895–1905*, Princeton, NJ: Princeton University Press, 1988.

—— "The Future of U.S.–China Relations: Is Conflict Inevitable?," *International Security* 30 (2005): 7–45.

Galtung, Johan, "A Structural Theory of Aggression," *Journal of Peace Research* 1 (1964): 95–119.

Gartner, Scott Sigmund and Randolph M. Siverson, "War Expansion and War Outcome," *Journal of Conflict Resolution* 40 (1996): 4–15.

Gartzke, Erik, "War Is in the Error Term," *International Organization* 53 (1999): 567–587.

—— and Kristian S. Gleditsch, "Why Democracies May Actually Be Less Reliable Allies," *American Journal of Political Science* 48 (2004): 775–795.

Gartzke, Eric, Quan Li, and Charles Boehmer, "Investing in the Peace: Economic Interdependence and International Conflict," *International Organization* 55 (2001): 391–438.

Garver, John W., *Face Off: China, the United States, and Taiwan's Democratization*, Seattle: University of Washington Press, 1997.

Geller, Daniel S., "Status Quo Orientation, Capabilities, and Patterns of War Initiation in Dyadic Rivalries," *Conflict Management and Peace Science* 18 (2000): 73–96.

Gibbon, Edward, *The Decline and Fall of the Roman Empire*, New York: Dutton, 1910.

Gill, Stephen, ed., *Gramsci, Historical Materialism, and International Relations*, Cambridge: Cambridge University Press, 1993.

Gilpin, Robert, *War and Change in World Politics*, New York: Cambridge University Press, 1981.

Goldstein, Avery, "Great Expectations: Interpreting China's Arrival," *International Security* 22 (1997/1998): 36–73.

—— *Rising to the Challenge: China's Grand Strategy and International Security*, Stanford, CA: Stanford University Press, 2005.

Gowa, Joanne, *Allies, Adversaries, and International Trade*, Princeton, NJ: Princeton University Press, 1994.

Gramsci, Antonio, *Selection from the Prison Notebooks of Antonio Gramsci*, ed. and trans. Quintin Hoare and Geoffrey Nowell Smith, New York: International Publishers, 1971.

Gries, Peter H., *China's New Nationalism: Pride, Politics, and Diplomacy*, Berkeley: University of California Press, 2004.

—— "China Eyes the Hegemon," *Orbis* 49 (2005): 401–412.

—— "Forecasting US–China Relations, 2015." Manuscript (Boulder, CO: University of Colorado, 2005).

Gurtov, Melvin, "The Taiwan Strait Crisis Revisited: Politics and Foreign Policy in Chinese Motives," *Modern China* 2 (1976): 49–103.

Haas, Mark L., "Prospect Theory and the Cuban Missile Crisis," *International Studies Quarterly* 45 (2001): 241–270.

Haas, Michael, "International Subsystems: Stability and Polarity," *American Political Science Review* 64 (1970): 98–123.

Hillgruber, Andreas, *Germany and the Two World Wars*, Cambridge, MA: Harvard University Press, 1981.

Hirschman, Albert O., *National Power and the Structure of Foreign Trade*, Berkeley: University of California Press, 1945.

Holsti, Ole R., "The Belief System and National Images: A Case Study," *Journal of Conflict Resolution* 6 (1962): 244–252.

Houweling, Henk and Jan G. Siccama, "Power Transitions as a Cause of War," *Journal of Conflict Resolution* 32 (1988): 87–102.

Hu, Angang, "The Chinese Economy in Prospect," in *China, the United States, and the Global Economy*, ed. Shuxun Chen and Charles Wolf, Jr., Santa Monica, CA: RAND, 2001, pp. 99–146.

Hufbauer, Gary C. and Yee Wong, "China Bashing 2004," *International Economics Policy Briefs*, No. PB04-5, September 2004, pp. 2–3; available at http://www.iie.com/publications/pb/pb04–5.pdf.

Hufbauer, Gary, Jeffrey Schott, and Kimberly A. Elliott, *Economic Sanctions Reconsidered: History and Current Policy* (2nd edn), Washington, D.C.: Institute of International Economics, 1990.

Huntington, Samuel P., *Political Order in Changing Societies*, New Haven, CT: Yale University Press, 1968.

Huth, Paul K., *Extended Deterrence and the Prevention of War*, New Haven, CT: Yale University Press, 1988.

—— "Extended Deterrence and the Outbreak of War," *American Political Science Review* 82 (1988): 423–443.

—— and Bruce M. Russett, "What Makes Deterrence Work? Cases from 1900 to 1980," *World Politics* 36 (1984): 496–526.

—— "Deterrence Failure and Crisis Escalation," *International Studies Quarterly* 32 (1988): 29–45.

—— "Testing Deterrence Theory: Rigor Makes a Difference," *World Politics* 52 (1990): 466–501.

—— "General Deterrence between Enduring Rivals: Testing Three Competing Models," *American Political Science Review* 87 (1993): 61–73.

Huth, Paul K., Christopher Gelpi, and D. Scott Bennett, "The Escalation of Great Power Disputes: Testing Rational Deterrence Theory and Structural Realism," *American Political Science Review* 87 (1993): 609–623.

Ikenberry, G. John, ed., *America Unrivaled: The Future of the Balance of Power*, Ithaca, NY: Cornell University Press, 2002.

—— "America's Imperial Ambition," *Foreign Affairs* 81 (2002): 44–60.

Inglehart, Ronald and Wayne E. Baker, "Modernization, Cultural Change, and the Persistence of Traditional Values," *American Sociological Review* 65 (2000): 19–51.

Inglehart, Ronald, Miguel Basanez, Jaime Diez-Medrano, Loek Halman, and Ruud Luijkx, eds, *Human Beliefs and Values: A Cross-cultural Sourcebook based on the 1999–2002 Values Surveys*, Mexico City: Siglo Veintiuno Editories, 2004.

Intergovernmental organizations data are available at http://cow2.la.psu.edu.

Iriye, Akira, *Power and Culture: The Japanese–American War, 1941–1945*, Cambridge, MA: Harvard University Press, 1981.

Jacobson, Harold K., *Networks of Interdependence: International Organizations and the Global Political System*, New York: Knopf, 1984.

Jentleson, Bruce W., "The Pretty Prudent Public: Post-Vietnam American Opinion on the Use of Military Force," *International Studies Quarterly* 36 (1992): 47–74.

—— and Rebecca L. Britton, "Still Pretty Prudent: Post-Cold War American Public Opinion on the Use of Military Force," *Journal of Conflict Resolution* 42 (1998): 395–417.

Jervis, Robert, *Perception and Misperception in International Relations*, Princeton, NJ: Princeton University Press, 1976.

—— "What Do We Want to Deter and How Do We Deter It?," in *Turning Point: The Gulf War and the U.S. Military Strategy*, ed. L. Benjamin Edington and Michael J. Mazarr, Boulder, CO: Westview Press, 1994, pp. 122–124.

—— *System Effects: Complexity in Political Social Life*, Princeton, NJ: Princeton University Press, 1997.

—— "Explaining the Bush Doctrine," *Political Science Quarterly* 118 (2003): 365–388.

—— *American Foreign Policy in a New Era*, New York: Routledge, 2005.

Johnson, Chalmers A., *Blowback: The Costs and Consequences of American Empire*, New York: Metropolitan Books, 2000.

Johnson, Alastair Iain, *Cultural Realism: Strategic Culture and Grand Strategy in Chinese History*, Princeton, NJ: Princeton University Press, 1995.

—— "Is China a Status Quo Power?," *International Security* 7 (2003): 5–56.

Kahneman, Daniel and Amos Tversky, "Prospect Theory: An Analysis of Decision under Risk," *Econometrica* 47 (1979): 263–291.

——, eds, *Choices, Values, and Frames*, Cambridge: Cambridge University Press, 2000.

Kahneman, Daniel, Paul Slovic, and Amos Tversky, eds., *Judgment under Uncertainty: Heuristics and Biases*, Cambridge: Cambridge University Press, 1982.

Kang, David C., "Getting Asia Wrong: The Need for New Analytical Frameworks," *International Security* 27 (2003): 57–85.

—— "Why China's Rise Will be Peaceful: Hierarchy and Stability in the East Asian Region," *Perspectives on Politics* 3 (2005): 551–554.

Kant, Immanuel, *Perpetual Peace*, trans. Lewis White Beck, New York: Bobbs-Merrill, 1957.

Kaplan, Robert D., "How We Would Fight China," *The Atlantic Monthly* (June 2005): 49–64.

Kegley, Charles W. and Gregory A. Raymond, *A Multipolar Peace? Great-Power Politics in the Twenty-first Century*, New York: St. Martin's Press, 1994.

Kennedy, Paul M., *The Rise of the Anglo-German Antagonism, 1860–1914*, London: Allen & Unwin, 1982.

—— "The First World War and the International Power System," *International Security* 9 (1984): 7–40.

—— *The Rise and Fall of the Great Powers: Economic Change and Military Conflict from 1500 to 2000*, New York: Random House, 1987.

Keohane, Robert O., *After Hegemony: Cooperation and Discord in the World Political Economy*, Princeton, NJ: Princeton University Press, 1984.

—— and Lisa L. Martin, "The Promise of Institutionalist Theory," *International Security* 20 (1995): 39–51.

Keochane, Robert O. and Joseph S. Nye, *Power and Interdependence: World Politics in Transition*, Boston, MA: Little, Brown, 1977.

Khong, Yuen Foong, *Analogies at War: Korea, Munich, Dien Bien Phu, and the Vietnam Decisions of 1965*, Princeton, NJ: Princeton University Press, 1992.

—— "Negotiating 'Order' during Power Transitions," in *Power in Transition: The Peaceful Change of International Order*, ed. Charles A. Kupchan, Emanuel Adler, Jean-Marc Coicaud, and Yuen Foong Khong, Tokyo: United Nations University Press, 2001, pp. 34–67.

Khoo, Nicholas and Michael L.R. Smith, "China Engages Asia? Caveat Lector," *International Security* 30 (2005): 196–205.

Kim, Woosang, "Power, Alliance, and Major Wars, 1816–1975," *Journal of Conflict Resolution* 33 (1989): 255–273.

—— "Alliance Transitions and Great Power War," *American Journal of Political Science* 35 (1991): 833–850.

—— "Power Transitions and Great Power War from Westphalia to Waterloo," *World Politics* 45 (1992): 153–172.

—— "Power Parity, Alliance, Dissatisfaction, and Wars in East Asia, 1860–1993," *Journal of Conflict Resolution* 46 (2002): 654–672.

—— and James D. Morrow, "When Do Power Shifts Lead to War?," *American Journal of Political Science* 36 (1992): 896–922.

Krish, Nico, "Weak as Constraint, Strong as Tool: The Place of International Law in U.S. Foreign Policy," in *Unilateralism and U.S. Foreign Policy: International Perspectives*, ed. David M. Malone and Yuen Foong Khong, Boulder, CO: Lynne Rienner, 2003, pp. 41–70.

Kugler, Jacek, "The Asian Ascent: Opportunity for Peace or Precondition for War?," *International Studies Perspectives* 7 (2006): 36–42.

—— and Douglas Lemke, eds, *Parity and War: Evaluations and Extensions of The War Ledger*, Ann Arbor: University of Michigan Press, 1996.

—— "The Power Transition Research Program," in *Handbook of War Studies II*, ed. Manus I. Midlarsky, Ann Arbor: University of Michigan Press, 2000, pp. 129–163.

Kupchan, Charles A., "Benign States and Peaceful Transition," in *Power in Transition: The Peaceful Change of International Order*, ed. Charles A. Kupchan, Emanuel Adler, Jean-Marc Coicaud, and Yuen Foong Khong, Tokyo: United Nations University Press, 2001, pp. 18–33.

Kupchan, Charles A., Emanuel Adler, Jean-Marc Coicaud, and Yuen Foong Khong, eds, *Power in Transition: The Peaceful Change of International Order*, Tokyo: United Nations University Press, 2001.

Kydd, Andrew, "Sheep in Sheep's Clothing: Why Security Seekers Do Not Fight Each Other," *Security Studies* 7 (1997): 114–155.

—— "Trust, Reassurance, and Cooperation," *International Organization* 54 (2000): 325–357.

Lacy, Dean and Emerson M.S. Niou, "A Theory of Economic Sanctions and Issue Linkage: The Roles of Preferences, Information, and Threats," *Journal of Politics* 66 (2004): 25–42.

LaFeber, Walter, "The Bush Doctrine," *Diplomatic History* 26 (2002): 543–558.

Lake, David, "Powerful Pacifists: Democratic States and War," *American Political Science Review* 86 (1992): 24–37.

Lampton, David M., *Same Bed, Different Dreams: Managing U.S.–China Relations, 1989–2000*, Berkeley: University of California Press, 2001.

Lardy, Nicholas R., *China's Unfinished Economic Revolution*, Washington, D.C.: The Brookings Institution, 1998.

Layne, Christopher, "The 'Poster Child for Offensive Realism': America as a Global Hegemon," *Security Studies* 12 (2002/2003): 120–164.

—— *The Peace of Illusions: American Grand Strategy from 1940 to the Present*, Ithaca, NY: Cornell University Press, 2006.

Lebow, Richard Ned and Thomas Risse-Kappen, eds, *International Relations Theory and the End of the Cold War*, New York: Columbia University Press, 1995.

Lebow, Richard Ned and Janice Gross Stein, "Deterrence: The Elusive Dependent Variable," *World Politics* 52 (1990): 336–369.

Legro, Jeffrey W. and Andrew Moravcsik, "Is Anybody Still a Realist?," *International Security* 24 (1999): 5–55.

Lemke, Douglas, *Regions of War and Peace*, Cambridge: Cambridge University Press, 2002.

—— "Investigating the Preventive Motive for War," *International Interactions* 29 (2003): 273–292.

—— "Great Powers in the Post-Cold War World: A Power Transition Perspective," in *Balance of Power: Theory and Practice in the 21st Century*, ed. T.V. Paul, James J. Wirtz, and Michel Fortmann, Stanford, CA: Stanford University Press, 2004, pp. 52–75.

—— and William Reed, "Regime Types and Status Quo Evaluations: Power Transition Theory and the Democratic Peace," *International Interactions* 22 (1996): 143–164.

—— "Power Is Not Satisfaction: A Comment on de Soysa, Oneal, and Park," *Journal of Conflict Resolution* 42 (1998): 511–516.

Lemke, Douglas and Ronald L. Tammen, "Power Transition Theory and the Rise of China," *International Interactions* 29 (2003): 269–271.

Lemke, Douglas and Suzanne Werner, "Power Parity, Commitment to Change, and War," *International Studies Quarterly* 40 (1996): 235–260.

Leng, Tse-Kang, *The Taiwan–China Connection: Democracy and Development across the Taiwan Straits*, Boulder, CO: Westview Press, 1996.

Levy, Jack S., "Loss Aversion, Framing, and Bargaining: The Implications of Prospect Theory for International Conflict," *International Political Science Review* 17 (1996): 179–195.

—— "Prospect Theory, Rational Choice, and International Relations," *International Studies Quarterly* 41 (1997): 87–112.

—— "What Do Great Powers Balance Against and When?," in *Balance of Power: Theory and Practice in the 21st Century*, ed. T.V. Paul, James J., Wirtz and Michael Fortmann, Stanford, CA: Stanford University Press, 2004, pp. 29–51.

Lieber, Keir A. and Gerard Alexander, "Waiting for Balancing: Why the World Is Not Pushing Back," *International Security* 30 (2005): 109–139.

Lindblom, Charles E., *The Intelligence of Democracy: Decision Making Through Mutual Adjustment*, New York: Free Press, 1965.

Lipset, Seymour Martin, *American Exceptionalism: A Double-Edged Sword*, New York: Norton, 1996.

Lo, Chi-kin, *China's Policy Towards Territorial Disputes: The Case of the South China Sea Islands*, London: Routledge, 1989.

Long, William J., *Economic Incentives and Bilateral Cooperation*, Ann Arbor: University of Michigan Press, 1996.

Luttwak, Edward, *The Grand Strategy of the Soviet Union*, New York: St. Martin's Press, 1983.

McDermott, Rose, *Risk-Taking in International Politics: Prospect Theory in American Foreign Policy*, Ann Arbor: University of Michigan Press, 1998.

MacFarquhar, Roderick, *Sino-American Relations, 1949–71*, New York: Praeger, 1972.

Mack, Andrew, "Why Big Nations Lose Small Wars: The Politics of Asymmetric Conflict," *World Politics* 27 (1975): 175–200.

Mahbubani, Kishore, "Understanding China," *Foreign Affairs* 84 (2005): 49–60.

Malone, David M. and Yuen Foong Khong, "Unilateralism and U.S. Foreign Policy: International Perspectives," in *Unilateralism and U.S. Foreign Policy: International Perspectives*, ed. David M. Malone and Yuen Foong Khong, Boulder, CO: Lynne Rienner, 2003, pp. 1–17.

Mansfield, Edward D. and Jack Snyder, "Democratization and the Danger of War," *International Security* 20 (1995): 5–38.

—— *Electing to Fight: Why Emerging Democracies Go to War*, Cambridge, MA: MIT Press, 2005.

Maoz, Zeev, *Paradoxies of War: On the Art of National Self-Entrapment*, Boston, MA: Unwin Hyman, 1990.

March, James, "Power of Power," in *Varieties of Political Theory*, ed. David Easton, Englewood Cliffs, NJ: Prentice Hall, 1966, pp. 39–70.

Martin, Lisa L., *Coercive Cooperation: Explaining Multilateral Economic Sanctions*, Princeton, NJ: Princeton University Press, 1992.

—— "Credibility, Costs, and Institutions: Cooperation on Economic Sanctions," *World Politic* 45 (1993): 406–432.

Mastanduno, Michael, *Economic Containment: CoCom and the Politics of East–West Trade*, Ithaca, NY: Cornell University Press, 1992.

Mearsheimer, John J., "Why We Will Soon Miss the Cold War," *The Atlantic* (August 1990): 35–50.

—— "Back to the Future: Instability in Europe after the Cold War," *International Security* 15 (1990): 5–56.

—— *The Tragedy of Great Power Politics*, New York: Norton, 2001.

—— and Stephen M. Walt, "An Unnecessary War," *Foreign Policy* (January/February 2003): 50–59.

Mercer, Jonathan, *Reputation and International Politics*, Ithaca, NY: Cornell University Press, 1996.

Midlarsky, Manus I., *On War: Political Violence in the International System*, New York: Free Press, 1975.

Modelski, George, *Long Cycles in World Politics*, Seattle: University of Washington Press, 1987.

—— and William R. Thompson, *Leading Sectors and World Powers: The Coevolution of Global Politics and Economics*, Columbia: University of South Carolina Press, 1996.

Moran, Theodore H., "Multinational Corporations and Dependency: A Dialogue for Dependistas and Non-dependentistas," *International Organization* 32 (1978): 79–100.

Morris, Morris D., *Measuring the Condition of the World's Poor: The Physical Quality of Life Index*, New York: Pergamon Press, 1979.

Morrow, James D., "The Logic of Overtaking," in *Parity and War: Evaluations and Extensions of The War Ledger*, ed. Jacek Kugler and Douglas Lemke, Ann Arbor: University of Michigan Press, 1996, pp. 313–330.

Most, Benjamin A. and Harvey Starr, *Inquiry, Logic and International Politics*, Columbia: University of South Carolina Press, 1989.

Moulder, Frances V., *Japan, China and the Modern World Economy*, New York: Cambridge University Press, 1979.

Nathan, Andrew J. and Robert S. Ross, *The Great Wall and the Empty Fortress: China's Search for Security*, New York: Norton, 1997.

National Material Capabilities (v3.0) are available at http://cow2.la.psu.edu.

Nye, Joseph Jr., *Bound to Lead: The Changing Nature of American Power*, New York: Basic Books, 1990.

—— *The Paradox of American Power*, New York: Oxford University Press, 2002.

Olson, Mancur, *The Logic of Collective Action: Public Goods and the Theory of Groups*, Cambridge, MA: Harvard University Press, 1965.

—— and Richard Zeckhauser, "An Economic Theory of Alliances," *Review of Economics and Statistics* 48 (1966): 266–279.

Oneal, John R., Indra de Soysa, and Yong-Hee Park, "But Power and Wealth *Are* Satisfying: A Reply to Lemke and Reed," *Journal of Conflict Resolution* 42 (1998): 517–520.

Oren, Ido, "The Subjectivity of the 'Democratic Peace': Changing U.S. Perceptions of Imperial Germany," *International Security* 20 (1995): 147–184.

Organski, A.F.K., *World Politics*, New York: Knopf, 1958.

—— and Jacek Kugler, *The War Ledger*, Chicago, IL: University of Chicago Press, 1980.

Overholt, William H., *The Rise of China: How Economic Reform is Creating a New Superpower*, New York: Norton, 1993.

Owens, John M., IV, *Liberal Peace, Liberal War: American Politics and International Security*, Ithaca, NY: Cornell University Press, 1997.

Oye, Kenneth, Donald Rothchild, and Robert Lieber, eds, *Eagle Entangled: U.S. Foreign Policy in A Complex World*, New York: Longman, 1979.

Pape, Robert A., "Why Economic Sanctions Do Not Work," *International Security* 22 (1997): 90–136.

—— "Why Economic Sanctions Still Do Not Work," *International Security* 23 (1998): 66–77.

—— "Evaluating Economic Sanctions," *International Security* 23 (1998): 189–198.

—— "Soft Balancing against the United States," *International Security* 30 (2005): 7–45.

Paris, Roland, *At War's End: Building Peace after Civil Conflict*, New York: Cambridge University Press, 2004.

Paul, T.V., *Asymmetric Conflicts: War Initiations by Weaker Powers*, New York: Cambridge University Press, 1994.

—— "Introduction: The Enduring Axioms of Balance of Power Theory and Their Contemporary Relevance," in *Balance of Power: Theory and Practice in the 21st Century*, ed. T.V. Paul, James J. Wirtz, and Michel Fortmann, Stanford, CA: Stanford University Press, 2004, pp. 1–25.

—— "Soft Balancing in the Age of U.S. Primacy," *International Security* 30 (2005): 46–71.

Paul, T.V., James J. Wirtz, and Michel Fortmann, eds., *Balance of Power: Theory and Practice in the 21st Century*, Stanford, CA: Stanford University Press, 2004.

Pew Research Center Public Opinion Polls are available at http://pewglobal.org.

Pollack, Jonathan D., "The Transformation of the Asian Security Order: Assessing China's Impact," in *Power Shift: China and Asia's New Dynamics*, ed. David Shambaugh, Berkeley: University of California Press, 2005, pp. 329–346.

Pollins, Brian M., "Does Trade Follow the Flag? A Model of International Diplomacy and Commerce," *American Political Science Review* 83 (1989): 465–480.

Post, Gaines, Jr., *Dilemmas of Appeasement: British Deterrence and Defense, 1934–1937*, Ithaca, NY, Cornell University Press, 1993.

Powell, Robert, "Uncertainty, Shifting Power, and Appeasement," *American Political Science Review* 90 (1996): 749–764.

—— *In the Shadow of Power: States and Strategies in International Politics*, Princeton, NJ: Princeton University Press, 1999.

Putnam, Robert, "Diplomacy and Domestic Politics: The Logic of Two-level Games," *International Organization* 42 (1988): 427–460.

Rapkin, David and William R. Thompson, "Power Transition, Challenge and the (Re)emergence of China," *International Interactions* 29 (2003): 315–342.

Rasler, Karen A. and William R. Thompson, *War and State Making: The Shaping of the Global Powers*, Boston, MA: Unwin Hyman, 1989.

—— *The Great Powers and the Global Struggle, 1490–1990*, Lexington: University of Kentucky Press, 1994.

—— "Global War and the Political Economy of Structural Change," in *Handbook of War Studies II*, ed. Manus I. Midlarksy, Ann Arbor: University of Michigan Press, 2000, pp. 301–331.

Ray, James L., *Democracy and International Conflict: An Evaluation of the Democratic Peace Proposition*, Columbia: University of South Carolina Press, 1995.

Reiter, Dan, "Exploding the Powder Keg Myth," *International Security* 20 (1995): 5–34.

Reuveny, Rafael and William R. Thompson, *Growth, Trade, and Systemic Leadership*, Ann Arbor: University of Michigan Press, 2004.

Rice, Condoleezza, "Promoting the National Interest," *Foreign Affairs* 79 (2000): 45–62.

Richter, Stephan, "Repeating History," available at http://theglobalist.com/nor/news/2000/07-11-00.html.

"Rising Oil Prices Will Impact Taiwan Economy: Economist," August 31, 2005, available at http://english.ww.gov.tw/.

Robertson, Esmonde M., *Hitler's Pre-war Policy and Military Plans, 1933–1939*, London: Longmans, 1963.

Robinson, Thomas W., "The Sino-Soviet Border Dispute: Background, Development, and the March 1969 Clashes," *American Political Science Review* 66 (1972): 1175–1202.

Rock, Stephen R., *Appeasement in International Politics*, Lexington: University of Kentucky Press, 2000.

Rosecrance, Richard, ed., *America as an Ordinary Country*, Ithaca, NY: Cornell University Press, 1976.

—— *The Rise of the Trading State: Commerce and Conquest in the Modern World*, New York: Basic Books, 1986.

Ross, Robert S., *The Indochina Triangle: China's Vietnam Policy 1975–1979*, New York: Columbia University Press, 1988.

—— *Navigating Cooperation: US–China Relations, 1969–1989*, Stanford, CA: Stanford University Press, 1995.

—— "Beijing as a Conservative Power," *Foreign Affairs* 76 (1997): 33–44.

—— "The Geography of the Peace: East Asia in the Twenty-first Century," *International Security* 23 (1999): 81–118.

—— "The 1995–1996 Taiwan Strait Confrontation: Coercion, Credibility, and Use of Force," *International Security* 25 (2000): 87–123.

—— "Navigating the Taiwan Strait: Deterrence, Escalation Dominance, and US-China Relations," *International Security* 27 (2002): 48–85.

—— "Bipolarity and Balancing in East Asia," in *Balance of Power: Theory and Practice in the 21st Century*, ed. T.V. Paul, James J. Wirtz, and Michel Fortmann, Stanford, CA: Stanford University Press, 2004, pp.267–304.

—— and Jiang Changbin, eds, *Re-examining the Cold War: U.S.–China Diplomacy, 1954–1973*, Cambridge, MA: Harvard University Press, 2001.

Rousseau, David L., *Identifying Threats and Threatening Identities: The Social Construction of Realism and Liberalism*, Stanford, CA: Stanford University Press, 2006.

Roy, Denny, "Hegemon on the Horizon? China's Threat to East Asian Security," *International Security* 19 (1994): 149–168.

Russett, Bruce M., "Refining Deterrence Theory: The Japanese Attack on Pearl Harbor," in *Theory and Research on the Causes of War*, ed. Dean G. Pruitt and Richard C. Snyder, Englewood Cliffs, NJ: Prentice-Hall, 1969, pp.127–135.

—— "The Mysterious Case of Vanishing Hegemony: Or, Is Mark Twain Really Dead?," *International Organization* 39 (1985): 207–232.

—— and John R. Oneal, *Triangulating Peace: Democracy, Interdependence, and International Organizations*, New York: Norton, 2001.

Russett, Bruce M., Harvey Starr, and David Kinsella, *World Politics: The Menu for Choice* (8th edn), Belmont, CA: Wadsworth/Thomson Learning, 2005.

Sabrosky, Alan N., "Interstate Alliances: Their Reliability and the Expansion of War," in *Correlates of War II*, ed. J. David Singer, New York: Free Press, 1980, pp. 161–198.

Samuels, Marwyn S., *Contest for the South China Sea*, New York: Methuen, 1982.

Sartori, Anne E., "The Might of the Pen: A Reputational Theory of Communication in International Disputes," *International Organization* 56 (2002): 121–149.

Sawyer, Ralph D., *Sun Tzu: Art of War*, Boulder, CO: Westview Press, 1994.

Schelling, Thomas C., *Arms and Influence*, New Haven, CT: Yale University Press, 1966.

Schroeder, Paul W., *The Transformation of European Politics, 1763–1848*, Oxford: Clarendon Press, 1994.

—— "Historical Reality vs. Neo-realist Theory," *International Security* 19 (1994): 108–138.

—— "History versus Neorealism," *International Security* 20 (1995): 193–195.

—— "Embedded Counterfactuals and World War I as an Unavoidable War," in *Systems, Stability, and Statecraft: Essays on the International History of Modern Europe*, ed. Paul W. Schroeder, New York: Palgrave, 2004, pp. 157–191.

—— "The Mirage of Empire Versus the Promise of Hegemony," in *Systems, Stability, and Statecraft: Essays on the International History of Modern Europe*, ed. Paul W. Schroeder, New York: Palgrave, 2004, pp. 297–305.

Schultz, Kenneth A., "Domestic Opposition and Signaling in International Crises," *American Political Science Review* 92 (1998): 829–844.

—— "Do Democratic Institutions Constrain or Inform? Contrasting Two Institutional Perspectives on Democracy and War," *International Organization* 53 (1999): 133–162.

—— "Looking for Audience Costs," *Journal of Conflict Resolution* 45 (2001): 32–60.

Schwartz, Nelson D., "Why China Scares Big Oil?," *Fortune* (July 25, 2005): 89–94.

Schwarz, Benjamin, "Comment: Managing China's Rise," *The Atlantic Monthly* (June 2005): 27–28.

Schweller, Randall L., "Domestic Structure and Preventive War: Are Democracies More Pacific?," *World Politics* 44 (1992): 235–269.

—— "Bandwagoning for Profit: Bringing the Revisionist State Back In," *International Security* 19 (1994): 72–97.

—— *Deadly Imbalances: Tripolarity and Hitler's Strategy of World Conquest*, New York: Columbia University Press, 1998.

—— "Managing the Rise of Great Powers," in *Engaging China: The Management of an Emerging Power*, ed. Alastair Iain Johnston and Robert S. Ross, London: Routledge, 1999, pp. 1–31.

—— and William C. Wohlforth, "Power Test: Evaluating Realism in Response to the End of the Cold War," *Security Studies* 9 (2000): 60–107.

Segal, Gerald, "East Asia and the 'Constrainment' of China," *International Security* 20 (1996): 107–135.

Servan-Schreiber, Jean Jacques, *The American Challenge*, trans. Ronald Steel, New York: Atheneum, 1968.

Shambaugh, David, "Containment or Engagement of China? Calculating Beijing's Responses," *International Security* 21 (1996): 180–209.

—— "China or America: Which is the Revisionist Power?," *Survival* 43 (2001): 25–30.

—— "China Engages Asia: Reshaping the Regional Order," *International Security* 29 (2004/2005): 64–99.

—— "The Author Replies," *International Security* 30 (2005): 205–213.

Shenkar, Oded, *The Chinese Century: The Rising Chinese Economy and Its Impact on the Global Economy, the Balance of Power and Your Job*, Philadelphia, PA: Wharton School Publishing, 2005.

Simmons, Beth A. and Daniel J. Hopkins, "The Constraining Power of International Treaties: Theory and Methods," *American Political Science Review* 99 (2005): 623–631.

Singer, J. David, "Reconstructing the Correlates of War Dataset on Material Capabilities of States, 1816–1985," *International Interactions* 14 (1987): 115–132.

—— and Melvin Small, "Alliance Aggregation and the Onset of War, 1815–1945," in *Quantitative International Politics: Insights and Evidence*, ed. J. David Singer, New York: Free Press, 1968, pp. 247–286.

Singer, J. David, Stuart Bremer, and John Stuckey, "Capability Distribution, Uncertainty, and Major Power War, 1820–1965," in *Peace, War, and Numbers*, ed. Bruce M. Russett, Beverly Hills, CA: Sage, 1972, pp. 19–48.

Siverson, Randolph M. and Ross A. Miller, "The Power Transition: Problems and Prospects," in *Parity and War: Evaluations and Extensions of The War Ledger*, ed. Jacek Kugler and Douglas Lemke, Ann Arbor: University of Michigan Press, 1996, pp. 57–73.

Slantchev, Branislav, "Military Coercion in International Crises," *American Political Science Review* 99 (2005): 533–547.

Small, Melvin and J. David Singer, *Resort to Arms: International and Civil Wars, 1816–1980*, Beverly Hills, CA: Sage, 1982.

Smith, Alastair, "To Intervene or Not to Intervene: A Biased Decision," *Journal of Conflict Resolution* 40 (1996): 16–40.

Stolper, Thomas E., *China, Taiwan, and the Offshore Islands: Together with an Implication for Outer Mongolia and Sino-Soviet Relations*, Armonk, NY: Sharpe, 1985.

Strange, Susan, "The Persistent Myth of Lost Hegemony," *International Organization* 41 (1987): 551–574.

Sutter, Robert G., *China's Rise in Asia: Promises and Perils*, Lanham, MD: Rowman & Littlefield, 2005.

Swaine, Michael D. and Ashley J. Tellis, *Interpreting China's Grand Strategy: Past, Present, and Future*, Santa Monica, CA: RAND, 2000.

Taliaferro, Jeffrey W., "Security Seeking under Anarchy: Defensive Realism Revisited," *International Security* 25 (2000/2001): 128–161.

—— "Realism, Power Shifts, and Major War," *Security Studies* 10 (2001): 145–178.

—— *Balancing Risks: Great Power Intervention in the Periphery*, Ithaca, NY: Cornell University Press, 2004.

Tammen, Ronald L., "The Impact of Asia on World Politics: China and India Options for the United States," *International Studies Perspective* (2006): 563–580.

——, Jacek Kugler, Douglas Lemke, Allan C. Stam III, Mark Abdollahian, Carole Alsharabati, Brian Efird, and A.F.K. Organski, *Power Transitions: Strategies for the 21st Century*, New York: Chatham House, 2000.

Taylor, A.J.P., *The Origins of the Second World War*, New York: Atheneum, 1961.

Tellis, Ashley J., Janise Bially, Christopher Layne, and Melissa McPherson, *Measuring National Power in the Postindustrial Age*, Santa Monica, CA: RAND, 2000.

Thompson, William R., ed., *Great Power Rivalries*, Columbia: University of South Carolina Press, 1999.

—— "The Evolution of a Great Power Rivalry: The Anglo-American Case," in *Great Power Rivalries*, ed. William R. Thompson, Columbia: University of South Carolina Press, 1999, pp. 201–221.

—— "Why Rivalries Matter and What Great Powers Rivalries Can Tell Us about World Politics," in *Great Power Rivalries*, ed. William R. Thompson, Columbia: University of South Carolina Press, 1999, pp. 3–28.

Thucydides, *The History of the Peloponnesian War*, trans. Rex Warner, New York: Penguin Books, 1954.

Trachtenberg, Marc, "A Wasting Asset: American Strategy and the Shifting Nuclear Balance, 1949–1954," in *History and Strategy*, ed. Marc Trachtenberg, Princeton, NJ: Princeton University Press, 1991, pp. 100–152.

—— *A Constructed Peace: The Making of the European Settlement, 1945–1963*, Princeton, NJ: Princeton University Press, 1999.

Treisman, Daniel, "Rational Appeasement," *International Organization* 58 (2004): 344–373.

Tuchman, Barbara W., *The Guns of August*, New York: Dell, 1962.

Tucker, Nancy Bernkopf, "Strategic Ambiguity or Strategic Clarity," in *Dangerous Strait: The U.S.–Taiwan–China Crisis*, ed. Nancy Bernkopf Tucker, New York: Columbia University Press, 2005, pp. 186–211.

United Nations, *United Nations Statistical Yearbook 2004*, New York: United Nations, 2004.

United Nations Development Programme, *Human Development Report 2000*, New York: Oxford University Press, 2000.

United Nations Educational, Scientific, and Cultural Organization, *UNESCO Statistical Yearbook 1999*, Paris: UNESCO Publishing and Bernan Press, 1999.

United Nations news releases are available at www.un.org/News/Press/doc.

Van Evera, Stephen, *Causes of War: Power and the Roots of Conflict*, Ithaca, NY: Cornell University Press, 1999.

Vasquez, John A., *The War Puzzle*, Cambridge: Cambridge University Press, 1993.

—— "When Are Power Transitions Dangerous? An Appraisal and Reformulation of Power Transition Theory," in *Parity and War: Evaluations and Extensions of The War Ledger*, ed. Jacek Kugler and Douglas Lemke, Ann Arbor: University of Michigan Press, 1996, pp. 35–56.

Vogel, Ezra, *Japan As Number 1*, New York: Harper & Row, 1979.

Von Stein, Jana, "Do Treaties Constrain or Screen? Selection Bias and Treaty Compliance," *American Political Science Review* 99 (2005): 611–622.

Wagner, R. Harrison, "Economic Interdependence, Bargaining Power, and Political Influence," *International Organization* 42 (1988): 461–463.

—— "Bargaining and War," *American Journal of Political Science* 44 (2000): 469–484.

Wallace, Michael D., *War and Rank Among Nations*, Lexington, KY: Heath, 1973.

Walt, Stephen M., *The Origins of Alliances*, Ithaca, NY: Cornell University Press, 1987.

—— "Keeping the World 'Off Balance': Self Restraint and U.S. Foreign Policy," in *America Unrivaled: The Future of the Balance of Power*, ed. G. John Ikenberry, Ithaca, NY: Cornell University Press, 2002, pp. 121–154.

—— *Taming American Power: The Global Response to U.S. Primacy*, New York: Norton, 2005.

—— "Taming American Power," *Foreign Affairs* 84 (2005): 105–120.

Waltz, Kenneth, *Theory of International Politics*, New York: Random House, 1979.

Wang, Jisi, "China's Search for Stability with America," *Foreign Affairs* 84 (2005): 39–48.

Wayman, Frank Whelon, "Power Shifts and the Onset of War," in *Parity and War: Evaluations and Extensions of The War Ledger*, ed. Jacek Kugler and Douglas Lemke, Ann Arbor: University of Michigan Press, 1996, pp. 145–161.

Weber, Max, *The Protestant Ethic and the Spirit of Capitalism*, trans. Talcott Parsons, New York: Scribner, 1930.

Wendt, Alexander, "The Agent-Structure Problem in International Relations Theory," *International Organization* 41 (1987): 337–370.

Werner, Suzanne and Jacek Kugler, "Power Transitions and Military Buildups: Resolving the Relationship between Arms Buildups and War," in *Parity and War: Evaluations and Extensions of The War Ledger*, ed. Jacek Kugler and Douglas Lemke, Ann Arbor: University of Michigan Press, 1996, pp. 187–207.

Whaley, Barton, *Codeword Barbarossa*, Cambridge, MA: MIT Press, 1973.

Whiting, Allen S., *China Crosses the Yalu: The Decision to Enter the Korean War*, New York: Macmillan, 1960.

—— "New Light on Mao; Quemoy 1958: Mao's Miscalculation," *China Quarterly* 62 (1975): 263–270.

—— *The Chinese Calculus of Deterrence: India and Indochina*, Ann Arbor: University of Michigan Press, 1975.

—— "China's Use of Force, 1950–96, and Taiwan," *International Security* 26 (2001): 103–131.

Wich, Richard, *Sino-Soviet Crisis Politics: A Study of Political Change and Communication*, Cambridge, MA: Harvard University Press, 1980.

Wohlforth, William C., "Realism and the End of the Cold War," *International Security* 19 (1994/1995): 91–129.

——, ed., *Cold War Endgame: Oral History, Analysis, Debates*, University Park: Pennsylvania State University Press, 2003.

Wohlstetter, Roberta, *Pearl Harbor: Warning and Decision*, Stanford, CA: Stanford University Press, 1962.

World Development Indicators are available at http://devdata.worldbank.org/dataonline.

Xiang, Lanxin, "Washington's Misguided China Policy," *Survival* 43 (2001): 7–23.

Yarbrough, Beth V. and Robert M. Yarbrough, "Reciprocity, Bilateralism, and Economic 'Hostage': Self-Enforcing Agreements in International Trade," *International Studies Quarterly* 30 (1986): 7–21.

—— *Cooperation and Governance in International Trade*, Princeton, NJ: Princeton University Press 1992.

Yeh, K.C., "China's Economic Growth: Recent Trends and Prospects," in *China, the United States, and the Global Economy*, ed. Shuxun Chen and Charles Wolf Jr., Santa Monica: CA: RAND, 2001, pp. 69–97.

Yergin, Daniel, *The Prize: The Epic Quest for Oil, Money, and Power*, New York: Touchstone, 1991.

Yu, Max Sung-chi, Alexander C. Tan, Tim Chen, and Karl Ho, "Is China an Upcoming Threat or a Peaceful Ascendance? The Determining Factor of Taiwan in Hegemonic Power Transition," presented at the annual meeting of the American Political Science Association, Washington, D.C., September 1–4, 2005.

Zagare, Frank C. and D. Marc Kilgour, "Deterrence-versus-Restraint Dilemma in Extended Deterrence: Explaining British Policy in 1914," *International Studies Review* 8 (2006): 623–641.

Zhang, Yunling and Shiping Tang, "China's Regional Strategy," in *Power Shift: China and Asia's New Dynamics*, ed. David Shambaugh, Berkeley: University of California Press, 2005, pp. 48–68.

Zheng, Bijian, "China's 'Peaceful Rise' to Great-power Status," *Foreign Affairs* 84 (2005): 18–24.

Zhu, Zhiqun, "Power Transition and U.S.–China Relations: Is War Inevitable," *Journal of International and Area Studies* 12 (2005): 1–24.

Zweig, David and Bi Jianhai, "China's Global Hunt for Energy," *Foreign Affairs* 84 (2005): 25–38.

Index